Singing Lessons

To Michael
love

[signature]

1

Nightfall

When I heard the news of my son's death, I was standing in the foyer of my apartment in New York among the paintings and the flowers and the photographs of my family, in the beautiful space I have called home for twenty-eight years. Louis was in Washington, D.C., making a presentation for the Korean War Veterans Memorial Wall. He had called at six that evening, saying he would take the noon shuttle and be home by two the following day. Meanwhile I waited for my son to call me back from St. Paul. I had left a number of messages for him. I worked for a while longer and ate a solitary dinner around eight. I was alone but contented, a normal, quiet evening.

My last.

The doorbell rang at around eight-thirty. I wasn't expecting anyone and a strange feeling came over my heart. I peeked out the keyhole and saw my brother Denver and sister-in-law Allison standing in the hallway. I let them in. There was a deep silence and I knew from my brother's eyes what had happened. He didn't even have to speak. He took me in his arms and my world changed forever. I heard a scream from some primitive place I had not known before.

I clung to my brother, slowly becoming aware of the scent of roses and violets from a bouquet on the hall table; there was a sweet, lingering taste of mint in my mouth; my eyes focused on a photograph of my brothers and sister in a silver frame next to the flowers. I heard the sound of a siren on a Manhattan street below, and then my eyes moved to a picture of my son as a child, his red hair cropped close to his head and his big blue eyes looking out at me. Our eyes held each other and I caught my breath for what seemed an eternity, knowing the world was turning to darkness and I would never see it or hear it or live in it the same again.

My brother and sister-in-law comforted me as best they could. I stood up. I sat down. I laid on the bed. Allison made tea. I wept. My brother had tracked Louis down in Washington and told him the terrible news and Louis had lovingly arranged for Denver to tell me about Clark's death in person so that I wouldn't have to hear it on the telephone. My mother had been called, my siblings—the family Clark had loved so much and who had loved him all now knew that he was gone.

I had thought we had won this battle, that the darkness had been averted. But it was not to be. Denver, Allison, my nephew Joshua and my neice Corrina and I flew to the Twin Cities the next day, where Louis joined us. The rest of my family arrived from far-flung cities to gather at the mortuary, putting their arms around me and each other; brothers and sister, mother, cousins, holding me close.

The tears for this terrible loss would keep coming in the days and years to follow, dropping like rain from the foggy valley through which I would walk, the valley of the shadow of death.

The world was suddenly the enemy, the place where this could happen, where it had happened. My knees wouldn't hold me, nothing could—but my loving family held me, and we held on to each other. None of us were sure we would survive Clark's death, floating on this new and terrible ocean that had sprung up around us, an ocean full of storm and sorrow.

In St. Paul, snow had fallen, a heavy white mantle covering every statue in the city, every tree, every lamppost. A whiteness and a cold penetrated my nostrils and my breath froze, holding back even my tears after a while. The weather seemed to foretell the end of a world. This must have been what it was like for primitive peoples, this disappearing of the sun, the brightness and light gone. The weight of my son's death, like the weight of the white snow, stilled every bird, froze all life. Nature wanted to stop, time wanted to stop, life had stopped. For my son, there would be no thaw.

January 16, 1992, Thursday. Bitter cold. Snow. St. Paul, Minnesota

The snow has fallen on the pine trees, and their branches bend, heavy with white drifts. I stand at the door of a long, narrow room covered with a green carpet, my fingers tremble and my knees shake. The walls of the room are hung with flowered wallpaper, a design of green ivy on a cream background. Far away, at the end of the room, is the end of the road, the end of my dreams; a body under a white sheet lies lengthwise on a marble slab and I struggle forward toward the ancient, familiar figure as though climbing a great mountain, as though swimming an endless sea. I walk against the wind, I fight tides. The distance I travel is the breadth of the known world, to the furthest galaxy, to the end of time, to the end of life.

There, I see my son's freckled face, his shining red hair in plaits falling from his high forehead. Red streaks line his pale skin, the mark of the carbon monoxide, the stamp of death. He is some warrior from another time. I kiss his forehead, cold as marble under my lips, and sink to my knees. My tears fall on my hands and on my shoes, then on the snow and on the coverlet of the bed in the hotel in which I lay, my eyes open, waiting, trying to keep breathing. I keep thinking, this is not him, there is some terrible mistake, he is not dead, he cannot be gone.

The next day, Clark lay under the aspen leaves, under the bed of white roses on the lid of the carved wooden casket. Under the baby's breath and intertwined white rosebuds, Clark kept his silent vigil at his funeral.

A suicide.

Louis talked to the press, keeping the newspapers and reporters at bay. He and my brothers handled details at the mortuary, letting me think I was making the decisions myself.

A woman at the mortuary, kind and gentle, told me she would take care of my son.

Alyson, my daughter-in-law, was very shaky and seemed to be in a daze, little Hollis was opened-eyed, aware of everything. She and her mother had discovered Clark's body, as he must have known they would. I knew both must still be in shock. All of us were moving through a dream. A nightmare. Our friend Terry helped Louis order flowers and put the obituary together. We chose an urn for my son's ashes and picked out the casket. The terrible chores. God must have lifted us through these because none of us could do this thing. Together we planned the funeral, Louis inviting Alyson and all of Clark's friends and family to speak. I didn't know if I could walk through this fire.

It was all such a waste, it was all such a tragedy.

❧♋

Louis spoke with tender words about his stepson. Then he invited everyone to share, Quaker-style. Nearly two hundred of Clark's friend's and family were there and many spoke of his loving spirit. The love for my son poured out in floods of emotion as Clark's friends memorialized my beautiful son. Everyone who loved Clark knew that he fought with his demons, knew that he had lived close to the angels.

After my daughter-in-law spoke, Rosalind, Clark's halfsister, stood, wearing my son's face, his fine bones, his gentleness, his beauty. She is tall like my boy, thin as he was, beautiful, her face pale under her pale complexion, her hair long and strawberry, as his had been. She talked of the secret suicide they shared, the death of their paternal grandfather Al. There was a sound, almost a sigh, in the room as she spoke.

"I see my father and his brother, as grandfather died, taking in that last breath, breathing in as he breathed out, and holding that breath for forty-five years. With Clark's death, that breath can finally be let out." Rosalind had earned the right to speak the truth, and truth was what was needed.

Under the white lilies and roses and aspen leaves atop his coffin, I seemed to see Clark's red hair shimmering all through the ceremony. At the end the bagpiper played "Amazing Grace." I sang "Amazing Grace" for my son for the last time.

At home in New York the mortuary sent me his clothes, the jeans they cut off him, the belt, the green and gray shirt, all smelling of carbon monoxide. They were in a brown shopping bag with his boots and his black socks. I wondered if my son had dressed for death. They gave me the leather briefcase in which were the keys to his desk at work, words to the last songs he had written.

It took me four years to get rid of the clothes. I gave them to a shelter. I could not, ever, look at them again, except a white cashmere sweater I have come to love holding next to my skin.

It was, for me, the saddest day of my life. It seemed to be the end of the world.

❦

Sometimes it seems to me the nightmare began the day I bought my son the Subaru. It was on one of my visits to Minnesota, a cold, bright winter day in 1987. The Twin Cities sparkled under that polished sky of the land of a million lakes, so clear and crisp it made your eyes ache. Our hearts were light and our voices filled with love and cheer. Life was so good.

The station wagon was a dark, almost charcoal color called umber—a solid car, good for the cold Minnesota winters. My son was bundled into a hooded, fur-collared parka and I was draped in my black cashmere coat with the purple lining, a coat I use every winter—warm as toast, comforting in hotel rooms. I spend a lot of time in hotel rooms, on the road, doing concerts. My son said he might have been a rock-and-roll singer but he knew from the life his mother led that it wasn't an easy one.

Clark was excited about the Subaru, looking at me from his clear, untroubled face with anticipation and pleasure.

I looked at him intensely as though to memorize his metamorphosis. He was about five nine, with freckles in a scattering across his nose and arms that deepened in the summer sun. He could never get a tan. At thirty-two, he was a lanky figure in the pictures from Holly's wedding, the replica of his father, Peter, even to the way his figure bends, just so, from the waist, leaning over to hear you speak, leaning back to laugh. It took my breath away when I saw that. My heart skipped a beat.

Clark had always had a soulful singing voice, dark and sweet, unique in the way he played the notes and the way his voice meandered over the words, lovingly. He had a great sense of humor and an infectious laugh. His intelligence, evident at an early age, illuminated a deep sensitivity to others' pain, and to his own.

He was a redhead, a shade of red that tended more to strawberry than firehouse. At times in his life his hair grew down to the middle of his back. He cut it at least twice in his adult life, severing the luscious strawberry hank in a twist a foot and a half long. For a while when Clark was in his late twenties and early thirties, he wore his beautiful hair short, chopped off at the root. At his death, he was wearing it long again, down to his shoulders. How could he do it, just like that? Grow his hair, cut his hair? Take his life?

Clark understood me as no one else could. He understood the celebration as well as the troubles that the journey of our lives together brought. We were bound so very tight by the good things, as well as by the demons. It was as if he had lived before, experienced many things, and could see beyond the moment with a clarity that was startling. At his darkest time, he could still be a shining light and a beacon of hope. Clark was the person with whom I had been through everything. I loved him more than anyone.

Many people loved him. Who wouldn't love him? Teachers he had in the schools he went to, friends I didn't know, peers he had helped, stop me in the street or in church or write to me and say how much he meant to them. He changed people, made them think, turned their eyes and their thoughts inward. He understood why life was funny, why loving animals is a requirement, why, as Norman Maclean says in "A River Runs Through It," fly-fishing is akin to religion. Fishing was in his genes, from his father, his uncles, probably his great-grandfathers, and he took to it with such zeal. In my mind's eye I see him, going up to the lake country in the Subaru, casting in his waders, walking through rippling waters, returning home with trout or bass, cooking them himself for Alyson and the baby. He would practically throw himself into the middle of a lake if that is what it would take to catch that fish.

❧◦❧

Clark always loved a good car and since he was healthy, he wasn't about to run this one into a mountain or drive it over a bridge embankment or roll it on a curve or put dents in the frame, as he had done in the terrible old days with my brother Dave's cars.

My son was a responsible man these days. He would soon be a parent. I was co-signing the loan for the station wagon that was going to get him around in the snows and the heat of Minneapolis with his wife and his baby. Those early, terrible days were only memories now, part of a story he might tell his child, the mesmerizing bedtime tale of how her father had come back from the grave.

It was a beautiful car, the Subaru. My son stroked the silky surface of the softly molded frame, complimented the paint job, checked out the tires and the big, generous backseat. We drove the car around the neighborhood for a while. On the way back to the office, we talked about Clark's job at the trade college in nearby Minneapolis where he worked in the computer repair shop. I knew he wanted to go back to school but was happy to settle for a good job where he was learning a lot about computer technology.

The computers, and the baby, and Clark's wife, Alyson, and the groceries and the fly-fishing rods for the northern Minnesota lakes would all fit into the Subaru, with room to spare. He looked at me and said, "Yes, this really is the one," as we sat in the office of the dealer, signing papers, talking and laughing easily over mugs of steaming coffee the salesman had brought, clutching sugar, milk, wooden stirrers, napkins and the co-signature papers in his hand. Nothing worth doing, Clark and I always agreed, could be done without a good cup of coffee.

I watched my son's face. His eyes were bright as he glanced at me over his coffee cup, skin shining with health, weight on his thin bones, life and hope and health in his body. How different from the pale, frightened boy who had traveled to Minnesota to find a new way of life. He laughed at something the car dealer said as he took the pen in his hand and signed his name. I signed on the dotted line as well. Clark was the proud owner of a brand-new, spacious, buttery-finished Subaru station wagon.

On my visits, my son would pick me up at the airport in the Subaru. We would hug each other, joyful to be in each other's presence. Clark was proud of the Twin Cities airport valet parking, unique in airports. He would pack my heavy luggage with its wheels, along with my computer and handbags, into the back of the umber station wagon and we would tool on down the highway that runs by the river, the great Mississippi winding south through Minneapolis, on down toward the Gulf of Mexico. On the drive, our voices rose and fell in pleasure. No one laughed at my jokes the way Clark did. We thought the same kind of things funny, the same kind of things sad.

We would arrive at the ramp to his tree-lined street, turning into the driveway of the house in Crocus Hill, where we would stop, perhaps admiring the new porch or the work Clark was doing on the house; hugs with his wife Alyson and kisses and hugs with the baby, Hollis; then Clark would pour me a cup of his black, strong-brewed coffee. We would visit, talking about the past, about the future, about the rich and wonderful present.

Louis and Clark became close in those years and sometimes he would join me in my visits. Clark and Louis talked as friends, and Clark would ask Louis' advice about work, about school. Sharing was important to both of them. The life we were living seemed to make up for all the sadness that had gone before. We had laughter, joyous laughter, like it was at the start when Clark was that little, bright redhead tucked into my backpack in Colorado, seeing a red bird and laughing. We had heart-to-hearts and shared each other's secrets, except that one that killed him.

❧

Once, just after my granddaughter was born, Alyson carried her to see me, at the hotel where I was staying in St. Paul, a tiny girl in a basket, with big blue eyes like her father's, and cherry lips like her mother's, laughing up at me. From the high hill in St. Paul I could hear the big bell of the cathedral tolling the time, chiming the hours. I felt the murmur of my genes, ancient voices in my blood, the purpose of my life, the completion of my role. My granddaughter's beautiful face looked up at me. "You can die now, she is carrying your line," the voice of my ancestors whispered. I was shocked to feel the primitive call from my civilized exterior. It is all genetic, all karmic, I thought, all this agony and all this joy.

It was heaven to have a loving relationship with my son now in this time of beauty, work, health, family.

All the things I had always hoped for Clark had come true.

The years were sweet and the time passed. I knew there was some difficulty in my son's marriage but neither Alyson nor Clark said too much. He was in therapy, then they were in therapy, which was good, wasn't it? I didn't want to pry. The ups and downs of married life came and went in my son's life, as they do in everyone's. What more did my son want? There was always that aching in him, that unsettled, unresolved itching to be somewhere and do something that he wasn't doing and couldn't even speak of. He played beautiful guitar. His wife Alyson and I bought him an electric blue Les Paul guitar and he played his songs to his baby daughter. He came to visit us in New York, to laugh and celebrate. Louis and I traveled with Alyson and the baby to Colorado, with my beautiful family, where we always feel our hearts are home.

Hollis turned four in October of 1991 and I was in St. Paul for her party, a joyous romp with a dozen children at the Minneapolis Zoo, where we ate chocolate cake and watched the seals and wore paper hats and looked out the big plate-glass windows at the dying, burning trees, at the beginning of the Minnesota autumn. Clark carried Hollis around on his shoulders. Blond, blue-eyed, and the spitting image of her father, Hollis had captured my heart. The little girl was filled with life and had a light, lovely quality about her, and from her emanated a sweet and untroubled sound. She and her father adored each other and she seemed to bring out in him his lightest, sweetest side.

But things with Clark were not good, no matter how it looked on the outside. My son's waters ran so still, so deep, so dark at times. Those of us who loved him seldom guessed how locked he was, behind that vulnerable, open, easy smile. Lurking beneath the surface like a big spotted rainbow trout, swimming in the shadows of a willow by the turn in the river, I felt murmurs in my blood, premonitions like sighs on dark and secret nights. These were thoughts that flitted like phantoms through the brain, and then hid in the light of the bright day's faith, a certainty that obscured the low, moaning, almost inaudible call I stifled with hope. I turned the volume down on the whispering discontent that throbbed beneath the reassurances and the lighthearted laughter, because I had no idea what my fears meant or, more importantly, what to do about them.

January, 1987

Dream of Clark (five years before his death).

I'm holding my son in my arms, inside a house. We see a tornado coming and I look for a place to stand where we will be safe. Clark tells me he is terminally ill.

Clark's keen mind, the fiery intelligence that led him when he was older to read Kierkegaard and Tolstoy and Yogananda even when he was nodding out on heroin, was a flame that caught the heart of all who knew him even casually, his light rubbing off on even the darkest thought. He was a kind soul, with a great heart to match his great pain. Beneath the slow and painful thawing of my frozen hope, it is this moan of sorrow that haunts me. Knowing my son is out of his terrible pain gives me consolation, for he could not bear his own deepest sorrows. That is the tragedy of the suicide, but also the one thing that makes life for the survivor bearable, to know our beloved is no longer suffering.

The contradictions are what ring now. Clark was like the sun, his spirit the song of a magical bird on a summer morning, a melody that is clean, cutting through all the other sounds of the earth, bright and warm. He was beautiful physically, but his soul was more beautiful. There was a kind of glow about him, even when he was having troubles, something fine and inspiring to others. He seemed to bring out the best in people. His laughter was full of lightness. Now I see this, that only a bird that can sing so sad a song can be as joyful.

In November 1991 Clark made what he would later call a halfhearted attempt on his life. Clark had started doing something again, maybe drinking, maybe drugs. He told me he had been depressed. When I told him I would come to Minnesota to help him, he asked me not to ride in on a white horse to try to save him, or tell him what to do. I knew that if he was using,

I couldn't help him and I backed off and respected his wishes. I later heard he resisted others' attempts to help.

When a friend who visited him at the hospital after that first attempt asked him why he had relapsed, he said, "I ran out of insurance." Meaning, he had cut back on twelve step meetings and talking to people who know what the solution was. He was back in denial. His addiction was on the front burner again and wanted him dead.

After a few days of observation, Clark was released. For the next few weeks he seemed to be doing better. The holidays seemed to go well for everyone, and Clark and I talked about my coming to Minnesota in January. He said he was feeling great.

The low moan roared in my ears, then settled down again.

ဘၟၚ

After my son's death Alyson gave me his notebooks and his songs. In his New Year's resolutions for December 31, 1991, Clark wrote a list of the things he was going to do—as all of us do on New Year's, looking for solutions. He would work hard every day and reduce debt, save money, he said, write music and play guitar and play more with his daughter; stop smoking. Clark had battled cigarettes for years, and for a time he wrote a wonderful letter called the "Grateful Ex-Smoker" that was filled with experiences he was going through in his fight to get rid of the "filthy weed," as he called it. He would work out regularly, he promised, clean out the garage, work on his diet, drink less caffeine. All the things we promise on the glorious eve of a New Year. Better ourselves, be kinder to those we love. He promised himself to find a hopeful attitude, go to sleep early, cook more interesting food, start writing, stop prying.

What he didn't write was "I will not take my life, one day at a time."

Clark forgot to mention that he was loving and compassionate, that he had made progress, against the odds, and had a steady, healthy life. That he had done well for his wife and his family and himself, he had a beautiful child who loved him, a huge family who loved him, friends who loved him. How could he not have noticed us in his life? How could he not have noticed all the good, and not have come to the conclusion that he wanted us more than he wanted death? He had some problems, but we all have problems.

On January 1, 1992, Clark called to tell me he had decided to go into a week of family treatment at the Hazelden Renewal Center. Hazelden is a place of peace and contemplation, group meetings and professional supervision structured to help the recovering alcoholic and/or family member living with the "ism" of alcoholism. I was overjoyed. My son was taking a positive action, in his own behalf, and that could only mean he was really dealing with his life in a healthy way. The low moaning hum settled back to a soft, almost inaudible sound like a feather, waking me in the night, so softly I didn't know it was there. It was silent but still hovering there in the dark.

I packed my bags for the yearly trip Louis and I make to the islands. I had thought of canceling the trip, concerned about Clark, but hearing the good news that he was taking steps for his health, doing the right thing, Louis and I left New York. I could relax. I could stop worrying.

Again.

A few days later, at ten o'clock on the morning of the tenth of January, 1992, I was standing on a tiled terrace outside our cottage, watching the morning sun as it slanted through an ancient fig tree whose branches sheltered lizards and aloe, seedling palms and banana quits, dancing shadows and skittering bars of sunlight. Blue water shimmered in the sunlight at the ocean's edge while I talked on the phone to Clark of everything, just as we always did. He sounded wonderful.

Paradise. Last stop.

I was drinking coffee out of a white porcelain cup with a gold edge, squinting in the sunlight. My son too, in that faraway city in Minnesota where fresh snow had fallen, was drinking his first cup of coffee. I felt the shadow lift, the humming sound fade into the background. Clark had stayed at the Hazelden Renewal Center for a week and was now out again, going to therapy, trying to sort things out.

I remember everything about that conversation. I was wearing a violet stretch bathing suit that clung to my still-white skin, and a wide-brimmed straw hat with a band of violet. I had the telephone receiver jammed against my ear, listening for clues, batting away tiny black flies. I shifted from foot to foot on the hot tiles.

"How are you, Mom, are you rested? Is your cold better?" Clark knew how beat I always was in January after a heavy year of concert touring.

"I'm better." The winter flu that had been dragging on during my concert season was drying out in the healing sun and I was feeling human again and ready for another year of life, of work and friends, of seeing my son and his family. "And how are you?"

"I'm good, Mom." Clark's voice sounded cheerful and calm, at peace, in spite of the fact that he and Alyson had decided they would try living apart for a while. He said he hoped they would not divorce, but also that he thought he might see a lawyer in case that was going to happen. The problems in their marriage had not gone away, but he seemed to be at peace with what they had decided to do about it.

I asked him if there was anything I could do, and he said that when there was, he would ask me.

How do you know when someone is at the edge, when the next breath will be the last, or near the last, when the last chance has been taken, the last bridge crossed? I listened for clues, but the sound of Clark's voice stilled the moaning hum.

"What are you going to do today?" I asked. Inside the cottage on the floor above me I could see Louis, padding about, getting ready to do some watercolors on the terrace, his body moving behind the slats of the shutters, a series of stuttering pictures, his lips under the wreath of beard smiling as he nodded to me from inside the room in quick poses, jerkily, like a black-and-white time and motion study.

On January 8 Clark had turned thirty-three, the magical age. Clark thanked me for the birthday gifts I had sent, a check and a watermarked tie from Florence, a dance of color.

"I've got some things to do," he said. "I trashed a hard disk at school, I have to talk to you about giving me some money to replace it," he said.

"Let's talk about it when I see you next week," I said.

Relief in his voice. "I'm going to the gym today," Clark said. Good! The gym meant getting rid of any lingering depression. Wouldn't it? "And I've got ten days sober and clean." He had had seven years of sobriety before his November relapse. I told him I was thrilled, which I was.

"I'll come out on Friday, honey," I said, hoping my offer would be greeted with enthusiasm. Today was a Friday. "I'll be there a week from today." I would get myself back to New York, and hop on a plane out to Minnesota.

"That's great," he said. "I've been wanting to go to the museum with Hollis, maybe we could do that." There was a pause and I heard water running. A banana quit flitted onto a branch above the telephone near where I stood, squeaking and bouncing on the tree, pure yellow and black. He chuckled then. "But I need my mom!"

Finally, I thought.

"I'll be there, I love you, Clark."

"I love you too, Mom." Those were the last words I heard him say.

He rang off, the sound of oceans and distance rolling in the telephone line.

I looked out beyond the fig tree, at the falling, rainbow-laden mist that drifted from the silver clouds above the water. I would work for a while, then go to lunch with Louis, and in a few days I would be on a plane headed home, and then to Minnesota to see my boy. He was doing fine, the crisis past. He had friends. He had the family given to him by God, and the one he was creating around him, both gifts, the ones we have at birth and the ones we find, collecting them as God brings them to us.

Like a fugue in slow motion, like a haunting melody that will not leave your mind, I play the scene over and over: the rainbow over the water, the mist in the air, each fig leaf, each word spoken, each wave in the sunlight, each gulp of strong coffee on my lips, the feel of each bare foot lifting off tile, the shift of weight from one foot to the other, the tapping with my yellow metal room key on the dusty red-brick wall, the hummingbird hovering over a red, long-lipped flower in a blazing green bush, drinking sweet nectar.

There will be a lifetime to remember it.

I should have been more worried about the lawyer, about the divorce. I still believed Clark and Alyson would work things out.

Sometimes I see myself putting on my ivory summer suit, packing my bags, climbing past passengers with reservations on planes leaving the Caribbean that day. I play the scene that way, some days. Some nights. I come home to New York and get on the next plane to Minnesota, and—and what? Save my son? Can we do that? Can people actually do that? Save each other? Mother? Son? Father? Daughter? Perhaps Clark would have stayed alive, for that week, for the time I was with him. Perhaps not.

Five days later, on January 15, just after one o'clock on a bright, sunny day in Minneapolis, while the birds sang on the bare trees and the Mississippi River ran its ice-laden course alongside the tree-filled park where his ashes would be scattered later that year, my son didn't check his telephone messages. I was trying to reach him to tell him what flight I was going to take to Minnesota, and when he could pick me up at the airport Friday in the Subaru. Later, we learned, he went to work in the morning and then had an appointment with his lawyer, and after lunch drove to the liquor store down the block from his house. He bought a bottle of cheap champagne. Odd. Clark had never really liked champagne. Counting days again, not far from his last drugs and booze, there were many friends he might have called, a community of souls in Minnesota, many of whom say my son saved *their* lives.

As far as we know, he didn't call anyone.

He drove to his house on the suburban, tree-lined street in Crocus Hill, the home he had been restoring with love and care and pride. The kitchen had a dark, mottled blue-gray marble counter, one of my gifts to the newly renovated house. Clark had put the counter in the previous winter with the help of my stepfather Robert, who had driven out from Denver with my mother Marjorie to give my son a hand. Robert is a skilled craftsman and he and Clark had had a fine time working together. There was an expresso machine on the counter, a new floor and dishwasher that shone in the kitchen, along with other generous gifts from Alyson's mother Sandy, and Clark's father, Peter, who had helped the couple make the down payment on the house. Everyone had pitched in, positive and hopeful of Clark and Alyson's happiness.

I wonder if he thought of any of us at all, but today I believe he was only trying to escape from the demon that was chasing him.

The garage stood next to the white gazebo under which Hollis's trainer bike, wagon, and other brightly colored toys lay. He parked the car in the garage between shelves of computer parts and projects in different stages and put the garage door down. He left the engine of the car running, plugged a length of hose into the exhaust of the umber-colored Subaru, and brought it around the car and in through the window. He switched on the ignition and while the engine idled, uncorked the champagne bottle and drank, breathing in carbon monoxide.

Most of this I know because Clark left a tape of his final message, speaking into the machine as he struggled to make this last act work. On the tape he made amends to all of us for what he was doing. He said to me, "Mom I love you, and you have tried so hard with me, and I'm so sorry." He left instructions with Alyson that the ignition of the Subaru needed checking.

Spiritual teachers say that every soul, no matter how determined, repents the taking of its own life. At the end, they would rather have lived, tried another way. For Clark, with his wild blue eyes like irises blooming in a field of white, with his beauty and his humor and his lyric songs, with his laughter and his love and his pure and gentle nature, it was too late.

On that shining day in the land of the lakes, with as much hope as most of us have and more trouble, perhaps, than many, my beautiful son ended his life.

Alyson sold the house after my son's death—and the Subaru. The car was almost paid off and I wrote a check for the balance, stunned with grief as the pen moved in my hand. Who is driving that car, who will be cooking in that kitchen that my son built with his hands? Who will be making pots of coffee and wiping that beautiful marble counter clean?

I went home to New York in a daze. Louis and I tried to pick up the pieces of our lives. Friends, tears, the wake. Like a sleuth searching for answers, I read letters and notebooks, looking for clues to how and why this could have happened. Why I hadn't predicted it, or foreseen it. I felt it was my fault, that I could have stopped my son from killing himself. Perhaps the fear of divorce had played a role in Clark's final choice, and there was something I should have done about that. A black hole of despair descended, through the numbness of the knowledge: the worst had happened, the worst was happening, the worst would continue to happen each and every day of my life. The snow is falling; the rain is falling. How could they fall? The sun is shining. How can it shine? How could I live if he was dead? Was his faith so great that he knew I would live through his death? How could he know that? The disbelief, like a howling wind in my head, tore at me. It was as if I discovered his death each day anew. Each morning the tragedy was as fresh as though it had just happened.

November 1, 1992, en route from Minneapolis to New York

Today we scattered Clark's ashes on the Mississippi River in St. Paul, down in a park called Hidden Falls. My daughter-in-law Alyson in black, her black hat buffeted by the wind, her words torn away from our ears, and my granddaughter Hollis's song, sung but unheard, the wind carrying her voice along the water to the high walls of Fort Snelling, her pretty voice absorbed by stone and the sound of the wind, her slight figure, wrapped in a black coat. A clear plastic umbrella showed her underneath its ribboned outline, a tiny survivor. All of us are now survivors.

We stood, our coats whipping around our legs, in a wind that howled and a rain that became colder and more fierce as the time went on, the wind battering rain against our bodies, hurling the ashes thrown into the air and the flowers, violet and golden mums on leggy stems, this way and that, all about us, as though Clark himself hurled the raindrops, shouting and laughing. "Is it cold enough for you? Here is Minnesota weather, here is more wind, more cold, more pouring, slanting rain! You call this cold?" His laughter was a red-headed, deep-souled, complete laughter. I could see him, with no gloves, having lost them somewhere, so like his mother, and his coat too thin, or wearing one of his great Minnesota down parkas, his face white. He would be cold too but wouldn't admit it for the world. My beautiful brothers were there, Denver and David and Michael, and my nephews, Matthew—looking like my son Clark's double—and Kalen, my sister Holly's oldest son. My life partner Louis and all Clark's Minnesota friends. No time to speak much, aside from a few mumbled words over the sound of the wind, my own words cut short. No singing, nothing but flowers in the gray wind, rain on our already wet faces and soaked clothes, our shoes in the river, our hearts flying into the wind with Clark.

I kept thinking, this is a dream, there must be some mistake. Gone, into the wind, into the river, into the grass, into the past, merged with my past and my future, all I have ever been or will ever be. My son's hair, my son's heart, burned now to ashes, on the river across from Fort Snelling, serenely ominous across the dark water, across from Hidden Falls.

We stood, our fingers numb with cold, trying to keep our faces warm, giving up, umbrellas no protection as the rain pelted us.

I imagine Clark's voice calling in the rain, calling against the wind.

ဆုပ္

On the first anniversary of Clark's death, January 15, 1993, Louis and I were in the islands once again. We brought flowers, wind-blown white roses and peach- and orange-colored trumpet flowers, wild bougainvillea, yellow geraniums and blue hyacinths, up to the statue of the Christ of the Caribbean—a white powerful adobe figure of the Savior with His face turned to the sea, His arms outspread toward the blue water of the Atlantic, guarding the boats and fisherman, the living and dead.

It was hot as we climbed the green, dusty, flower-dotted trail to the statue. There were some others that day, a few tourists in sunglasses and bright yellow print shorts, three children in fuchsia shirts and Lycra bathing suits, their shrill voices calling to one another. We stopped before the Savior and followed his gaze, looking out at the blue sea and the whitecaps and the sky dotted with clouds. The tourists and the children evaporated down the hill and when they had left we knelt in the grass beneath the statue and held hands and prayed for Clark's peace and for his daughter's happiness, and for our family's healing.

Late that afternoon, after the thunder showers, a rainbow appeared outside the window of our room. It stretched from the sun setting in the sea to the trees at the end of the island. The arc of the rainbow hovered over the spot where I was standing when I last spoke to my son, when he said, "I love you, Mom," and where I told him that I loved him.

Forever.

At midnight I woke from a dream and looked out the windows at the white moon's silver broken path upon the sea. The wind was blowing the leaves of the fig tree and the waves were bobbing, phosphorescent in the moon's light. In my dream I had been trying to persuade Clark not to die, arguing with him, trying to convince him that he didn't *have* to die, he didn't *have* to end his life.

My son smiled and looked at me with love in his eyes, the twinkling light of his angelic spirit.

"Mother," he said, "death is not an ending."

O God of the sun and the moon, of rivers and water-falls and tears, God of thunder and of lightning, of the quickening of life and the ending of life; God of the plains and the mountains, of the rushing rivers that flow north to south and east to west, God of the prairies green in spring and gold in autumn, God of birth and death, of love and war, of fear and prayer, of holiness and evil, of the flowers that bloom and the aspen that cover the mountainside and shiver in the wind like handfuls of gold; O God who made the earth and the stars, You who can do anything, accept my son into your loving arms, take him and show him your mercy, your tenderness.

Help me through the nights and the days, You who drive the sun and the moon and the ocean tides. Help me cry my tears and still be breathing when the dawn comes. God help me to live for I cannot. Help me to do what I cannot do. I have seen blackness, give me the light. Help me to see that light in the shining sky. You have shown me the darkness, now show me the day. Heal me, O God, and hear my prayer.

Take the dark pain away, and show your face of light.

2

My Father

I can always remember myself singing.

Naked, in a washtub in the sunshine on the lawn in front of our house in Seattle, I sang "Row, row, row your boat" and "Frère Jacques," cheered on by my enthusiastic parents. I joined my mother's sweet voice, humming along with her on the lullabies, and I piped in when my father's baritone voice sang me to sleep, harmonizing with "Kathleen Mavourneen" and "Danny Boy." I then sang those lullabies to the billy goat who was tethered down the dirt road from my grandparents' farmhouse. My mother says I was practically born singing.

Every morning started with music. I listened to birds sing; the song of meadowlarks, the music of robins, the tangled, lacy songs of the purple finches. I was a bird too, singing whenever I was sad, singing whenever I found anyone to sing with. I loved to harmonize with my father and my siblings. It was natural for us to sing, like walking, like smiling, like speaking.

I was born on the first of May, 1939, at eleven-thirty in the morning, at Maynard Hospital in Seattle, Washington. My father, who could smell and feel and touch and hear, could not see. He looked at my face with his hands and named me Judith, after the biblical queen who cut off Holofernes's head, freeing the tribes of Israel.

My father was twenty-eight when I was born and already he had a great career. He was one of the pioneers of the golden age of radio. His music, poetry, philosophy and good humor rode out over the airwaves to the ears of hundreds of thousands of people, giving them what my dad liked to think was a "great edge" to each day as they listened to his songs and humor.

Daddy loved Seattle, and, although he could not see it, he appreciated it for all its charms. The city was named for Chief Seattle of the Yakima Indian tribe; city of light and clouds, crisp apples, bridge to the San Juan Islands; yet to be the home of grunge music and good coffee; city of independent-minded sons and daughters of immigrant pioneers. The city of fishermen of sockeye, silver and king salmon, and of the Pike Street Market: and the gateway to Canada, the Bering Strait and Russia.

Seattle is a city where river and bay run with barges of big pine trees cut from the mountains, a city on hills of passing shadows from thunderclouds about to burst. It is a land where green and blue glass globes adrift from Japanese fishing nets smash upon the shores, leaving burnished chunks of glass among the white and sparkling sand. Sometimes they land perfectly on beaches where children find them and bring them home, smiling at their luck. It is a land of whales passing to and from their nurseries and feeding grounds, singing their ancient songs; where dolphins dance among the myriad islands.

Seattle is a city of dancing light and music—sparrows and bluebirds, larks and robins, and the songs of the ferry and tugboat horns and the deep, sonorous calls of big ships in the harbor. It is a city of smells—pulp from the lumber mills, pine from the forests along the water and up into the mountains, the smell of apple cider, the smell of smoked and fresh salmon, fresh as the sea. It is a city of music: lumberjacks' folk songs, fiddles from the logging camps, Irish melodies sung by young girls with long hair and guitars in bars along the waterfront on Pike Street; rock and roll on the radio and in the uptown bars; Norwegian melodies and English roundelays; the Chieftains and English music hall ditties and Broadway songs; garage bands; music playing in the renovated coffeehouses along the routes of long-forgotten trolley car lines. It is a city where the traffic whizzes by on the vast freeways and the buses, cars and trucks honk or stand patiently in lines hundreds deep for the ferry boats to Bainbridge and Vashon islands, their passengers drinking out of Starbucks coffee cups, listening to National Public Radio by the hour. It is a land of rain.

My first memory of my father is his singing. He would warm up in the morning as he showered, his voice mellifluous as the water that poured across his bare, strong back and down his sturdy, five-foot-seven frame as he stood behind the plastic shower curtain in the tiny bathroom that was shared by Mother, Daddy, and me, aged three. He would turn the taps off hard, tighten a terry cloth towel around his middle, step over the shower stall nimbly with his lovely feet, scrub his hair dry and comb it back from his face, looking in the mirror as though he could see his own reflection. Twirling his shaving brush in the round, smooth wooden bowl of soap, he would lather his face and then shave, razor in one hand, the other trailing two fingers behind as the lather disappeared to check the smoothness of his cheek. He would lean down, still singing, traces of shaving cream on his fingers, and run his fingers over my face, calling me "Dreamboat," roughing up my hair, still vocalizing, spinning a melody off with a good, clear sound.

"Cleanliness is next to godliness," he would sing, some melody conveying the words to my ears. Then he would put in his glass eyes, blue eyes that had been especially painted by hand in the factory in Colorado where he and my mother ordered them by the dozens. They arrived in little segmented boxes, like eggs. Sometimes one would slip out of his fingers, break and fly across the bathroom floor, scattering blue and white splinters of glass on white tiles, and he would curse and splash Old Spice on his face to sting the nicks from his shave. He checked his very delicate feet as he sat on the edge of the tub, to be sure a snippet of glass hadn't gone astray. He had lovely feet, so much nicer than mine, with their bunions and sprawling, wide toes; my father's feet were something beautiful to see.

Years later he caught a nasty case of athlete's foot at the mineral spa in Glenwood Springs and the doctors, after the foot powders and antibiotics had failed, treated the fungus with X-ray therapy. The X-ray got rid of the fungus all right, but in the process burned the bone of Daddy's right foot and he had to have his little toe amputated, a complicated job of removing quite a few tiny bones. This small, painful amputation took him by surprise, kept him in the hospital for a few days, put him on a cane, and threw off his balance. Those things he got over, but I think the thing that really burned him up was losing the symmetry of those lovely feet.

After Daddy shaved, he would practice the piano, running his fingers over the black and white keys, in much the manner in which he ran his fingers over the pages of the braille books when he read to us, softly, deftly. He would rehearse for his daily radio show or for the concerts he did on the road in schools in a dozen states in the Northwest and the West. I learned from my father that one must focus on making music, on reading, on living, on getting through the world. My practice time was in the afternoon, but his was in the morning, and my memory is filled with the lyric singing of "Oh, what a beautiful morning" and "Grab your coat and get your hat," and "O-o-o-o-oklahoma, where the wind comes sweeping down the plains."

"I'll take you home again, Kathleen," he would sing, striding into the kitchen to join us for breakfast, moving his hands about the table, finding the salt, finding his plate, telling my mother, when she tried to help him butter his toast or pour his juice, "I'll do it myself, Marjorie." I remember his perfect posture, his erect stride. My mother used to refer to Daddy as "your father." "You can do that only if your father says it's all right." "I'll have to ask your father." "When your father comes home, he'll hear about that." Sometimes that meant a strapping, for we were disciplined, and that was the way it was.

Daddy's shins were battered from running into sleds and wagons left unattended on the sidewalks in front of our many houses, and the inevitable curse, "Goddamn it! When will you kids learn to put your toys away?" accompanied the mounting scars. He once tried to play the guitar, but had to give it up because the strings made calluses on his fingers that made it hard for him to read braille. I remember his fingers slipping ahead on the bumpy braille pages to see what was coming next—like scanning a page with your eyes—his fingers becoming eyes, ears, senses, making up for everything. Almost everything.

The fact that my father was blind shaped my psyche at a very young age, teaching me that I was different. Other children did not have disabled fathers. Other children did not know about avoiding the pitfalls—offering too much help, offering none, walking a very thin line, having to see for my father, yet feeling at times that I was invisible because he could not see me.

But my parents thought I could do anything I put my mind to, even if it meant cutting off Holofernes's head.

I learned quickly from my father that you don't have to see to believe.

My siblings and I talk about Daddy sometimes, wondering, since he is gone, if he really *was* bigger than life, larger than imagination, just as we experienced him to be. Blind, he saw. Awkward, his grace overcame. Disciplined, he faltered, to try again. We come back to the feeling we all have, that our father was magnificent, flawed, a genius choked by his own inability to get out of the quagmire that pulled him down at times, yet flying with us, leading us with his vision, his insistence, to heights we had no idea we could even dream of.

Daddy had the philosophy that anyone could change the world simply by being a part of the solution. He was an optimist to the bone. Often he led discussions of the writing of Emerson and Mark Twain and, when he discovered him, Dylan Thomas. We discussed world politics, art, overcoming handicaps, being a good citizen, voting, putting your money where your mouth was, speaking out against violations of civil rights at all levels and how to get a good trim on the hedge or find out if your automobile mechanic was doing the job you paid him to do. Daddy talked to us about sharing our good fortune with those who were less fortunate—a New Deal philosophy was his ideological meat and potatoes and became ours.

I remember my mother, young and slim in her ankle-length tweed skirt, graceful patent leather heels and white silk blouse with a tie in a bow at the throat, the scent of Chanel No. 5 in her hair that was pinned up in a Gibson girl, kissing me on the cheek as she waited for my father, who was tying his tie, dressed in his best dark suit, smelling of aftershave and looking clean and hearty. I remember my mother playing the piano then, and reading me stories. She had a quick, constant energy, as my father did, and that I seem to have inherited from both my parents. I ran wild circles around my mother, and she regrets that she had to put a leash on me when we went to the grocery store or walked around the block, because I would be gone in an instant when her back was turned. It was the beginning of my trying to see what was around every corner and pursue every dog, cat and shadow.

My mother and father were gay and young, brash and as successful as success went in the late 1930s, a pair of idealistic people who had grown up knowing this was the greatest country in the world, the land of opportunity, the land of possibility. They had grown up in the Depression with the faith that life would always get better.

Daddy had been born on a farm in Nez Perce, Idaho, in 1911, to farming parents. His father, Frank, was a handsome, musical, magical man who looks, in his photographs, like my brother Denver. Frank Collins was an Irishman and Daddy loved and admired him so much that he considered himself entirely Irish and named his firstborn son Michael Collins. There were also Booths and Petersons in his family; his maternal grandfather, Charles Booth, had come from England to Canada in 1857, crossing a sea filled with whales and dolphins that he described in the journals he kept of the trip as covering the water to the horizon. Charles was a successful banker with a big prosperous farm. Daddy's mother, born to Charles and Laurie Booth, in Nez Perce, Idaho, loved books and dug flower beds out of the dry Idaho earth on her husband's acres and raised chickens and cows and tended her patch of vegetable garden.

At the age of four, when Daddy lost his sight completely, he decided he was not going to live down on the farm nor keep his light under the bushel. He crawled and fought and kicked and struggled his way to success, determined to get out, up, and away from his roots as fast as he possibly could. But he would remember where he came from, and the dignity of his parents and their struggle. It would inform his own.

My father's mother Ethel knew he was losing his sight slowly from birth, till he could not see the barns, nor the sky, nor the birds. He could still hear their music, and he could hear many things the rest of us could not.

Great-grandfather Booth found my father out in a field one day, clapping his hands. He asked the four-year-old what he was doing.

"I'm listening to the barn," Daddy said. He had found the radar by which he would navigate from his dark life on the farm to other shores, to the light of radio waves, where no one needed more sight than Daddy had.

My ancestors were preachers and teachers, sea captains and writers, home-makers, beekeepers, bootleggers, fiddlers and visionaries who all struggled for a better life, worked hard, and believed that theirs was the greatest country on earth. They were good people, like my great-grandfather Booth, who, after his bank was robbed by a partner, sold his prosperous farm and moved to a smaller one in order to pay back every cent to his investors. There were missionaries on my mother's side: Aunt Belle Cope and Uncle Harry Pilley went to China and hunted souls and butterflies until the Chinese Revolution sent them fleeing back to the port of Los Angeles in 1947. There were rail-road men, ranchers and Quakers, men and women who went to church and prayed for their sins.

When Daddy was seven and his brother Frank was eleven, their father Frank died. After his death, my grandmother Ethel married a man who, according to Daddy and all the other relatives I have talked to, was well-off and disliked both of Ethel's boys. Daddy was sent off to boarding school in Gooding, Idaho, a place he called the "menagerie," home to a hundred children who were disabled in some way: blind, deaf, maimed, crippled. The children bonded in their difficulties. Daddy learned to find the humor is his predicament. Once, when he was sitting under a tree eating fried chicken sent by his mother, a chum who was sighted said that the chicken, perhaps truly delicious, was also covered with green mold, provoking gales of laughter in both boys. He would tell us of the blind and deaf boy in his dormitory who howled all night, with what might have been fear and might have been habit. One night Daddy stealthily dropped water into the boy's open mouth. The puzzled boy lay in silence for what seemed a long time before he began his heart-rending call again, expressing what the others could only feel. Daddy told us of a day when the deaf children asked him to take them ice-skating. A teacher, suddenly remembering that Daddy couldn't see, chased after the delinquent children, but too late—they were already happily skating on the ice behind a joyous Charlie Collins. The same radar that had found the barn on the farm was what he used to make his way in the world.

When Daddy's brother Frank was sixteen, he, too, became blind. It is a strange coincidence since the blindness in the brothers was apparently caused by different conditions: glaucoma in Frank, mysterious infection in Daddy. Ethel and her new husband, Mac MacCready, had a child named Billy, who became, in that family of blindness, the favorite son, for his vision was perfect.

Daddy learned the piano. His teachers loved his bright, eager spirit, his quick talent, and his beautiful voice. He continued his musical studies and his industrious reading of braille books in another school in Boise, Idaho, where upon graduation from high school he was given a scholarship to the University of Idaho at Moscow.

It was at college in Moscow, Idaho, that my father truly blossomed. He became the traveling correspondent for the *Moscow Bee* in 1933, covering the World's Fair in Chicago. He and his friend Glee Melcher didn't have the money for a car, or a bus ticket, so they rode the rails to the fair—first to Minneapolis where a friend put the two short-time hobos up for a few weeks. My father must have loved doing this. He always refused to use a guide dog and insisted on going everywhere on his own, using the sound of his shoes on the pavement to tell him where he was. He could never wear sneakers, they muffled the sounds he needed to hear where he was.

Daddy also tuned pianos during that two weeks in Minnesota, making a few bucks, and then their friend John Spaulding drove Daddy and Glee down to Chicago in his Model T. My father drove while John put his hand on daddy's knee to signal him where to turn. John, who is eighty-nine and still fit as rain, said recently that Daddy did quite well driving that Model T, even learning to pass cars!

Daddy wrote the paper of the exhibits at the fair, and of working on a showboat at night, where he met John Charles Thomas, the great singer, and Joan Crawford, who was just starting her career. She would come down at night and sing along with Daddy on the old standards.

Back at the University of Idaho, Daddy was pledged to the Phi Gamma Delta fraternity, where he became something of a hero. He quickly found an audience for his music, and his ability to entertain, to read, digest, debate and generally fit in won him a crowd of bright young men and women. He was always up for antics, for a gag, and, as on the road with John Spaulding, his fraternity brother Holden Bowler put him behind the wheel of another Model T and guided him as he drove around the campus. "Driving by braille," Holden and the Figi fraternity brothers called it. Holden became another lifetime friend and my godfather.

Daddy worked terribly hard at life, struggling through it all as though he could see, as though he was like everyone else. He didn't let his blindness make him different. This was his enemy and his friend at the same time, this effort to prove he was like all the others. Because he wasn't. He was brighter and more perceptive than most people, both enormously talented and enormously sensitive. He was blind, but that wasn't his problem.

His problem was that he thought you wouldn't love him if you knew.

He told me many years later that he had intended to be a lawyer, but that the pay for making music, the money for the dance bands, was too alluring. The scholarship he had been offered at the University of Idaho law school was not enough to support him. He would have to work, and music was the only thing he really knew. He graduated cum laude and headed for Seattle, where he intended to make his mark in radio, the new media.

One of my great-great-great uncles on my mother's side, Gilbert Cope, compiled a family tree in 1861, in which he includes a moving poem. I still feel a connection with my ancestor's words.

> From the eternal shadow
> Rounding all our sun and starlight here
> Voices of our lost ones sounding
> Bid us be of heart and cheer.
> Through the silence, down the spaces
> Falling on the inward ear
> Let us draw their mantle o'er us,
> Which have fallen in our way—
> Let us do the work before us

Cheerily, bravely, while we may.
E're the long night silence cometh
And with us it is not day
Watch and pray.

My ancestors on my mother's side arrived in Tennessee in 1691 from England by way of Pennsylvania. They came with the wave of religious-freedom-seeking immigrants led by William Penn. Most were Quakers, at least for some of the years before they became Methodists. Gilbert Cope, who wrote the poem, was a poet. One of my great-great-grandmothers, Mary Ann Brown, was a quilt maker. My cousin Betty recently gave me one of Mary Ann Brown's quilts, a lovely thing of rust and violet and deep blue velvet oblongs and triangles, odd-shaped pieces of worn, delicate fabric. The embroidery of birds and flowers among the stitching is worn and the quilt smells of smoke, from some distant pipe-smoking ancestor. It is a delicate scent and reminds me, like the madeleines of Proust, of memories I did not even know I had: of my mother's family, the Copes and the Byrds, fighting on both sides of the Civil War, sometimes brother against brother; of the story I have been told of my grandmother Byrd's father taking her in a carriage to see General Ulysses S. Grant, who bowed and took off his hat to the pretty four-year-old in her frilly dress and velvet muff; of the South after the Civil War.

Mother's mother, Agnes May Cope, married Oscar Byrd in 1904. Oscar hailed from a branch of the family tree that spawned politicians, missionaries and bridge builders who had immigrated to Virginia and then Tennessee. These were English and Irish Protestants. In 1916, Oscar headed west to Utah and then Idaho, looking for work. He took a job with the railroad, leaving his wife and their three children behind in Tennessee. Agnes, who didn't intend to lose her husband, went after him and caught up with him in Nampa, Idaho, where Mother was born. When Mother was six months old, Oscar got a job with the National Lead Company and moved his family to Seattle. Growing up, Mother spent her summers on Vashon Island, riding on the ferryboats, running through the long green fields of grass by the blue sea, pulling berries from the wild, tangled blackberry bushes, growing brown in the summer sun with her siblings and her cousins.

Oscar and Agnes raised Rhode Island Reds in Seattle and had a fine garden: vegetables, apple trees, roses, lilies of the valley and blackberry bushes. I remember playing the upright black Steinway piano in my grandmother's house, watching the bluebirds nest outside the dining room window in the apple tree. I remember that Grandmother smelled of lavender bath salts and had skin as soft as butter. She was the first person I ever heard sing "Amazing Grace." She was shocked, I remember, when I brought my friend Walt Conley, a black folksinger in Denver, to dinner on Thanksgiving in 1959. But she served him graciously, recovering her composure.

Mother was the seventh of nine children. One boy died in infancy. Her oldest brother Robert was a sea captain on a freighter that ran from Seattle to Hong Kong and Singapore. Her brother Frank fell down an elevator shaft when he was fourteen; my mother has told me that she still shudders when she walks by an open-mouthed hole in the sidewalk with its steel door flipped up. Herbie lived in Los Angeles and worked for a milk company. Another brother, Shannon, was seventeen when mother was born. He joined the Merchant Marines and one of Mother's memories of Shannon is his riding his motorcycle to the house while on leave. She remembers Shannon as mysterious, a loner, elusive. He worked up in the lumber mills in Port Angeles. Later he moved down to Los Angeles when mother's sister Louise was living in Southgate. He got odd jobs, doing what he could. One week he failed to show up for dinner, didn't make contact for months, then decades. Louise and my grandmother tried and failed to locate him. One of Mother's cousins tracked him down a few years ago and was able to locate his daughter Virginia. She learned that Shannon had died in 1989, still in Southern California.

I have often wondered if, had I not been tethered to the piano, I might not have wandered off, like Shannon, lost to my own family, lost in my own dreams. I remember Shannon's daughter Virginia used to braid my hair and play with me and Phillip, Aunt Ethel's boy. They lived in Ethel's farm on

Lopez Island. When Phillip was thirteen, he was killed when the gun with which he was knocking cherries out of a tree went off. Aunt Ethel never got over Phillip's death.

Ethel had other children, but she was fragile and spent some time in an institution for depression. Mother says it was because no one understood her sister's sensitive nature. I wonder if it wasn't because of Phillip's death. I thought after Clark's death that I couldn't survive in the world without being put somewhere safe. But Ethel was a survivor, and she and Mother's other sisters, Jeanette and Louise, are all alive today.

The Byrd girls are all survivors.

In 1937 my mother was in school at the University of Washington, sharing a room with her best friend, Eline Taylor, when she met Daddy on a bus in Seattle. She noticed that he was blind and asked if she could help him down the stairs. He brushed her off, always furious that anyone would think he needed help. But he must have sensed that she was beautiful and invited her for a Coke. He told her she could hear his radio debut the following Saturday night. My mother and her best friend Eline sat down by the radio that Saturday and my mother says she started crying and fell in love when my father sang the old Buddy Green song, "Once in a While," in that lilting baritone voice of his.

Both my father and mother had high standards and personal integrity. I learned from them that the responsibility of all of us is to try to give back to the society in which we have had so much good fortune. Daddy was always doing fund-raisers. If it wasn't for the Salk vaccine, it was the Salvation Army, the poorest children in the city, as well as those less fortunate than we. He also contributed to the basket in church. He believed in tithing, and I also observed his acute sense of not taking advantage of his position, as in the time he refused to use the blind fare to which the bus driver said he was entitled. I learned from my father that it was not all right to act like a star just because you are one—and he was one. The people in the cities in which we lived respected my father and stopped him on the street to tell him how much they admired him. He greeted them all warmly, without exception. They wrote him fan letters and told him he was the greatest. It never went to his head.

For four years I was the only child. We lived in a little white shuttered house on a hill in Seattle, near my maternal grandparents. I remember sliding down the green square of front lawn on the snow that had fallen during a rare winter storm, and a Christmas when I saw Santa put my doll under the tree. I remember having a high fever when I was sick with the measles. There were a lot of Mother's family about, and lots of nights of music and drinking with Holden Bowler and his brothers, Dritch, Ned and Bruce, and sister Merideth, and my parent's other friends in Seattle. From my very earliest years I remember hearing Holden singing with Dad. Holden had a magnificent voice and sang once at Carnegie Hall. My father would play "Richard of Tauntan Deen," "Kathleen Mavourneen" and "Danny Boy." I didn't know these were folk songs, I thought they were just songs, like "How Are Things in Glocca Mora" and "My Funny Valentine." Those Figi boys sang, and they laughed, and they knew how to drink.

At home in Seattle, for the first four years of my life, I remember being loved and fussed over by my parents, my relatives and my parents' friends. Daddy's radio show ran for two years and then, when I was three, he went on the road for National School Assemblies doing concerts from Seattle to Santa Fe, from Dakota to Del Mar, California, from Cody to Death Valley. I was on the road with my parents for the first season, when Mother was doing the driving. Riding in the backseat of the Buick, which Daddy had named Claudia, I learned how to be happy and creative on the road, in the big backseat of the car, reading and singing rounds with Mommy and Daddy, making pictures and amusing myself. In a rainstorm once I told my parents that the windshield wipers said "Daddy works, Daddy works." I learned to love the feel and smell of travel, to take in a breath of the pine forests and tilt my face into the sun on a bright day in the desert, to take the moments as they came, treasure them and move on to the next. I learned from my father how to live the gypsy life, the life of a troubadour.

There is still nowhere I feel safer than in a car or a plane, watching the scenery pass, listening to music on tape, writing in my journals and reading. There is a peace, a feeling of being watched over, taken care of, yet free of any encumbrance. Traveling through the world, safe in my haven, free of worry, the trees and the rivers passing, the shadows of clouds, the chill of winter snows. Time stands still inside the windows, in my moving kingdom.

I took to the singing. I had a sense of melody, and harmony, and we always sang songs in the car, tooling along through the Rocky Mountains or over the Cascades, watching the scenery outside while my mother drove and Daddy backseat drove. He talked over the map, urged me to read aloud the Burma-Shave signs along the sides of the highway, separate signs planted a few feet apart that told a story or homily, one line on each sign, such as the following, which I made up:

> *A man may think his life is fine*
> *He scrubs his car and drinks his wine*
> *Until his wife finds someone who*
> *Knows how to stop and what to do—*
> *Get Burma-Shave!*

The messages were always a bit sexist, somehow slightly off-color, and very amusing. They were interspersed with views of trees, fields, and long narrow roads with few cars.

After my first year with my parents on the road, Daddy hired a young man named Glenn who drove him over the narrow two-lane highways to the audiences who waited for him in a dozen states. After Glenn came on board, we stayed home in Seattle and got letters from Daddy on the road when he traveled all over the Northwest and the West. He wrote to us from the wide prairies and deep forests, inns and small hotels, deserts and watering holes where he sang for his supper, and ours, at schools and colleges.

My parents had decided by the time I was four that I should study music seriously. They understood my love of melody and appreciated that I adored being trotted out on the stage at Daddy's concerts, bowing and singing a song as he accompanied me on the piano. I sang "Animal Crackers in My Soup" and "I'll Be Home for Christmas" as Daddy sat playing for me, his head nodding, his glass eyes open wide, shining out as though he were sighted, his head bobbing to the music, his dark, wavy hair shaking.

Many of my father's letters survive, written from the road first to me and my mother, then to me, my brother Michael and Mom. He would send me little bars of hotel soap with the name of the hotel stamped in the middle; miniature milk bottles in tiny racks; chunks of mica and minerals from the local regions. He typed on sheets of hotel stationery, telling us of the smell and the feel of the towns, the weather, the people. My father liked people, loved conversation he heard in the small-town diners and in gas stations and post offices. He would strike up a friendship with a long-distance operator when he was calling home on some late night from Fresno or Billings; when he got home, he would repeat the slang and the drawl of whatever local accent he had encountered, always reproducing accurately what was different in the speech, what was peculiar about the local humor. With his amazing powers of observation, he would describe the cooking, how the applesauce tasted, the roast chicken, the way the water tasted, full of minerals in Lincoln, clean and fresh as rainwater in Colorado. He would describe the smell of dust in the prairies and the smell of rain in the mountains. What sounds came through those letters: train whistles on lonely prairies, barking dogs, howling winds, rippling rivers.

En route—near Albuquerque, N.M.

Dearest Marjorie and Judy,

Claudia is doing 50 and better, and has been rolling tirelessly all day. I do not mean without tires, I mean without getting tired! . . . This highway goes on and on like a brook, broad and straight, and running west. We are among the mountains for the first time in many weeks, and have seen a few cactus plants. Glenn is feeling fine and singing "Easter Parade" over and over again. It is not hot today but I have a headache. Nothing serious . . . New Mexico, with its reasonable prices, friendly people and flat roads, is getting under my hide, in the spring at least . . .

On May 25, 1943, when I was four, my beautiful brother Michael was born. I remember my mother had been looking ill for a while. She went to the hospital and was gone for a few days and when Grandma Byrd and I went to get her, she was standing there outside the hospital with this little bundle in her arms, wrapped in a blue wool blanket with a silk lining, and she looked so very beautiful that I wondered what had happened to her. I peeked inside the blanket. Bright blue eyes just like mine looked back at me. My new brother and a new world of sharing my parents.

Daddy was on the road when Mike was born. His letters continued to arrive, now addressed to the three of us, telling of his anxiety about the possibility of taking a new job in Los Angeles. It would mean leaving his beloved Seattle.

Dear Marjorie, Judykins and Mikey,
. . . The big bad bogie of Los Angeles and my fight for life there begins
to loom. I've a world of confidence in my ability and my lucky star, but
cutthroat competition, shallowness, hard-boiled stuff, and show business
scare me . . .

Me too, Daddy.

Daddy took the new job in Los Angeles. Six weeks after Mike's birth, Mother, baby Mike and I took the train south where Daddy was staying with Aunt Louise in Southgate, near Los Angeles. A new leaf, a new start, another rung on the ladder of the dream. We moved from rainy Seattle to a white, stucco house at 11572 Mississippi Avenue in West Los Angeles, where Daddy had a contract to do a radio show every day from the NBC studios on Sunset Boulevard in Hollywood. Daddy was happy, he smiled all the time and strode around the new house with his shoulders thrown back. Life was good. He was on top of the world. When Daddy was on top of the world, so was everybody around him.

Mother missed her parents and siblings in Seattle, and I remember once she baked them an anniversary cake. Lovingly packing each layer separately, she carried the cake north on the train from Los Angeles to Seattle, along with my brother Mike, who was only a few months old, and me, about four and a half. Back home at her parents' house, she assembled the cake, all four layers, decorated with flowers and leaves that she had drawn herself in sweet, colored frosting. Across the top she had written, "Happy Silver Anniversary, Agnes and Oscar, thirty-five years."

Our little house at 11572 Mississippi Avenue had two bedrooms, but it was dark, with its white stucco walls outside, and shadowed rooms inside. Mother says she still has nightmares about having to move back to that house. There were wildcats who lived under the house and basked in the sun under the poinsetta tree. I used to try to catch them under its red blossoms and they scratched me with their sharp little claws and ran like small balls of lightning through the yard and out under the fence to our neighbors'. I wanted them to get along with Fluffy, our gray Persian. Fluffy had her kittens on my bed, the safest place to hide from Koko, the cocker spaniel. When I woke up and saw six balls of fur being washed by their mother's tongue, I told my mother that Fluffy had fallen apart. We named two of the kittens Nip and Tuck.

There was a walnut tree in the backyard and "When you cracked those babies, the flesh was sweet and snappy," my father said. The house had a red tile roof, and there were peach-colored roses blooming by the fence, the gift my brother Michael had wanted as a birthday present when he was barely walking. That rosebush was so endearing, so Michael. When we were growing up we had an intense rivalry. My status as an only child had been changed. I beat him up whenever I could, until he got too big to bully. He wore glasses and although he had braces on his legs for a year due to rickets, he gave me a run for my money. He was tough. He once cracked me over the head with a hoe when we were all out in the backyard digging up the crabgrass under the walnut tree. I ran into the house, wailing that my little brother had crowned me. Mother followed, skeptical, but seeing blood, told us we had to be friends.

When I was in my thirties I remember sitting on a ski lift in Aspen with Michael and making amends to him for being so mean when we were little. He laughed it off, but it was an important amend. We are friends and my oldest brother, a doctor of speech pathology, lives in Madison, Wisconsin. He says that the fact that he had a stutter when he was young led him to his profession. When he was growing up he played the cornet. Now he is an avid golfer. He and I talk about books and music. He turns me on to new things that I haven't heard. I admire his professional life and the way he lives his personal life. He grew up with grace and intelligence and I love and treasure him. He is married now to Kathy and has two stepchildren, Nick and Stacey, as well as a son, my nephew Matthew, who is in his late twenties. He plays golf all over the world. His goal is to play every great course. He has cats, a big fluffy Persian named Smoke, a black shorter-haired cat named Spook, and a bouncy, orange and white Persian named Gismo.

I remember skipping rope and swinging on the bars and playing jacks at the schoolyard on the blacktop playground, roller-skating and chewing Fleer's Double Bubble gum, scraping my knees on the sidewalk in spectacular falls. I remember my first friend, Catherine, a blond thin girl who lived near my school. A jacaranda bloomed across the street from our house. Its purple blossoms fell on the lawn and a fig tree grew in the yard of Mrs. Woodruff on the corner. The tree was off limits, but I climbed it and hung upside down and one day slipped and plunged to the ground from a high branch. I was afraid if my mother found out I was in that tree she would kill me. I ran home and threw myself at her feet, gasping for the breath to tell her I was dying. When I was almost five, I started piano lessons and after that, played the piano each and every day after school.

Mother became pregnant again and in December, 1946, she gave birth to my brother David. David was so laid back he would fall asleep in his high chair, his blue eyes closed and his pink cheeks flushed under his head of white-blond hair. He still is easygoing, handsome, and talented, and he works with wood and builds houses. He has a heart of gold, a love of nature, a quiet and solid personality. I would trust him with my life. He lives out in Bainbridge near my sister Holly now but is planning to move back to Colorado. Everyone in Colorado seems to know and love David. He taught skiing in Vail in the sixties and seventies and built fifty-two houses, including a huge lodge that used to be owned by Ross Perot. David is extraordinarily good at what he does and inspires confidence in all who work with him. In the Northwest, where he tools around in one of those big, marvelous trucks I will someday have, he listens to National Public Radio and plays

Bach cello suites really loud on the radio. He has become more politically informed, I am convinced, than I am.

Now, we were three, and Daddy worked to keep us in music lessons and shoes, Christmas trees and clothes. Mother worked just as hard, as she said, raising four children; me, my siblings, and my father.

My father was the first and the most powerful influence on my music, and on my personality—what I think is funny, how I cherish poetry, the things I am passionate about. What he did, what he said, the songs he sang, were all memorable. He had a vibrant, contagious love of life. He gave me the inspiration to study, to learn, to want to be the best at what I did. He taught me that there is a power in the universe that will support my intentions. He loved and supported my music, and, along with my mother, engendered in me a belief that I can be successful at anything I do. I know that, as I enter the fourth decade of a successful performing career, it is my father whom I have to thank for my optimism, my wonder at life, my continuing hope, the fact that I am surviving my son's death. He believed in people. He believed in his children. He believed in me. That was the greatest gift of all.

Before I suffered a major catastrophe, I had no way of understanding the depth to which the soul is shaken, the exterior shattered, the interior made vulnerable and raw. Perhaps this is the way the wound works: to open us up so that we can feel and experience the depths, and having gone there, climb to heights we could never imagine.

In the beginning I was in shock, but soon the shock began to wear off and I was like a creature with no skin, no protection. The slightest thing set me off into tears, emotions whirled me about like a tornado. I didn't understand just how long it was necessary to talk, to cry, to be in the pain that comes with such a loss. People sometimes tried to speed me through the grieving, uncomfortable with the feelings it brought up in them, uneasy in my presence.

Traumatic loss cannot be fixed. Each one of us must go through the process into healing. As long as we need to talk about our loss, just so long must we do it.

I pray for the courage to let this great wound heal, the strength to keep it clean by shedding my tears, rending my heart, screaming and shouting and shaking my fist at the universe, if that is what it takes. I must not be afraid to do this.

God understands our curses as well as our prayers. I must talk until words are still, until my grief is bearable and no words will suffice but "Unto You, my God, I surrender."

3

Halfway to the Sky

"Rise and shine," Daddy would call, his voice hearty, his mood buoyant. He would knock outside our bedrooms, pounding as though he would break down the doors of heaven. "Arthur, Angus, Brighteyes, Dreamboat, HolDol," naming his children in his own oblique, wondrous language. We groaned and opened our sleepy eyes, not nearly up to our father's insatiable enthusiasm for each new day. He celebrated each new day, singing at the breakfast table, getting ready for a morning at the radio station, smelling good and looking fine, shoulders back, glass eyes bright, suit fitting his trim figure to a tee. On a weekend, "Out to do chores," "Help your mother," "Get you kids on track." Mowing the lawn with his feet bare so he could feel where he had already mowed.

The next day he might be sitting in his big easy chair with the braille writer propped in his lap, his head lifting and nodding as his fingers flew over the keys, and he might have only one drink all evening, into which he had poured a jigger or two of whiskey and smashed a couple of ice cubes with the back of a sterling silver spoon. "Oh no, not another one!" my mother would lament when he got the angle wrong and turned the smooth silver hollow into a dented wreck. The "ice thing" was my father's attempt at perfect geometry. He always believed he could hit the exact spot where the curve of the spoon would make contact with the flat surface of the ice. When he succeeded, he would beam, shattered ice sprinkling into the glass and over the kitchen floor. After Daddy's death, my stepfather Robert had all Mother's silver spoons returned to their smooth, original shape.

But my father could also be drunk, morose, plunged by his demons into the darkest of places, unpredictable. He could be angry. Terrifying.

He was, when sober, insightful, intelligent, funny, witty, fun to be with, impressive. He had an admirable knowledge of the world, he knew politics and history. He read extensively in the fields of history, biography, and literature, and would smoke a pipe of Old Briar tobacco and philosophize with great passion, and great compassion.

I can see Daddy enthusiastically touching the cloth on my new party dress, feeling the cashmere on his new sweater, tapping the Old Briar tobacco down in his pipe, snapping a Diamond blue-tipped wooden match into flame with his thumbnail, puffing between sentences as he talked with my godfather Holden, or some other friend. Daddy would slap his open palm down hard on his easy chair in frustration over the mess in Indochina, the State of the Union, the treachery of Joe McCarthy. I see him laughing most heartily at his own jokes, as when he told my mother he had gone out "just to warm the car up for you, Marjorie!" after he had put the Buick through the brick wall of the garage. He would hike in the mountains on the way to Fern Lake with a walking stick, the only time I ever saw him use anything or anyone to help him get anywhere. Mother held the stick, Daddy held the other end, and thus he made his way up the mountain. I can still see him getting ready to go out with my mother for an evening, sparkling with energy and enthusiasm, radiant, adoring, celebrating, welcoming life.

Two hours later he might be shouting at mother, screaming at us, giving me an out-of-proportion-for-the-infraction whipping. Other times we would find him weeping in despair over his lost youth, his broken promises, his vanished dreams.

Over the years my father's drinking worsened. He would be perfectly fine for weeks or months, and then come home drunk one night and start chasing my brothers down the stairs to the basement to fight them, man to man. He might be charming, friendly, and then turn into a monster none of us knew.

Mother was puzzled, perhaps astonished over what, those days, no one knew enough to call a disease of the body, the spirit and the mind, the disease from which my father was suffering. She didn't leave him, although some of my parents' fights were about her threats to go. Often she took us kids to the park on early summer evenings when things got bad. She would pack us up into the car and drive away from the house, dusk falling, the light pale in the sky and, it seemed to me, holding back the tears for our parents and for us. We children would be silent as Mother drove and Claudia, our big black beautiful Buick four-door sedan, would, like a migrating bird, find its way to the park. There, Mother would buy us popcorn and sweets, pleasures that would stick bitter in our throats, pleasures that could not take away the sadness.

Other cars repeated the slow ride in the waning light, though after Claudia, Daddy gave up naming our cars. Dusk in a city park, warm air still hanging in the trees, voices of children calling, tulips on their long stems glowing red and ruby, violet and white, catching the last light of the sun, the smell of popcorn and the distant call of a wild animal, longing for his uncaged home somewhere, these still fill my heart with sadness for my mother and father, who had no idea that alcoholism, like the monster that it is, with its many faces, was loose in their home, in their lives, in the lives of their children.

Mother went to church, she sorted out the pain my father caused her, she did what she had to do. Her father, she told me later, had been an alcoholic, so she understood that the man waiting at home, lights out as evening progressed into night, stillness surrounding him, his children and wife having fled, that man was not her husband, but a stranger.

Mother drank Presbyterians, cocktails made with bourbon and ginger ale, usually becoming fondly reminiscent and sometimes very funny. She would giggle like a schoolgirl and at times would be able to laugh with Daddy. It didn't last long, but there would be interludes of lightheartedness at cocktail hour.

Daddy went further and my mother had no way of keeping up. There were times, in desperation, when she would lock up his booze. Then we would hear Daddy downstairs in the middle of the night, breaking the lock, padding around, making speeches to himself, muttering as he was pouring Jack Daniel's over ice, chuckling in amusement about his family's attempts to curb his God-given right to drink, getting his "spirits."

His behavior, when drinking, was unpredictable. He had a roving eye which, for a blind man, was quite a feat, but it got him into hot water at times since he cared not that whatever skirt he chased might be attached to a husband. And he expected my mother to forgive and accept all.

Perhaps I knew my father was ill. It was impossible not to appreciate his valiant struggle—going on fasts, going on the wagon, making pledges and promises. But nobody was talking about the gorilla. Nobody even knew there *was* a gorilla in our lives.

❧

Music gave me shelter from the pain of thinking it was my fault, that I had done something to cause what sometimes happened to my father. Music helped me make sense out of this transformation from loving, supportive, wonderful man to total stranger.

As soon as I could walk I would toddle over to the piano, reach up and poke my fingers on the keys. There is a photograph of me in my little white dress, a frilly thing; my hair is short, curly blond, my eyes as wide as saucers, with a glint in them, as I stand on my tiptoes to reach the keys on the piano in my grandmother's house. I wanted to play music practically from the time I was born. I fell in love with the piano, with all it could do for a song, for a melody.

Glorious music was everywhere in our home; it poured out of my father's voice and his piano playing; it poured out of the phonograph. Sounds of Rodgers and Hart, Rodgers and Hammerstein, the Gershwins, and Cole Porter, songs that Daddy learned from listening to the ten-inch red vinyl records that must have been expensive, but were recordings he could not afford to be without. The house was filled with the songs from *Annie Get Your Gun* and *Guys and Dolls*—"I've never been in love before, now all at once it's you, it's you forevermore"—and from *Finian's Rainbow*—"Look, look, look to the rainbow, follow the fellow who follows a dream" and *South Pacific*—"I'm gonna wash that man right out-a my hair and send him on his way."

My mother loved music too and had studied the piano when she was growing up, and once had even gone to hear Rachmaninoff play and excited me with the story of being in his presence: of the long, lank figure bent over the piano in his dark suit, of his extraordinarily long fingers, of the power of his playing. She too played sometimes when I was little, but more and more she didn't—there was too much to do, no time for Mother's music, with the children, with my father.

I remember my father getting drunk and dancing in the streets when the Second World War ended. Everyone else was drinking and dancing too, but not as much or for as long as my father. My uncle Elmer sent me a Christmas card in 1944 with Santa Claus drawn in ink, a card from the PX. It said he would explain more about why he had to be there when he came home. Elmer sustained a "golden injury" in the last months of the war and my aunt Jeanette expected him to come home from the hospital in Germany. When she received the telegram that he was dead, she didn't believe it. They came to tell her that he had unfortunately not been wounded badly enough. He had been sent back to the front and there, before the war ended, he died, leaving Jeanette a widow with two children, my cousins, Tommy and Pam.

During the years between 1945 and 1948 I walked to my school on Sawtelle Boulevard in West Los Angeles, about a mile from home. To get there I walked past Mrs. Woodruff's scary house that was dark and mysterious inside, past the fig tree in her yard, past the sweet green grass with the leaves like four-leafed clovers growing in the vacant lot on the corner, past kumquat trees in the yards of pretty pink and white stucco houses, past the homes of Spanish and Mexican and Japanese children I knew from school and played with at home. I'd buy Double Bubble chewing gum and pencils with bright pink erasers, to which I was unaccountably drawn. Sometimes I walked with Marva Dawn Pincock, our blond, pigtailed next-door neighbor who used to get into fights with my brother Mike in which they would bite each other, not so playfully. We walked past the chain-link fence that surrounded the Lark Ellen Home for Boys, a place of lost and found male children with whom I went on my first hayrack rides and had my first kisses. I don't remember the name of the first boy who kissed me, but I remember the smell of the hay and the taste of the apple cider, the pumpkins and the twirling girls in colored skirts, boys in cotton shirts and blue jeans, all of us bobbing for apples in the big oak barrel, coming up with wet faces and apples gripped in teeth that, in my case, already needed the attention of what would become a lifetime of the brotherhood of dentists.

Ours was a strict home, run on timetables of when to be "up and at 'em," as my father would say, when to do homework and when to be in bed. So I guessed, on the evening of that first kiss as I closed my eyes and my seven-year-old date said "Guess what this is?" and pecked me on the lips, that this was a forbidden fruit. Halloween witches were already flying, and kissing, which I knew could make you pregnant, was the most outrageous thing I had done so far. At eight, I knew it was a pleasure that would have its punishment. Shaking my long brown braids and batting my blue eyes and grinning, I said, "Well, I guess I know what that was, but you tell me," avoiding his lips in case he had other questions in mind.

At school my favorite teacher, Mrs. Munch, had a hive of live bees in a glass case in her office. The insects flew in and out through a hole in the window.

And always, I played the piano.

I studied piano with Mrs. Munson and took the bus from West Los Angeles to Santa Monica, and always spent my change from my bus money on candy—jawbreakers and Sugar Babies and Bazooka bubble gum and Heath bars.

From our little house at 11572 Mississippi Avenue in West Los Angeles, we would drive to Malibu beach early on a Saturday when Daddy didn't have a radio show. There was nothing at Malibu but beach then, and, it seemed to me, a million white sand dollars. The Malibu mountain range rose up above us and my father swam the surf in his shorts and we ran on the beach screaming with joy, and my mother cooked eggs and bacon in a skillet over a little fire that burned in the sand like a sparkling star. The water was very blue, and driving there and back we could look out over Los Angeles and see all the mountains with snow on the tips.

I remember picking black raspberries from a tangle of bushes that grew across the street from my best friend Maria's house. The smell of the berries was sweet and heavy. My mother would make a pie with the berries, covered by a crisp, flaky crust. Mother taught me how to bake, slicing into the mixture with two knives, moving in opposite directions, cutting the butter and flour into tiny pieces that would make a flaky, beautiful crust.

At the end of 1948 Daddy lost his job in radio in Los Angeles. He was quickly offered a new job in Denver, Colorado, as the voice of King Soopers grocery stores. His new boss, Lloyd King, was a kind of bigger-than-life CEO, and his was one of the first of the big supermarket chains.

Daddy rented us a red brick duplex in East Denver on Willow Street. Mother packed us kids into our Buick, Claudia, the steady and faithful chariot of tours and piano lessons, benefits and trips to the beach, and drove David, Michael and me from Los Angeles across the desert, up over Rabbit Ears Pass into the "Queen City of the Plains," golden capital of Colorado.

Lloyd King treated my father well, and Daddy was happy. King's friend Harold Walter Clark was the head of the agency that represented King and had offered daddy the job. Hal became daddy's first friend in Denver.

Nine years later, my son Clark would be named after Harold Walter Clark.

Hal was courting Margaret Taylor, a widow with three children. Margaret's husband, Al Taylor, had died a year or so before we arrived in Denver. There was a mystery in the air about Al, in the way people spoke in hushed tones about his death. Daddy later told me Al Taylor had killed himself in his garage, in his car, dying of carbon monoxide poisoning. For many years, no one in the Clark or Taylor families ever talked about this secret.

Suicide. A man I never knew had taken his own life. I was nine years old and this knowledge took hold of my imagination as though it were my own trouble, my own inheritance.

∽∾

My love affair with the Rockies began as soon as I set eyes on the great Rocky Mountains. On that wide, flat plain that butts up against the peaks of the Never Summer Range, Longs Peak, the President's Range, we settled in to live and worship, a mile high, our lungs improved and our sights enthralled with the beauty of the purple mountains, their magic and their majesty. I lived with the mountains in my view every day as I walked to school, looking up at their grandeur on the western horizon.

On weekends the whole family would head up the canyon to Idaho Springs or Estes Park where we would picnic by a rushing mountain stream, or a gurgling, whispering river. There would be smells of ozone and green grass, chortling water, mayflies dancing in the light above the river, Daddy stretched out on a red wool blanket eating Mother's deviled eggs. She would hard-boil them, cut them in half, scoop out the yellows, and mix them with mayonnaise and salt, pepper and paprika. They melted in your mouth. There would be potato salad with sweet pickles and fried chicken and homemade brownies for dessert and Kool-Aid in the big green Thermos. When I was older I would go ice-skating with friends from church in Evergreen; I remember skating behind a Jeep on a frozen lake, holding on to a rope, going like a bat out of hell, screaming with pleasure.

With the new start my father had been given when we moved to Denver, my parents were happy. Daddy loved his new job. My brother Michael was five, David two, and Mother was pregnant for the fourth time. On January 25, 1951, she gave birth to her third son. My father, overwhelmed with his good fortune in Colorado, named the baby Denver John.

My beloved youngest brother was always artistic. In high school he skied and read voraciously, as all my siblings did. He did some acting when he went to Mt. Herman, a prep school in the East. He decided, after being in the movie *Doc*, with Stacy Keach and Harris Yulin, that he wanted to work on the other side of the camera, and is now a director of photography. I see him often, we talk a few times a week, and I depend on Denver for a continuity that has always been there for me, since he was a little boy. We like the same kinds of things. He usually shoots for me when I am doing a television special or a video. Talented, handsome, funny and engaging, Denver is a shining light in our lives.

&

I don't know how she found the time, but my mother made all my clothes for many years. The moments we spent shopping for fabrics and buttons were incredibly precious to me. I loved the colors—blues, purples, florals—and textures. The corduroys, nubby or fine, were my favorites, for the light turned violet to silver on their surfaces, changing in every angle. We bought trims—silver rick-rack for my blue crushed cotton "squaw" dress; brightly colored buttons, white and black from seashells and carved bone and pearl; matching shimmering silk liners for hems of skirts and pants; matching threads from the rolls of color on the wall, stacked in boxes and in drawers that opened like rainbows under your eyes.

My parents worked very hard for everything they had. The work ethic was in their blood, and I was taught work would better my spirit; work would save my soul. In a way, we worshiped all week at the feet of work. We only worshiped the other God on Sundays.

"Money isn't everything," Daddy would say. There was a great deal of success in his life. When lean times came, he kept a bright optimism going, knowing he would bounce back. I knew that was the way it was supposed to be, the ebb and the flow. Daddy said the universe would provide, and it did. Sometimes feast, never famine. Always work.

We had fine food, good clothes, a lovely home, books—those were the things that counted, books and talk and music and, well, books! You talked of books and that was the coin of the realm. If you spoke of art and made music there wasn't much else you needed. My father thought great fortunes corrupted the soul.

My parents always had a few treasured, favorite possessions. My mother had a fur coat, a diamond ring. My father bought silver flatware for Mother when she had finished making a glorious tablecloth, crocheted over many years, lacy snowflakes emerging from the silver needle and white thread that flew between her fingers while Daddy read aloud to us kids before bed or we all watched *Omnibus* on the black-and-white television set on Sunday afternoons. Mother's fingers flew like the wind, working her way to her prize, the silver that would adorn her handiwork, sterling on white lace. We used both at every Sunday dinner. My mother treasured her glass bowls and Limoges plates, her collection of owls, in glass and stone and ceramic. She loved the polished wooden Buddha her cousins Harry and Belle had brought from China and her beautiful silk blouses and suits and high heels and coats in which she looked so lovely. But she didn't have hundreds of suits, and I don't think she would have wanted hundreds. One of my saddest memories is of my mother coming home one afternoon to find that, in an attempt to iron her one silk negligee, I had burned a hole in it the size of the iron. My mother didn't say anything, she didn't discipline me, but I could feel her heart crack and I felt ashamed of my error, and so sorry.

My father chose fine clothes, a few but of the very best quality. He chose carefully, feeling the fabric, knowing the cut was classic. Cashmere and wool, silk and fine cotton. He had a few carefully polished, lovingly cherished pairs of really good shoes, and ties, handkerchiefs and cuff links, and a good watch on a fine silver fob. My brother Michael has the watch now, and the fob, and I see my father's hands in his as he winds the stem tenderly. The Meerschaum pipe, too, carved and aged, in which the fire in Daddy's Old Briar tobacco smoldered softly. Catching a whiff of sweet pipe smoke can still run shivers of memory up my spine.

We were not rich, yet we had great wealth, and much that money could not buy.

❧❦

In the late forties and early fifties swimming pools were closed all over the country. It was the time of polio and parents shielded their children from all possible sources of the disease. Soon after moving to Denver I started to have what my mother referred to as "growing pains" in my left leg. I had been tested for polio the year before, when we lived in Los Angeles, taken to a clinic for the famous long needle thrust into the spine. The spinal tap, made hilarious by the film of the same name, is far from funny. The results of that first spinal tap in 1948 were negative. This time it was positive. I was nine.

I was put in the hospital for two months, the first in isolation. I could not see my mother, Daddy, or my brothers. All my mail and even my flowers were put through a sterilizing machine that turned everything black. My one and only small roommate, a baby, died one night. Suddenly there was silence where before he had been crying. He was whisked away in the night without a word.

I missed my mother terribly, and my father, but I read and drank juice in the mornings and mused as I stared out the window at a hedge where sparrows occasionally hopped and chirped and watched people walking by. I lost weight and read a lot of Jack London—*White Fang* and *The Call of the Wild*. I thought about survival, about how you had to know how to survive. I knew I could. I never thought for one instant that I would die of polio. My faith was firm.

After the first weeks of aching hips and legs before I was diagnosed, I don't remember the pain. I was given painkillers and folded within a cocoon of doctors and nurses, far from my family, free from worry, free from anything but my thoughts. I could survive with my thoughts. I learned that I liked being with myself, thinking want I wanted to think. I dreamed my mother had tied a sheet down on the ground with four stones so that it wouldn't blow away. But I liked the silence.

After the month-long isolation period was over I was much better and was transferred to a ward for another month, where I learned to walk again on crutches and to fashion things with string and colored plastic. I made slippers and place mats and was thrilled to see my parents, at last, visiting me, although I couldn't see my brothers. I came home, shaky and having slid back the grade I had skipped when we moved to Denver, and continued to regain my strength, and to heal.

When I came home I got to sleep and drink soup and be coddled by my mother, a wonderful treat. I don't know how she did that, with so much to do. I remember lying in bed with my arms around the bunch of flowers Mother and Daddy had given me—anemones, purple, pink and red—and they became my favorite flowers next to lilies of the valley. The flowers and the languid mornings in bed and the tender loving care from my mother brought a respite from playing the piano for a few more weeks.

In those weeks, I remember my friend Wilma Zimmerman and I going down to the river. In the winter, we had stepped back and forth across the patches of melting snow, our pants legs wet in the freezing water. Now, we explored the river's path out to the edges of East Denver and wandered too far, usually, getting back late, risking a spanking, a warning, a scolding, but my mother was treating me gingerly. I took full advantage of the lenience the polio had given me. I always wanted to explore, go further than was safe or advisable. Wilma was a daring friend, and my mother, who was still worried about my illness, told me I should be careful. Wilma did things I wasn't supposed to do—she walked on narrow ridges above the river, poked holes in thin ice, ran across the highway to beat the traffic. All the things I wanted to do, I did when I was with her.

Sometimes, though, I was haunted by fears and apprehensions. The pain of an animal dead in the street or the death of someone I had known, my great-grandmother or, later, the death of my godfather Holden's son, who was killed in a hunting accident, all seemed to me unbelievably cruel and unnatural, not the workings of a just God, if there was a God. I knew there must be, for there was music. But the disparity between what should happen and what did happen was too great. I took my pain to the piano. I put my sorrow into the music. And my joy. For there was much joy, as well. I knew somehow that the contrast between the pain and the joy were valuable, impenetrable, vital. I knew I had to experience them all.

I sang easily and naturally. As far back as I can remember, when a song claimed my soul, like "Where or When," the lyric seemed to become soldered to my flesh, like some tattoo, some lifelong wound.

At all my family's houses, there was music underneath everything. In Seattle and Los Angeles and Denver, on Mississippi Avenue in West Los Angeles; behind the white lace curtains my mother washed and pressed carefully crisp; before and after the trips we took to Malibu in Claudia the Buick for our breakfasts on the beach on Saturdays; between the meals we shared together; while playing braille Scrabble so my father beat us all except when he let us win; beneath all this simple life there was a magical world happening. The hunting of the song was what earned the bread on our table and put the shoes on our feet, paid for my piano lessons and Michael's cornet lessons and skates and bikes and sleds. It put the gas in Claudia the Buick. My father sought for great songs, hunting them as I would later, searching them out, shaping their nakedness around his beautiful baritone voice, singing them in the shower, showering his radio audience with their beauty. I learned from a master hunter of songs.

My parents wanted me to have good teachers. My first teacher gave me the rudiments, but she was old and soon retired. Next was Mrs. Munson in Brentwood, who used to give presents of books about opera and the lives of composers to her students when they performed particularly well. I was given a book I couldn't wait to tell my parents about. It was, I said, the story of the "Battered Bride." My parents hid their smiles and corrected me. The book, they said, was called *The Bartered Bride*. Battered, bartered, it was all the same to me. Mrs. Munson would from time to time invite me to come and listen to one of her "older" students practice. I usually found this boring, but at the same time I felt special to be singled out to sit at the feet of a wunderkind whipping out scales and exercises at lightning speed, working on "La Campanella," or bringing the slow movement of a piano concerto into smooth, easy performance. Mrs. Munson was always telling me it was not the speed that was important, but the concentration.

The repertoire I played at a young age consisted of Schubert sonatas and Mendelssohn pieces, fugues and waltzes by Chopin, and Czerny pieces to emphasize technique. I always spent a good portion of my practice session doing scales and exercises, the metronome keeping me in pace. I loved the big chorded passages in Chopin, the way my fingers could fly over the keys, making the music. For me, playing has always been deeply satisfying, gratifying. Melody seems to soak up all the bitterness and pain of the world.

Sometimes when I practiced scales I put a book on the shelf of the piano and played while I read *The Count of Monte Cristo* or a Nancy Drew mystery.

ꗺꗺ

While I was in the hospital Daddy had found me a new teacher, Dr. Antonia Brico. She was to move into our lives with the force of a hurricane.

My first meeting with the intimidating Brico, a large, fierce-looking woman with a European demeanor, was at Brico's studio in downtown

Denver, a magnificent structure carved out of the quarries in Marble, Colorado. The massive walls were covered with climbing ivy and inside the wooden carved door of Brico's studio stood a pair of matched nine-foot Steinway grand pianos, harp to harp against one end of the room, flanked by photographs, statues and death masks of Sibelius, Beethoven and Bach. A Persian carpet stretched from the pianos to the end of the room.

I appeared that first day with my crumpled music under my arm, my oxfords scuffed, my pigtails unkempt from a day in school. Between my parents, I entered the doors of Brico's awesome studio and passed through the photograph-filled room to sit in front of the keyboard of one of the Steinways. I adjusted the height, put my fingers on the keys and played for Antonia. From that time, my music merged with hers and I adored at the feet of a woman who was a true pioneer, a true champion, a true warrior.

Dr. Brico was not impressed with my technique, but she told me and my parents that if I cooperated, she could change all that. I quickly found a way to please my new master, working desperately hard to become what she told me I could become. Brico was a slave driver. I would come to my lessons sometimes shivering in fear, for she was a demanding teacher.

On Saturday mornings during my lessons the studio would be filled with the scent of grapefruit and pungent tea. Brico would take out her long pair of scissors and clip my nails. Then I would play Chopin while Brico spooned ruby-colored segments out of a round of citrus, carrying them to her lips while listening and muttering, between bites, about my performance. Among the statues and death masks, there were photographs of singers and instrumentalists signed "To Antonia, with love." Sometimes if I had a late lesson on Saturday I would stay for lunches where, over sliced chicken and yogurt and cucumber salad and apple tarts, she and I and one of her faithful cooks and companions, Mrs. Page in the early years, or Elizabeth Jans later, would listen to the broadcasts of the Metropolitan Opera from New York. I sang in the choruses of Brico's productions of *Don Giovanni, Eugene Onegin* and *Fidelio*. Once, when Arturo Toscanini came to conduct in Denver, Brico brought me to the rehearsal. She and Toscanini were friends and he had called her to be his ears and eyes with the Denver Symphony. I followed Toscanini around, carrying his music, and listening to the two conductors laugh and speak together in German. It was heady, it was exciting to be an aspiring pianist in the company of the great conductor. I was practicing the Mozart piano concerto that I would later play with Dr. Brico's orchestra, and Toscanini encouraged me, saying I would do well.

After my lessons and sometimes on Saturdays I would pour over the five-inch-thick books of clippings of reviews and articles, photographs and pictures from newspapers from all over the world that contained the story of Brico's life. From the headlines and the articles, I knew my teacher was a star, an internationally known conductor whose career had ended here in Denver, teaching me. I wondered how that miraculous event had occurred, giving me the gift of her genius. I learned her amazing story.

Brico was born in Rotterdam in 1903. Her mother was from Amsterdam and at the age of nineteen had had a fling with an Italian sailor. After the sailor departed the next morning, never to return, her mother found herself pregnant. Brico's grandfather found out about the pregnancy and threw his pregnant daughter out of the house, telling her never to come back. Antonia's mother traveled to Rotterdam, where she got a job as a housemaid. When the baby was born her mother put her into a convent because she couldn't afford to raise her. After three years, she found a foster home for the baby girl. It was then that Antonia's grandfather became gravely ill and was told he was dying. He sent for his daughter and granddaughter in order make his peace on his deathbed. But it was too late for little Antonia. Her foster father, a baker, had heard of the great earthquake in San Francisco. He thought the need for his services would make his fortune. By the time of the reconciliation of her grandfather and her mother, little Antonia was sailing for San Francisco.

Brico's foster parents shouted at and physically and emotionally abused her. Antonia's foster father drank and her mother believed in mystics and psychics. She would take Antonia to séances and the psychics would invariably see, as they gazed at little Antonia, something musical.

"They would see Liszt, or Beethoven standing behind me," Antonia told me. Thereafter, the foster mother made sure that little Antonia had music lessons, and the child found her solace in the piano, quickly getting scholarships and attention in school. Not really knowing the truth, she told everyone who would listen that she believed she was not her parents' child, and couldn't believe true parents would treat a child in the way she was treated.

At thirteen Antonia went to live with a friend from school whose parents saw the brutality in the family and gave Brico a home. Months went by, and Brico refused her foster mother's pleas to come home. One day her stepfather, sober for a change, gave her the birth certificate from Rotterdam, telling who Brico's real parents were. Brico was confirmed in all her fears. But at least she knew where she had come from, and that she had a family in Holland, although it would be many years until she was reunited with them.

Brico first began to yearn for a career as a conductor when she went to the park in San Francisco, where she saw Karl Muck conduct. "What he does with a wand, a little stick!" she said. She burned with a sudden desire. She, too, would be a conductor. It was the one thing she knew she wanted in life. She worked as an usher at the performances where Muck and others conducted, thereby getting a ticket free. She would take her portable camp stool, and after seating the paying audience, Brico would set up the camp stool firmly in the middle of the aisle at the foot of the stage, score in hand, and follow the music through the entire performance.

Karl Muck, introduced to Brico at a university gathering, was amused to see in person the "camp stool girl," as he fondly called her. Her reputation for devotion to music accompanied Muck to New York, where he told other musicians who were headed for San Francisco that there was this most gifted musician who always brought her camp stool to the concerts. He intervened with the famous pianist Stojovsky, who arranged for Brico's scholarship at Juilliard after her graduation with honors from the University of California at

Berkeley. But both men, and everyone else, male and female, refused to give Brico any encouragement in her pursuit of becoming a conductor. Karl Muck said privately that Brico's dream of conducting was crazy and that to even imagine such a thing, for a woman, was impossible.

In New York Brico spent hours practicing the piano at the Steinway Piano Showroom on 57th Street. The manager, a sympathetic friend, would let her in at odd hours of the day and night, because Stojovsky did not approve of all the hours of practicing Antonia thought she needed and would not let her use the piano in his home. It was during those years, encouraged by a friend in New York, that Brico discovered her family in Holland. They had all assumed she was dead, and were overjoyed to find her. She went to Holland for a tearful, happy reunion.

In 1923, despite the conviction of everyone that women could not become conductors, Brico was chosen as one of four American music majors to study conducting in Germany at the Academy of Music. Following her graduation in 1929, she made her debut conducting the Berlin Philharmonic to rave reviews in the *Paris Match* and the German papers and she came home to a royal welcome. "Cinderella Returns!" the papers in the United States proclaimed. The Los Angeles and San Francisco symphonies fought to be the first to showcase her with their orchestras; she went on to conduct in New York, Chicago, Boston and other cities. Europe flooded her with invitations. Press clippings began to mount, rave reviews flew into her thick press books. Sibelius invited her to conduct his orchestra and his compositions in Helsinki, Finland. They became close friends and for twenty years she conducted in Finland and in other European cities, at the request of the composer.

The girl they once called "Cinderella" was now my teacher.

In spite of her successes, she told me of the terrible prejudice she found in conducting circles, including Denver, where she had moved when offered the possibility of the position of conductor. When she arrived from

New York with her pianos and her statues, the orchestra had reconsidered, and hired a man

"In Denver," Brico told me, "there is a club called the Cactus Club, a very exclusive male club. The orchestra president said to me, after he had broken his promise of making me the Denver Symphony's conductor, "Why, we couldn't have a woman conductor. She couldn't be a member of the Cactus Club!'"

In the next thirty years, during the entire time of his tenure as conductor of the Denver Symphony, Saul Caston, the man who got the job, did not once extend an invitation to Brico to guest conduct the Denver Symphony.

Brico started her own orchestra, the Denver Businessmen's Symphony. It was a first-rate orchestra. With this instrument, Brico performed many concerts every year and made a solid reputation in Denver for her operas and symphonic performances of Beethoven, Mahler, Sibelius, and the other great composers.

All during the years I studied with Brico and for many years after, I kept the riveting and inspiring story of her life alive in my heart. In 1972 I produced and co-directed, with Jill Godmilow, a documentary film about Brico's life. When it was released, *Antonia: A Portrait of the Woman* had a tremendous and positive impact on Brico, bringing her many new opportunities to conduct in the United States and Europe. The film was nominated for an Academy Award and won the Christopher Award, as well as being named a top-ten movie of the year by Tim Cox in *Time* magazine. Brico was back on top, conducting all over the world. She returned to New York for Mostly Mozart, made a recording for Columbia Records, and was applauded, reviewed, appreciated and celebrated not only for what she had done as a conductor, but for what she had achieved as a woman.

❧❧❧

Not long after I started taking lessons from Brico and began to play complicated and difficult pieces by Chopin and Debussy, she convinced my parents I needed a grand piano instead of our little upright Mason & Hamlin (a good piano, by the way, just not a grand). That was when the Baldwin came into our Willow Street living room, almost dwarfing it. Playing it was the difference between driving a bicycle and getting behind the wheel of a Cadillac. It was so very wonderful, my heart leaped out to hear what my hands could do on that instrument.

I sang in the choirs in school and church. But the pristine world where my teacher, the pioneer conductor and pianist, lived, was extremely narrow. It could not embrace Rodgers and Hart, only Beethoven and Bach and Rachmaninoff, whose statues glared down, it seemed to me, from marble pedestals at my eleven-year-old pigtailed person with my scruffy oxfords. I played Mozart as though they knew things I didn't and suspected that I was not truly "serious" about my classical music. I yearned to be up to it. Brico had decided I had what it took and she put all her efforts, as she constantly reminded me for the next few years, into bringing all of my latent potential to the surface.

But no matter how appealing the melodies, no matter how demanding the fingering, the technical aspects, the loveliness of the sonatas, and the fugues, I was still playing music without words. I know that I needed to talk, to tell stories.

There was a lot to do in our house besides practice. I changed diapers, did dishes and walked and bottle-fed and lullabyed my siblings—the best of children: Michael was seven, David four, Denver John a few months old. Between baby-sitting and ironing and going to school, I played the piano, practicing every day after school. Michael was taking cornet lessons by that time, and so the house was filled with music—my father was playing Irving Berlin and Rodgers and Hart while my brother Mike was playing Schumann trumpet solos and I was whirling through Czerny and Chopin. After school every day, and on Saturdays and Sundays, I was at the piano, usually for several hours. I asked my mother recently whether she had to get after me to practice, and she told me that I went to the piano naturally, without being forced, but she always reminded me to wash my hands before I played!

Daddy and I had to share the piano and I think now of how hard that must have been. He might have been eager to sit down when he came home from work in the afternoon and just noodle, or write his own songs, which were very good. But there was his daughter, hogging the instrument. He was a musician and the breadwinner, but he didn't ever have a room of his own. I never heard him complain, but now, looking back, it seems to me it was a very great price for him to pay.

Daddy had many famous guests on his radio show, among them Bob Hope, Red Skelton and George Shearing, who was also blind. George and my father hit it off and George came to dinner a few times when he was in Denver. The first time, my mother prepared lamb with garlic. It turned out George was allergic to garlic, but he ate salad and vegetables and Mother's delicious pie, and seemed quite contented. After dinner, he played me the lush "Laura," with its elongated ninths and intricately woven jazz chords. I had already begun to noodle, to play simply for my own amusement, which, many years later, would lead me to the composition of songs. George Shearing inspired me, and his chords were new and exciting.

Brico couldn't tolerate my playing this kind of jazz. She said it would ruin me to play in this way, nosing around the piano, finding melodies, discovering myself. She never encouraged me to play by ear (which was what my father did all his life and what I would come to discover was my real strength). Her students were also discouraged from playing or listening to anything that deviated from the classical forms.

Funny. When my granddaughter first started playing the piano, I was amazed to find the instruction in her practice book to "make up your own songs." My God, that was sacrilege to Brico. I could have wept, for a moment, over what I had missed growing up! Nevertheless, I played every day, without fail, even when I wasn't in reach of a piano.

In the spring of 1951 when I was eleven, Brico decided I should start working on the Mozart two-piano concerto. She wanted me to play it with another young pianist, Danno Guerrero. We would play together, with her orchestra. However, when she heard that I was going to be away from the piano for two weeks on a trip to Idaho to see my great-grandparents, she nearly had hysterics and arranged for my parents to buy me a cardboard piano keyboard on which I could memorize the Mozart concerto. She admonished me to practice and memorize, as though I were home playing my own piano.

This trip was like something out of *The Wizard of Oz*. I had a parakeet I called Merry Christmas, Chris for short, because I got him on Christmas morning, and Daddy had hung a square cage on upholstery hooks to the roof of the Buick, securing the little bird's traveling home in the soft cloth. The blue parakeet sang happily in his cage, said "My name is Chris," "Drop dead, Koko," and "Birds can't talk," jumping about, whistling on the mountain passes to the squeal of Claudia's tires, singing all the way to Idaho, while my brothers cried or slept or laughed. I sat with the keyboard spread out over all our knees in the backseat, memorizing Mozart. Mother drove and Daddy did his usual passenger-seat driving, commenting on the terrain after Mother described it, singing songs, smoking his pipe, the smell of Old Briar tobacco drifting out of the windows as we tooled over Berthoud Pass, out onto Highway 61, and north to the Idaho hills. Denver John was a few months old and Daddy would often hold him in his arms.

It was on that trip that I saw my great-grandfather Booth for the last time. Daddy adored his grandparents, Charles and Laurie Booth, and we visited them on their farm in Idaho a few times. There is a home movie from 1939 made by one of Daddy's cousins, of Mother, in her slender skirt with her hair piled up in curls; Daddy in a suit, thin and young, standing next to Great-grandpa Charlie Booth, his pipe between his teeth; and Great-grandma Laurie Booth in her flowered dress and low-heeled shoes with glasses on her nose. In this early home movie Daddy is holding me in his arms, I in my white dress, about seven months old.

Great-grandfather Booth had a hundred smooth silver dollars in a blue velvet pouch that he would let me play with, pouring them out on the flowered Oriental carpet, rolling them through my fingers, studying the figures and words coined on their shiny surfaces. They were magical, those silver dollars. Great-grandpa also had a gambling machine, a miniature of the ones in the casinos in Las Vegas. When you pulled the handle, pictures of green grapes and red flowers, hearts, oranges, blue birds and red roses rolled till they stopped. I was sure real oranges and roses would appear from somewhere if I won. "Win or lose, place your bets," he'd say and we'd bet. Then he would slip the silver dollars back into the velvet pouch, smoothing his fingers lovingly over the faces.

Great-grandmother Laurie had died after a stroke and long years as an invalid. On that last visit he had placed a picture of Pier Angeli from the cover of *Time* magazine on the pillow where Great-grandmother Laurie's head had rested all those years when she was paralyzed. He said Pier reminded him of his wife when she was young.

The day we left Idaho, I said good-bye to this fine, loving old man, knowing I would never see him again. He was frail, and thin, yet full of grace and wonder at life. His bees still thrived, his farm still flourished. He waved at me as we drove off, as the little blue parakeet sang in his cage in the ceiling of the Buick and the figure of Charlie Booth disappeared in the distance.

❧

By the time we got home from this trip, I had indeed finished memorizing the Mozart and, the following year, Danno and I, as promised, played the two-piano concerto. On a snowy night in February 1953, I put on my white organdy dress and my black patent leather shoes and played Mozart. Outside of Phipps Auditorium and all through Denver and the Rockies, the worst blizzard in ten years howled. When we finished playing my father was yelling bravo and clapping like mad and it didn't matter much that the audience was tiny because of the storm. I had done it. I felt as though I had climbed a great mountain.

After my debut, I continued to sing in Brico's opera productions with the Denver Businessmen's Symphony. I went to master classes, swinging my brown oxfords and trying to absorb the meaning of Beethoven, impressed with the information that the great composer had been deaf. Brico, with her scowl or her grand, smiling, European approval, spoke of technique, devotion, timing, determination. In my lessons she constantly told me I didn't practice enough, I wasn't devoted enough, but she believed in me anyway. She knew I felt passion for Chopin and Debussy. I memorized the Rachmaninoff Second Piano Concerto. I wanted to play these compositions not only for my teacher, whom I adored, but also for myself. They were breathtakingly beautiful and it was thrilling to play them.

It was not that Brico was cruel, exactly; yet she made me suffer, thrusting upon me her longing that I *be* better, and *do* better, knowing I could, and telling me I should. She used a kind of emotional blackmail on me. She was so wonderfully joyous when I practiced constantly and faithfully and came up to her standards, telling me how proud she was of me and how I had proven she was right, that I could be great, she knew I could, if I would only keep my nose to the grindstone. When I didn't live up to her expectations, there were many tears. I can remember so many times leaving the studio with my shoulders drooping, my spirit crushed, a deep depression overlaying the brightness of a summer day in Denver. Everyone else seemed so happy, so untroubled. Something was being demanded of me that I couldn't accomplish. I was often miserable. I determined, of course, to do better, to do better for her. For me, but especially for her.

When I was fourteen we moved, Baldwin piano and all, to a stucco, whitewashed house on Oneida Street with a wide, almost Spanish porch where I would stand in the cool Colorado mornings, gazing at the Russian olive tree that grew in the side garden, waiting for my favorite male high school friend, the tall, handsome, blond Randy Robinson, to pick me up in his yellow Jeep to drive me to East High School. I was learning to smoke cigarettes and play the guitar and date boys. I also fell in love with the movies, that magical world on a Saturday night, and I went to see *Orpheus* and *Beauty and the Beast* with John Gilbert, a platonic friend who was the son of the Unitarian minister in town. I also went to the movies with Dave Larson, my first real "swain," as my father called the boys who took me out. We would neck passionately in the last row of the theater and I would come home sweaty and guilty and slip up the stairs to my room, past my sleeping parents.

My mother was pregnant again.

Our next house, on the corner of Emerson and Marion streets in East Denver, was a one-story, brick, five-bedroom structure, with a basement filled with skis and ice skates, rakes and bicycles, bunk beds and a freezer full of the fruits and vegetables my mother had gone to Durango in the autumn to pick and brought back to Denver to cook and freeze. Daddy was doing his radio shows every day as well as selling insurance. It was a good choice, for he knew everyone in town. Ironically, Daddy died with no life insurance.

Mother cooked and cleaned for Daddy and my three brothers, Michael, Denver, and David. Mother held down a good job at Neusteter's selling women's clothing. At night she cooked splendid meals. Smells of garlic, roast beef, steamed dumplings and chicken, fresh baked bread, apple and lemon meringue pies and crisp bacon constantly filled our kitchen. My mother was a wonderful cook who taught me the magic incantation, "First you take an onion."

❦

By the time I was fourteen I had spent ten of my fourteen years preparing to have a career as a concert pianist. I was a perfectionist, as my father was. He expected everything to be just so, he wanted us to be good, to be successful, and he told all of us children so. The perfectionism that drives me is something I know I inherited from my father.

I was in the middle of learning a piece by Liszt, a whirlwind of a piano piece called "La Campanella," filled with twirls that must be performed at lightening speed, dizzying eighth-notes in vibrating clusters, floods of arpeggios that dazzled the listener and threatened to overwhelm the fingers. I had memorized all of the piece. I would practice slowly, my father hovering, listening, fascinated, impressed, and making his own plans. He began to hint, then to insist, then to command, that I get the piece ready for an appearance he was making at the Denver Coliseum, a very special appearance at which he intended to make his little Judy the highlight of the evening. I begged off, saying the Liszt was not ready, not up to speed, that it would be weeks before I could put all the black and white notes into any semblance of one piece, put any real class or feeling into the music, that I would have to practice for many weeks to do this. He refused, he insisted, I rebelled, I cried, I fought.

I didn't want to disappoint my father. He had had many disappointments, including waking up one day when he was four, living on the farm in Idaho, and realizing he could no longer see the color of the sky, the color of the wagon, the color of the wind. For that, somehow, I believe I also felt responsible, as well as for Daddy's drinking. I collapsed into depression. The dark folded over my soul and the night breathed monstrous suggestions into my ears.

On the next quiet day in my family's house on a sunny afternoon while I was ironing clothes, when everyone for some reason was away, I took a hundred aspirin and thought about my funeral, and how miserable my family would be.

I wept, and ironed, and took more aspirin, and wept and ironed some more. Soon my mood began to change from remorse and resignation to the distinct sensation that I was going to vomit. I began to be frightened, not of death, but of throwing up.

I called my best friend Marcia's mother, whose husband was a doctor. Mrs. Pinto told me to put my finger down my throat and throw up, and that she would send Sherman over as soon as he came home.

I did as I had been told and was lying with a cold wash rag on my face when Dr. Pinto arrived. My mother came home, took one look at me and, after watching me retch over the toilet bowl, put me right to bed. Dr. Pinto said I would live. Like many doctors, he didn't ask me any questions that counted. Like many patients, I didn't offer any explanations. My mother suspected that I had wanted attention, and she was right. She had a drama on her hands every day of her life, with four, and soon, five children to raise, with all the dreams of her own that had been shelved or shattered, as well as with the chaos of our house. She didn't have time for this. But I *had* wanted everyone to listen, to know what I was going through. I didn't realize, and neither did anyone else, that I was at the beginning of emotional problems that would take years to heal.

And I *did* get a certain attention to my needs.

Daddy wrote me a letter the next day in which he confessed to demanding too much of his children. My parents didn't send me to a psychologist. That wasn't the thing to do in 1954. You shoved your apprehensions beneath a quilt of beautiful colors and went on with your lives. There were things we didn't talk of, and this was one of these things, best left to sort itself out. It would, I am sure they thought. Everything did, after all.

On December 23, 1953, my beloved sister, Holly Ann, was born. Her entrance into our lives seemed to make everyone happier. Holly Ann was proof that there was a divine spirit in our lives. I was fourteen years older than she, but she is my friend, and has been through all we have been through. I am blessed.

Holly and I are very close and I see her a number of times a year. I speak to her on the phone as many times a week as possible with our schedules and see her as often as I can. Holly is an artist in everything she touches. Her paintings are rich and wondrous, her piquecette work—polished stones and sea glass embedded in teapots and mirrors, tables and tiles—is uniquely beautiful. Everything she does is filled with a sense of color and light.

In high school, my girlfriends Marcia and Carol and I formed the "Little Reds," our first dramatic effort being to set the story of Little Red Riding Hood to dance and music. I narrated the story sitting at the piano, playing the themes as my friends danced out the drama. Marcia was Little Red Riding Hood, Carol was the wolf, and Susan and Peggy took parts as the soon-to-be-devoured grandmother and the heroic woodchopper. I played the piano, making up the themes for the characters, and telling the story. We were a hit and performed *Little Red Riding Hood* all over Denver for months.

By that time I was breaking Brico's rules regularly. All along I had been singing music that my father sang on the radio, sometimes going on the radio with him to perform "My Funny Valentine" and "Dear Hearts and Gentle People." After that summer I spent a few months singing with a local musician named Jack Blue who had a dance band that played for parties at the Air Force base, the Denver Country Club and the Brown Palace Hotel. Dressed in a fluffy dress like the ones worn by Dorothy Collins on *Your Hit Parade,* I sang "Blue Moon," "Funny Valentine," "They Can't Take That Away from Me," and George Shearing's "Laura." That wonderful job ended when they found out I was too young to sing in bars.

On Friday nights, my first flame, Dave Larson, and I were dancing cheek to cheek to "Earth Angel" and "Rock Around the Clock." It was during that winter I heard "Barbara Allan," sung by Jo Stafford. The song was to change my life. I began to discover folk music and realized that some of Daddy's old Irish ballads like "The Kerry Dancer" and "When Irish Eyes Are Smiling" were also folk songs. One afternoon I heard "The Gypsy Rover" on the soundtrack of a movie called *The Bold Black Knight.* I got the record and learned the song and called Carol and Marcia and sang it to them. They choreographed the story, that of a young princess who leaves her father's castle to run off with a romantic, young gypsy rover, who turns out to be a prince in his own right. I began to learn as many folk songs as I could from recordings, from other singers. My father rented me a banged-up National guitar to see if I was really serious, and after I started to play songs and work on finding my way on the guitar, he bought me my own. I was on a new path, singing songs that spoke to my soul, singing melodies that moved me, stirred me, spoke to that lonely pianist who had been spending her afternoons practicing the piano.

Brico was furious. I had finished memorizing the Rachmaninoff Second Piano Concerto and Brico told me that as soon as I was ready, she wanted me to perform it with her orchestra. I loved that piece and wanted more than anything to play it with the orchestra: the big, lush chords, the runs, the sweet second movement with its melodic central theme. The music of Rachmaninoff called me, but the call of folk music was stronger. I knew I could not do both, and I told her I was not going to continue with my lessons.

We were both upset. The scene at Brico's studio was tearful and extremely hard. I left Brico behind, with regrets that still haunt my dreams, but with great joy as well. I knew I had found the music I loved. It wasn't Daddy's music, those lush and rich songs from the Broadway theater, and it wasn't Brico's, with those cold marble statures staring down at my drooping shoulders. It was something of my own.

❧

After my singing profession had become successful, with many recordings to my credit, Brico attended one of my sold-out concerts at Boettcher Hall in

Denver. After the concert we embraced backstage. She took both my hands in hers and looked wistfully at my fingers.

"Little Judy," she said, "you really could have gone places."

Years later, as I was making the movie about the life of my teacher, I discovered that she had made her living in college playing jazz, ragtime and popular songs, sitting in the window of a music store in Berkeley, California. At the end of a week of intense and emotion-filled interviews in her living room, with the marble faces of the composers staring down in disbelief and horror, a sheepish Dr. Brico played a few riffs of "Whispering," just as honky-tonk, down-and-dirty as you please. To me it was the ultimate victory, tinged with the greatest sadness. If I had only known that contrast was part of her personality when I was a sad-eyed student! But there are things we are not meant to learn until we learn them.

The last time I saw Dr. Brico she was in a nursing home in Denver, Colorado, called Bella Vita, out on Highway 25, far from her beloved Helsinki, her haunts of Berkeley and Salzburg, her beloved home in the old brownstone in downtown Denver. She was very ill, but took my hand in hers and gave me a glimmering, weak smile.

"Have you clipped the nails, little Judy?" she asked, studying my fingers with her hands. Across the room from her bed was a large framed photograph of Yogananda, her guru and friend, whose dark eyes glowed in the soft light of the room. I had learned it was Yogananda who helped Brico get to conducting school in Germany and told her she could do anything she put her mind to. She became a lifetime devotee of the Indian teacher and told me she had found him in New York just in time, when she was drinking and spiritually lost.

Elizabeth Jans, Brico's faithful companion, cook, housekeeper and friend, told me Brico had been waiting to say good-bye to her friends, who were coming from all over Europe and the continent to have one final loving moment with their great teacher.

Her last words to me were, "You must practice, little Judy, you must always practice!"

Thanks to my father's friendship with an eccentric entertainer called "Lingo the Drifter," who had moved to Denver in the early fifties with no last name and a backpack full of songs, I learned more songs and met more local folk singers. Lingo would come to the house and he and my father soon became close drinking and musical buddies. I started learning Woody Guthrie and Pete Seeger songs.

Lingo had come to Colorado in 1953. He was single, and mysterious. He wore a felt cowboy hat and dressed in buckskin and Levi's, and he carried an old beat-up guitar around his shoulder on a worn-out string. He seemed to know every folk song there was and started the folklore society in Denver in 1953. He had a radio show on a Denver station and became a regular at our house, stopping by for bull sessions, good Sunday dinners, whiskey, Old Briar tobacco, and conversations with my father and with me, the budding folk singer. He was extremely well-read. Daddy convinced Lingo to go on the game shows in Los Angeles, and one day we tuned in to listen to his guest spot on a Hollywood quiz show. When Lingo started answering questions, my father slapped his hand on the chair in which he was sitting and said, "Goddammit, Marjorie, he doesn't know the answer to that! This show's got to be rigged!" Lingo took the money he made on the quiz shows and bought some land up on Lookout Mountain. He built a cabin and hosted the Saturday night folk parties to which all of the aspiring and fortunate singers in Denver hoped to be invited: home brew, borscht, and good old music, long nights singing to the stars, coming home at dawn.

Years later in Chicago when I did his radio show, Studs Terkel told me Lingo's name was Paul something and that he had lived in Chicago up until the time his child and wife were killed in an automobile accident, at which time Paul headed for the West, becoming Lingo the Drifter. I learned "Maid of Constant Sorrow" from Lingo, certainly "The Lavender Cowboy," and possibly "The Bonnie Boy Is Young." He knew all the songs, and if he didn't, he could find you somebody who did.

I did baby-sitting, sold Christmas wreaths, and, at Brico's request, was still teaching a few piano students. One of them, Hadley Taylor, was the child of Margaret Taylor, who had married Hal Clark shortly after we moved to Denver. Hadley had two older brothers. At our lessons at her house in East Denver we would giggle and gossip about the possibility of my meeting Gary or Peter. The long-schemed plan was that Peter would drop by my house one night on his drive to school at the University of Colorado to "return" a book I had left at Hadley's. When Peter visited me briefly that first night, I was in a robe with my hair in a towel. We spoke only three or four words, but I thought him appealing. A month or so later, Hadley got me a job at Sportsland Valley Guest Ranch on the other side of Berthoud Pass, where the owners needed help. Peter volunteered to drive me the two hours up over the pass and to the valley near the Winter Park ski area.

Peter was two years older than I, with sandy brown hair and blue eyes and a tall, lanky figure. He had a good sense of humor. I liked him immediately. He was comfortable and easy and smart. He loved books and poetry and wanted to teach English literature and study Blake. His intelligence attracted me almost as much as his handsome frame. I was smitten, and managed to speak a few words to him on the drive to the mountains that morning. His friend Patti Gwen Huffsmith, who had a boyfriend up in the mountains near the ranch, was with us in the front seat but it didn't prevent us from finding each other's eyes in the rearview mirror. I let the feeling of intimacy and delight wash over me. I was not even sixteen, but by the time we got to the ranch, I was in love. It felt different from my earlier crushes. This, I suspected, was the real thing.

At the dude ranch there were a dozen swabbies, like me, cleaning, washing dishes, making beds, sweeping and, somewhat unsuccessfully in my case, waiting on tables in the American-style dining room of the ranch. After pouring coffee down the shirt of one of the patrons, I was put on duty upstairs cleaning bathrooms for the guests, who spent their time in the nearby mountains riding horses, fly-fishing, hiking, and going on cookouts with the wranglers.

Peter stuck around a couple of days and by the time he had left, I knew the feelings I was experiencing were mutual and that we had both fallen in love.

At the ranch that summer I revelled in the childhood I had never had. I played games and romped, rode horseback and swam in the nude, went out dancing and sang songs around the campfire, things I hadn't done very much when I was younger. Hadley and I screamed with laughter while cleaning cabins far enough away from the main lodge so the owners wouldn't hear us or see us smearing each other's faces with Bab-O the foaming cleanser or chasing each other into the icy river with broom handles, screaming wildly as we floundered in the freezing water. My friendship with Hadley let a child loose in my life, one who wasn't always and only having to perform, having to be so grown-up.

Peter would come up over Berthoud Pass for weekends and we would go dancing at Wally's Bar and Grill down the highway from the guest ranch and drink 3.2 beer and drive into Grandby with the rest of the gang, shouting Hank Williams songs at the top of our lungs and going to the movies, singing rounds, kissing by the gas pump in the moonlight, talking about our rebellions from our teachers—I from Brico, he from his professors who wanted him to go right on to graduate school from college. We were young dreamers, we told each other, idealists.

At the end of the summer I started back to school at East High. I was a junior. Peter was a sophomore at the University of Colorado in Boulder but he drove to Denver nearly every weekend, and we walked and talked, and he and my father discussed great books, and we had meals at each other's houses.

It was 1956 and I was learning folk songs and going to the Friday night parties on Lookout Mountain. My husband-to-be studied William Blake and read Camus and Dylan Thomas with my father. America was in that quiet time between the Korean and Vietnam wars, and Peter and my father talked about the mess the French had gotten themselves into. (The first U.S. casualty in Vietnam would be a soldier killed in a bomb accident in Saigon in 1957, the following year.)

The next summer I was at Sportsland Valley again, this time with more songs and more experience. Peter was often at the lodge, and when he was away, we wrote letters to each other. At the end of the summer I started my senior year at East High School in Denver and Peter joined the Naval Air Cadets. Peter and I wrote letters almost daily. We seemed to know we were meant for one another.

Between my father's love of books and the wonderful teachers I had in junior high and high school in Denver, I had a good liberal arts education. I also had a fine musical training with Brico. These were teachers with great love of literature and music and the ability to communicate to young and eager minds. My father and one of my teachers, Jack Shearn, read books together and talked over politics and life in general. Jack was our neighbor for a time, and I remember those nights of ideas discussed among burning meerschaum pipes and glasses of dark, burning whisky—it was art, music, ideas, and of course, booze.

Irish embryonic fluid.

∫❀

I started drinking when I was fifteen. My family thought children should learn to drink at home, moderately, so that they learned about alcohol in a safe place. Sometimes I might be allowed a tiny glass of Spanish sherry, smoky and sweet; or a mug of 3.2 beer, the low-alcohol "horse piss," as my father called it, that was sold in Colorado; perhaps a watered-down bourbon with soda or a small glass of wine with dinner.

There were nights to come when I drank more than a moderate little glass.

One of the first times I remember getting roaring drunk was with some girlfriends driving down to Colorado Springs, where we had gone to hear the Naval Air Cadet Choir sing. I was the one drinking most of a quart of Gilbey's gin, hogging the bottle, not wanting to let it go. We were all giggling and having a grand old time on the weaving drive back to Denver, but I was the one who got sick. My mother told me she never drank gin. It had always made her sick, and I had obviously inherited her allergy. So from that time on, I never drank gin.

I drank tequila, the wormwood in its teeth, the hangover in its vapors, in Mexican restaurants in Denver and Central City as I grew older; and margaritas, the lime and ice tangy on my tongue; and cool vodka drinks. Once, in a plaster cast up to my hip, I got so drunk that I fell in the pool at my brother-in-law's wedding. I had to go to the hospital to have the cast replaced, laughing all the way as though at a good joke. I drank rum in the eggnog Daddy made at holidays; Manhattans served in lovely slanted crystal glasses, red cherries at the bottom of the glass; ice-cold vodka martinis, with pearl onions and only a whiff of vermouth. I soon discarded the cherries, the olives and the pearl onions. *Jim Beam, Jack Daniel's, GlenLivet,*—these words were to become as familiar to me as *table,* or *chair.*

Later, I would drink anything you were serving. I would water your booze, and hide my own, though there was often no one to see me do it. Alcohol smoothed the rough edges. I learned to make home brew in Colorado, a strong dark ale that I bottled in batches that sometimes blew up in the cellar or the closet because I added too much sugar. There was always some good whiskey around when I lived in Boulder and I would have a beer or a tall drink while I cooked dinner. We would drink on weekends and during the week. The cocktail hour was a regular ceremony. When I was working I would drink during my shows, usually sipping Pernod or Scotch or Manhattans.

Drinking came easily, as painlessly as breathing, like something natural, preordained. Everyone around me drank. Even as a young girl, alcohol took all my inhibitions away, made me feel I could do anything. Drinking became a part of my life, much as my blue eyes and my ability to sing. Drinking was like the music in my soul, like my love of my family. When I had a few drinks I was no longer awkward, no longer fearful. Drinking moved me to spiritual heights which, though short-lived, were enough to make me know that I needed alcohol, that I deserved it, that I would make it my business to get it in every situation in my life, for the next two decades.

Alcohol gave me a feeling of peacefulness, a feeling I was all right, a feeling that I might be normal, like everyone else. Drinking gave me something that seemed to accompany the holy feeling of music. Music gave me angel's wings. But alcohol let me fly—until it let me crash.

Alcohol kept me from acting out my suicidal impulses again. I began having terrible anxiety attacks in my early twenties and I used alcohol to keep the anxiety medicated. I didn't take drugs, at first. They were too much trouble. Booze was legal. I didn't want to look as though I had a problem and I was under the impression most people around me drank as much as I did. Yet, even early in my drinking life, when I was in a restaurant or a bar and a drink was served, I couldn't wait for the next to be ordered. My eyes would follow the waiter, keeping track of the other glasses at the table, waiting for an opportunity that wouldn't look out of line with what my companions were doing. There were the first feelings of shame over my drinking.

I knew even from the beginning that I had a problem. I would spend the next twenty-three years trying not to let it show. As the years went by, I developed an aching, vaguely paralyzing feeling about my drinking. It was more than a passion. I had begun to worship a false god in secret, making blood sacrifices that I could tell no one about. I knew there was something wrong with the picture of a talented, fortunate young woman with the world in front of her and a blossoming career who dreams not of professional and personal fulfillment, but of having enough money to buy a lodge in the mountains, fill it with alcohol, and quietly drink herself to death. On some mornings of remorse, I felt a sense of foreboding, heard a whisper from the cloud of Irish whiskey, or some warning spoken by a ghost of my Irish ancestors.

I can remember distinctly someone referring to a relative who drank: "He has the *failing,* you know." There was a click in my gut. Every Irishman knows about drinking and the path to hell. They know about those who have this problem. They know about "taking the pledge," and most people know there are those who look for God in a bottle, calling it strength or spirit. They know the "failing" is out there, and people fear it and hold up a cross or a fist to stop its coming to them.

Most people I knew seemed to be happy when they drank. There were those, however, who spoke in hushed tones of the curse of drink. The Irish knew about alcoholism; some kind of search for God, some kind of fall from Grace. The signs were there early, if you knew what to look for. "She has it, you know dear." I stayed away from people who were on to my secret. I couldn't have told you, not for decades, what it was exactly that I suspected they knew, but in my bones *I* knew I was in deep trouble.

No one seemed to know in those days that the "failing" was not a moral issue, but a disease. We made no connection, it seemed, between what happened when Daddy drank and *what* he drank. Perhaps we could connect the dots from bottle to action, but what could we do about it? Someone who drank, drank. There was drama, there was chaos. We might have seen the outline of the bottle behind the behavior, but what was to be done if we did? No one talked about treatment in those days. I never heard anyone say that my daddy belonged in a rehab center. No one had ever heard of such a thing. The closest you would hear would be that somebody had to go into a sanitorium to "dry out." And there was that article in the *Saturday Evening Post* by Jack Anderson about the guys down in Akron, Ohio, who had found a cure. Daddy thought they were religious fanatics, and when he once went to one of their meetings, in the fifties in Denver, never went back because of the "God" stuff.

But Daddy could dry out on his own, and sometimes he did, for weeks at a time.

Of course, on my best days, the failing didn't bother me. I was sure I would be able to drink like a lady, drink with class, that I would stop before there were real problems.

I swore I would never drink like my father.

❧ Valentine's Day, my son's anniversary. Nine years ago today he landed, dazed, bottomed out after years of drinking and drugging, at a treatment center in Minnesota where he made the start on his new life. The new day brought him sobriety, self-respect, a life of service in his community, friends, renewed ties to his family, and a good relationship with God. It also brought him a family and a life in the community.

Treatment works. Staying in a program of recovery works. Clark's death by his own hand after years of sobriety does not mean his life was wasted or that his struggle was not valiant and successful. He brought good things into his own life and the lives of all of us, his friends and his family.

Einstein said you can live as though there are no miracles, or as though everything is a miracle. I must learn to live without Clark's heart, beating and alive. On this Valentine's Day, when I would have celebrated with him, I must try to find the celebration in his memory, the goodness, the courage he showed nine years ago when, against the odds, he won the day and the miracle came.

Does the miracle ever stay? Do we have to go on winning some new miracle every day? On this day of the anniversary of the heart, my heart aches for my son. I miss him. I yearn for him. I know that his heart is with God, guiding him through the realms of the next stage of his journey.

4

Reaching for the Stars

*I*t was during these years that my social conscience, which would be so much a part of my journey in the revolutionary sixties, was being honed. At home, I had the example of my father's political sensibility. Now, at East High School, more texture and belief systems were being added. We attended speeches about civil rights and listened to Steve Allen, the entertainer, speak about the nuclear threat and the Committee for a Sane Nuclear Policy. My social studies teacher, Mr. Lindbloom, brought us propaganda films made in Nazi Germany and we discussed the evils of fascism. We read and talked about women's rights and the suffragette movement. We were encouraged to picket and protest, to get into political activities both at school and in our communities. Our school was diversity oriented and elected a black head boy and a Jewish head girl in a school that was predominantly white Anglo-Saxon Protestant. Both these young people were undeniably gifted with leadership qualities, but that might not have mattered if the group conscience of the school had not chosen to elect them. My own personal friends were artistically inclined and rebellious. We read Albert Camus and talked about Algeria.

With my best male friend, John Gilbert, a wonderful and gifted actor who went on to become quite well known in Seattle, I went to avant garde movies and fought the system. We smoked in the restaurants around the corner from our high school, drank beer in the graduation parade while driving one of the truck beds for the floats. They were innocent rebellions. We talked about deeply philosophical matters. We read Rimbaud and Valéry and knew about the dark lives these poets led, with their drugs and their wild dreams. The drugs gave them freedom to be artists, we thought. We went to see *Cyrano de Bergerac* and wept when the cruel forces turned against Jose Ferrer, hunting down the artist.

The sixties and its social and musical revolutions had not yet started, it seemed, except in the dark clubs in the big cities, where poets and beatniks were reading and railing. But I was already participating in the change. I was singing folk songs, learning that it was important to rebel against things you felt were unjust, and feeling I had a voice in the changes that were about to happen in my country and in the world.

They say when you change yourself you change the world. I wouldn't learn much about changing myself until later in my life. At this time, I was sure I could change the world, and wanted to. The world, after all, was unjust and needed changing.

In this heady climate I spent no time thinking about a "career." There were no courses for women in my high school about how to turn your passion for medicine or literature or music into a lifelong career. I was driven, but knew not where. Fate moved the figures on the board and I followed.

In my junior year in high school the father of a friend submitted my name to a contest called "Stars of Tomorrow." The contest, sponsored by the Kiwanis Clubs of Colorado, Arizona, New Mexico and Kansas, was held in a big auditorium in downtown Denver. I sang a traditional song called "Pretty Saro," on which I accompanied myself with guitar. I was surprised when I won the contest. There were other very talented kids competing, including a young woman who played marvelous classical violin. For years after, I heard from Daddy that her father was plain stunned that his daughter had been beaten out by a "hillbilly."

The Kiwanis gave me five hundred dollars, out of which I bought a dress and an airline ticket to Atlantic City and paid for my hotel room. The International Convention of Kiwanis Club members was held in the same hall that hosts the Miss America contest to this day.

I went to Atlantic City at the end of the following summer. The air was damp and smelled of salt and I stayed at the Marlboro Blenheim hotel and walked the boardwalk and ate Taylor's Pork Roll and dried my gloves on the windowsill. I had white gloves for traveling, and carried my guitar in a plain old cardboard case. On the big Monday night at the auditorium of the Convention Hall, I was on the program in the section called "Talented Youth," between Lois Miller and Gene Sullivan playing the "Mighty Organ," and the "Swingin' Subteens" of Huntington, Long Island, followed by Miss Alabama of 1955, Patricia Huddleston. I sang "Pretty Saro" again, as I had in the contest. I played my guitar, my head thrown back. I stood out, to say the least.

Folk music had arrived on the American music scene.

After the show I went up to New York and met up with Peter, who had a few days' leave. Peter was in the Naval Air Cadet program in Pensacola, Florida, by then. He flew into New York and we visited my mother's college room-mate, Eline Taylor, and her husband Paul in Stamford, Connecticut. Peter and I got a taste of what it might be like to live in New York: we drove into the city from Stamford, following the Hudson River along the West Side Highway, the same highway that today I can see out my window through the trees in the winter, and on which I hear the traffic between the leaves in the summer. We went to see *Damn Yankees* with Gwen Verdon and *Separate Tables* with Eric Portman. We ate in great restaurants and I was hooked. I promised myself that someday I would live near that flourishing green mass of trees along the river. Peter and I had a romantic couple of days at Eline and Paul's, necking on the couch when everyone else was sleeping.

Back in Denver I finished my senior year in high school, learning more folk songs and getting better at what I have come to love the most in life: singing, playing the guitar, and collecting songs. There were more nights in the mountains at Lingo the Drifter's log cabin where I met with other Colorado singers. We listened to Lingo spin his tales, and gazed at the stars in the black sky. They sparkled like diamonds above Denver, the city with such grace so far below on the plains.

My family always supported me. As my brothers grew older, they were turning into a handsome trio, talented, smart and good-looking. They were all gifted. They did well in school and worked, as all of us did. Holly was the baby, toddling in her little dresses, with a look on her face that said my mind is made up. Later, she, as I had, would get jobs baby-sitting for children in the neighborhood. The boys delivered the *Denver Post*. For many years they kept the best paper routes in the family and like Saturday pilgrims as they reached ten or eleven, they would get enough sales points selling the *Denver Post* to win trips with the Eskimo Ski Club train that went to Winter Park on weekends. There, my brothers all learned to ski down the trails in elegant curves.

They drove fast cars, crashed the Cherry Creek Country Club dances and dated good-looking Denver girls who showed up at the house sometimes for dinners, eyeing my brothers with sly looks under long lashes, girls who wore cashmere sweaters and pearls and looked comfortable in their clothes and in their skin. Young Denver women in love. Some of these girls my brothers married. I still run into wonderful-looking women all over the country who say, "I knew your brother, Denver," or Michael, or David, sometimes all three. At the mention of my brothers' names, their eyes go moist. My handsome brothers' pasts are filled with beautiful, smitten western maids.

After graduation, I got a job in another mountain lodge in Colorado on Grand Lake. At Lemon Lodge, cleaning cabins and riding horses with the cowboys, I waited for Peter to come back on his holidays from the Navy, which were few. One morning I discovered the dead body of a friend's mother in one of the cabins. She had taken an overdose of sleeping pills. It was a deeply upsetting experience and I called my parents and they drove to Grand Lake to calm me down. We talked about suicide, including my own attempt. There was a lot of sharing between my parents and me.

That summer I also had a few dates with cowboys from Grand Lake, but my heart was true blue. At the lodge, I would sing for the guests around the fireplace every song I knew, playing all night if I could: "This Land Is Your Land," "The Bonnie Ship the Diamond," "Shenandoah."

In the autumn I went on scholarship to a school in Illinois that I remember mostly for its loneliness out on the Great Plains. MacMurray was two hours south by train from Chicago, in the town of Jacksonville, Illinois, a coeducational Presbyterian institution where chapel was required and alcohol was forbidden. I quickly became a beacon of sobriety, smoked like a fiend and was on the freshmen's honor role committee. I once remember being partly responsible for getting someone thrown out of school for drinking in her room—something I would have loved to do, but didn't.

I used to sing in the smoker, gathering around me a group of young women from all over the country who piped in with their voices on "This Land Is Your Land." I missed my home and my family and longed for my mother's cooking. Once more I played guitar for the school shows and wished I were in Colorado.

I had a job in the library to earn my scholarship. Occasionally Peter would get out to see me and we would meet in Chicago. They had something in the Windy City that I had never seen before, a club where they served alcohol and played folk music! We sat in the dark of the Gate of Horn. Peter bought me one drink and one for himself and we nursed them all night and listened, spellbound, to the singing of Cynthia Gooding, whose records on the Elektra label I had bought and loved and by whom I had been inspired. Someday, I promised myself, I would do this, sing in a club where people could come and hear me.

By the time I was eighteen there was a quiet musical revolution going on in the country, one that was growing slowly. Radio stations in Colorado were playing the Kingston Trio and Harry Belafonte and even the Weavers, who had been making music, and incorporating their politics into their lively, energy-filled songs, for decades already. There were little shops in most big cities where you could find guitars and copies of Sing Out!, the Bible of the folk movement, a broadside filled with songs, stories, and the political drift of the new folkies who were always gathering in cities from New York Island to the Redwood Forest. The pulse of folk was folks themselves—the problems of workers, the feelings of people. The folk movement was tapping into a furnace of youth and energy that was burning with desire, with stories to tell, with tears to shed and with a pulse of life about to burst into new musical and art forms, working melody into politics, heart and soul.

In March 1958, I returned to Colorado for spring break. Peter had dropped out of flight school for medical reasons—during wing-tip-to-wing-tip formations, he broke out in a painful rash over most of his body. He finished his tour of duty with the Navy on what he referred to as a "tin can" in the Pacific. After he entered the winter semester at the University of Colorado, we drove into the mountains and went skiing at Arapahoe Basin on a blizzardy, cold weekend.

When I returned to MacMurray, I discovered I was pregnant and was filled with total panic. What in the world was I going to do with a baby? I agonized over my situation, managed to slip through the rest of the term with decent grades, and over the telephone across the miles, Peter and I worried over our dilemma. I was not at all sure I could handle having a baby. Peter had taken the summer off and was looking for a job in Estes Park. I was home in Denver and we spoke on the phone, trying to decide what to do. Peter said he would come down to Denver the next day and talk about our choices. We knew we had only two.

God intervened, I believe, in my life, as He always has. Peter was headed back from Estes Park to my godfather Holden's cabin near the Longs Peak campground. Blinded by oncoming headlights, Peter rolled the car he was driving. He walked away from the accident without a scratch. Shaken up, he came home to Denver where he told his stepfather Hal and my godfather, Holden, that I was pregnant. Their advice, men-to-man, as it were, was that Peter and I announce that we were married.

Which was exactly what we did. It was a relief to celebrate my new state instead of hiding it. We told my parents, who were excited for us, although I know my father couldn't have cared less if we were married or not. He was only happy that I was happy—and that he was going to be a grandfather!

I became, as if overnight, a happy, serene, contented and completed woman. The acceptance I felt was total. Peter and I had been together for a long time, and knew each other very well. We wanted the same kinds of things. My anxiety level dropped. I stopped worrying about what would happen to me, to my life, to us. I embraced approaching motherhood as my natural, predestined state.

We moved into my godfather Holden's cabin in Estes Park and started looking for work. We had only been there for a few days when Peter applied for a job with Jim Bishop, whose family had been in the lodge business since the turn of the century. Jim ran Bear Lake Lodge in Rocky Mountain National Park and also a little treasure of a place called Fern Lake Lodge. He needed a couple to run Fern. The "man," he told Peter, had to run "power and lights"; bring water down from the springs above the lodge and chop wood for fires: the "woman" had to bake bread and pies on a wood stove. Food, as well as a bottle of booze or two, would be brought in by pack mule once a week. There was a telephone but no electricity, and we would be responsible for making lunches for a few dozen hikers a day. Jim was offering in return for our running the lodge all we could eat and drink and three hundred dollars for the two months we would be at Fern. We accepted immediately and went to live at Bear Lake Lodge.

We had to wait for the snow to melt and spent the last two weeks in June at Bear Lake before we could make the climb to the top of Fern Lake trail. It was spring in the Rockies and around Bear Lake there were wildflowers of every description—purple lupine and red and yellow Indian paintbrush; violet, yellow and blue and pink columbine; and yellow and blue Johnny-jump-up, blooming in the meadows and ravines, springing up from the mountain streambeds, blossoming along the rugged trails. The meadows were carpeted in wildflowers. The smell of pine and ozone from the little streams running into the lake from glaciers high in the mountains was heady and sweet. Those smells, and the sound of rippling water and the calls of bluebirds and Clark's jays, the big gray and white camp-robbers, still make me heady with pleasure. I felt as though I had fallen into some exotic dream.

At Bear Lake Lodge, next to Bear Lake with its sparkling alpine waters, I learned from the pastry chef to make bread and he taught me how to bank a wood stove and keep the fire going, slow and steady. Peter did chores around Bear Lake Lodge until the snows on the upper trails were gone and then we filled our packs with food for a week, and, carrying most of what we owned on our backs, started up the mountain, each loaded with a fifty-pound pack. It was a bright, sunny day, July 5, 1958.

Fern Lake Lodge was a pinion pine structure that had once been host to dozens of year-round guests. In its heyday, the lodge sported three cooks who baked and cooked on wood stoves; a team of mules that hauled guests and their steamer trunks, skis, gaming tables, vegetables, sides of beef, furs, parkas, pajamas and whiskey up the winding trails in the snows of winter and heat of summer. By the time Peter and I got to Fern Lake it had been shut down on and off for many years. Few people wanted to run an isolated, remote lodge whose financial rewards were meager and whose distance was far from most of what people call civilization. For us, it was perfect. We were thrilled by our good fortune.

The old pine lodge had floors which my father identified as "puncheon" when he came up on his first visit. He reached down with his fingers to feel the rounded, cut-off logs, held together with tar. In the big kitchen there were utensils and porcelain, wood stoves and Coleman lanterns. There were a dozen cabins scattered about the lake and among the woods. The cabins had not been used for years. In each one stood two single beds, springs bare and sagging, and an antique, perfectly preserved Franklin stove. Quilts and pillows were stacked in the storage bins, canned goods lined the shelves, and mysterious utensils for baking and straining, peeling and whipping, scalloping and chopping, stood gathering dust on the vast wooden shelves that lined the huge kitchen. There was a big radiator that was strapped inside the top of the fireplace in the living room. Spring water ran through it and when the fire was burning it heated the water on its way back into the kitchen. In the coming months we washed dishes and, a few times a week, stood under a metal spigot for our hot showers, our feet in a washtub under the scalding, steaming water.

In a few days, a pack horse arrived with our groceries for the week, the promised whiskey, and my guitar, strapped to the mare's flanks. By the time our first pack mule delivery arrived, our routine had already been established. In the morning I baked bread and pies on the wood stove, getting ready for the lunches we would serve; the smells of fresh baking pie crust and homemade bread filled the air, drifting down the mountainside. I made cherry and apple pies, sandwiches from homemade bread with sliced ham, Spam, chicken, cheese, lettuce and tomatoes when we could get them. Tuna was popular, and I added chopped, sweet pickles and mayo to the salad as my mother had taught me.

Peter chopped wood and carried water from our spring up the mountainside. The smack and ring of the ax as he swung on kindling filtered in among the call of jays in the early light. In the cool mornings, after breakfast, we smoked cigarettes and drank good, strong coffee and played chess in the sun at one of the big wooden tables on the porch of the lodge, waiting for our first customers. With my pies and bread in the oven, my chores done, and Peter's chopping and readying the fires and getting the water drawn from the springs, everything was prepared for our guests.

In the silence, we would hear the voices of the hikers coming down from the highest lake, Odessa, and across the green valley to Fern Lake. We knew they would be with us in about a half hour, and scurried to finish; bread sliced, plates laid out, drinks ready. We made a traditional raspberry drink from a powder, adding crystal water from our spring, and a lemonade, tangy and sweet. We set places at the tables. The smell of smoke from the wood fire in the fireplace drifted up the piney trail, tantalizing and enticing. Water was on the boil for tea and you could smell my good coffee, an eggshell dropped in the grounds to settle them in the old-fashioned pot that steamed in the coals of the fireplace, ready to be poured into cups to go with the homemade apple pies. I always heated the coffee cups with hot water, as I had seen the waiter do at the diner the morning after Peter and I had spent our first night together.

Our luncheon guests hiked up the trails from Grand Lake in the morning, taking on the challenge of a nine-mile, round trip hike ten thousand feet above sea level. Their faces, delighted with their victory over the rugged terrain, greeted our lodge, and us, with pleasure. I still have the guest list from that summer. People came from all over the world to our hideaway in the Rockies. We met Stanley and Marion Fletcher and their children, Amaryllis and April, and John Clark, a tall, dark-haired man who was the ranger at Longs Peak for many summers. Through him we met many people in the Park Service in Rocky Mountain National Park. Fern Lake was very much like the European camping lodges, we were told by our foreign hikers.

There was a special quality about our life there that people felt. We made it comfortable for our guests. Fern Lake Lodge had everything: unique people who were willing to travel a long way to get to us, a stripped-down lifestyle that suited our rebellious and nature-loving spirits, and some of the most beautiful scenery in the world—tall, powerful mountains, a crystal clear mountain lake, the smell of pine in the air, the call of birds. Wild martins and deer drank at the river's edge and waterfalls tumbled down beside the mountain trails.

The place was a paradise.

After Peter and I served lunch to our hikers, I would bring out the guitar, and we would sit with our guests on the front porch, talking and singing songs. My mother often came up the mountain with Holly and Daddy to visit us and she always asked whether it upset my stomach to cook. I never had a moment of physical discomfort when I was pregnant with Clark. Emotional and mental twinges, perhaps, but I was physically healthy as a horse during my pregnancy. I was becoming more and more visibly pregnant. There is a photograph of me on the porch, guitar in hands, short hair, eyes closed, stomach—you can tell how happy I felt.

In the middle of July, I cooked up a lot of pies and bread to take care of our guests, and our friend Judy Holland hiked up the six miles from the moraine road and took over running the lodge for the day. Peter and I hiked down to Judy's car, which she had kindly left us, and drove to Fort Collins, where a judge married us. It made all the males in Peter's family happy, but it didn't change anything for us.

Peter and I tried to lease Fern Lake Lodge. Jim said he thought ten thousand dollars would do it. We envisioned places we could borrow the money. But that year "Project 66" took away our chance for a mountain life at Fern Lake. The project was intended to remove all commercial enterprise from all national parks. Along with the tourist traps and eyesores on the highways in the park, "Project 66" removed Fern Lodge and plans to lease it again were abandoned. Although the lodge still stood for many years, eventually the park service tore it down. Only a potato slicer of which I was inordinately fond, an old Coleman lantern that my brother Denver now has, slices of puncheon pine from the floor of the lodge, which my stepfather Robert had framed for each of us children and my mother, and a few long building nails that I found among the pine needles and brought out on a trip there in 1986 made it down the mountain with us. People scavenged in the years after the lodge was closed up. They broke into the big wood doors and cracked through the isinglass-like windows, pried open the sheds and stripped the quilts and the bedding out of the cabins. Jim hauled all the charming old Franklin stoves and the big, well-preserved wood stove from the kitchen down to Bear Lake Lodge and used them till Bear burned down a few years later. He used mules to bring down the radiator from the back of the fireplace.

The last time I was at Fern Lake, nothing remained of the old lodge but pine needles, moss and memory.

Back in Boulder, we moved into a basement apartment on Walnut Street and Peter registered for school. Mrs. Tingly was our landlady. She was a creaky and pleasant widow of about eighty who baked casseroles and homemade cookies and brought them downstairs to us. I started going to a gynecologist in Boulder. Dr. Lockwood and I talked about natural childbirth. Peter and I settled down in our little apartment. Every morning Peter got up at four-thirty to deliver newspapers, the only job he could find that fit into his school schedule. I got a job filing papers in the administration office, alphabetizing the names of students. I also started taking a typing course at night. The university still thinks I was a full-time student, but I never reached those exalted heights.

Why I didn't think about making a career of music at this time has always haunted me. I don't know if it was the times or the fact that women didn't have jobs in professions other than nursing or teaching; that most of my peers weren't keeping jobs after they were married; or that all that drama in my childhood had blinded me to what was in front of my eyes. Perhaps I had settled into marriage with the attitude my mother had carried into hers—that I would give up my own dreams for those of my husband. But at that time, I wasn't aware of any dreams other than giving birth to my baby.

The winter was long, and my due date came and went. Over the holidays Peter joked that the baby was never coming at all, that the pregnancy was all in my imagination. I began to think so to, but a few nights later I knew this was for real.

On January 6 my contractions started for real and Peter took me to the Seventh Day Adventist hospital in Boulder, where they served no meat, no alcohol, no tobacco, and no coffee. About halfway through the labor the nurses came in and drew a long red line across my stomach where the doctor planned to do a Cesarean section. My labor went on, and then for some reason the doctor decided he should try for a mid-forceps delivery. Today this is considered dangerous for the baby's brain—the forceps can be too tight, and can cause severe damage. After twenty-eight hours of labor, Clark was born with red hair, tiny fists waving. I looked at his beautiful face and his blue, blue eyes and felt love and apprehension—for his fragility, for his strength—the feelings most mothers have, I think. Clark opened his mouth, breathed, and cried a healthy, hearty sound. He weighed nine pounds and two ounces, and I was exhausted.

Clark was beautiful, of course. Peter and I knew he was brilliant just by looking at him, and he had another considerable trait: by the time he had been home a few days, he was sleeping through the night. He was a good baby, and he was the first grandchild in both our families. All four grandparents were wild for him. After the first few days it seemed as though I had always been a mother. He nestled in my arms as though he had always been there and stared at me with his round blue eyes when I sang him lullabies. I loved him with all my heart.

My mother had been good with all her babies. She had been one of nine, and I was one of five siblings, so we both always had infants to cuddle and play with and talk to. I had no fear of babies. I loved the touch of my son, his tiny fingers, his voice that cooed and gurgled and obviously wanted to communicate. I had taken care of my brothers and sister and, after the first shock of realizing my son was mine alone, and not anyone else's, I had a calm and very natural relationship with him.

One weekend before Clark was born, Mother drove to Boulder and we spent the day talking, just being together. Mother had written me a letter about my father's behavior, which had become more erratic, threatening the health of our relationship. She talked about my father's temper, his chasing other women, and her total faithfulness. The conversation explained a lot to me; why she put up with my father's behavior when he was drunk, and why she had never left him. During that day I came to understand that she loved my father totally and would never have betrayed her marriage. That afternoon, when I was nineteen and pregnant with Clark, sealed our friendship. Now Mother looked at my tiny baby in her arms and, when he began making faces that the doctor had assured me were gas, said, "No, he's smiling." And so he was. His smiles were as angelic when he was a baby as they were when he was grown. His smiles could melt your heart.

Peter continued his job delivering the *Denver Post,* rain or shine, going out on cold winter mornings. It was hard, and it seemed we never had any money. I wouldn't earn enough to hire a baby-sitter for Clark if I worked at the university in the filing job I had held until he was born. I really didn't know what we were going to do. I couldn't do anything but play the guitar and sing songs.

One night Peter turned to me as we were getting ready for bed.

"Why don't you get a job doing something you know how to do?" he asked. "Then I can quit this job and concentrate on studying, and take care of Clark at night." I talked to my father about it, and he called Al Fike, an old friend who was a performer at a lot of clubs in the area. Al arranged for me to have an audition at Michael's Pub, a college hangout in Boulder.

The night of my audition, I dressed in black tights, a black top, and black boots. My hair, which Peter had cut by putting a bowl on my head and cutting around it, was short and dark brown. I sat hesitantly on a stool, gripping my guitar in front of a room filled with cigarette smoke and tables of college students. Pitchers of beer banged down on two dozen tables and loud talk and laughter filled the room. Mike announced me, the spotlight hit me, and I started to sing. I don't remember my first song, but slowly the room quieted, smoke rose from cigarettes now poised between fingers in midair, beer glasses came to rest on tabletops, drops of perspiration slipping down their sides. I met the eyes of a hundred or so students and sang every song I knew.

When I had finished singing, the owner, Mike Besessi, clasped my hand in his and shook it hard. He told me he hated folk music, but said that in my case he would make an exception. I was hired on the spot for a hundred dollars a week to sing five nights a week, two shows a night. He said he would throw in free pizza and all the 3.2 beer I could drink. It was March 1959.

Peter was delighted not to have to get up at dawn and go out into the cold. He was as good as his word, staying home at night, studying, taking care of Clark, feeding him and putting him to bed. I spent my days with my bright, red-headed baby. I took Clark everywhere in a pack on my back. We hiked and shopped, did the housework and rehearsed my songs. He listened, eyes bright, and cooed to the music.

I continued to sing at Michael's Pub in March, April and May. I began to draw an increasingly larger crowd. I was learning, getting a feel for the pace of a show, changing songs around, learning new ones. I was growing as a performer as I sang every night, and my son was growing too. When school was over for the summer, my job was over too, but in July 1959 I was offered a job at the Gilded Garter in Central City.

Central City is a silver mining town above Idaho Springs. It has nightclubs and an opera house. On the floor of the Opera House Bar is the "Face on the Barroom Floor," painted by a miner as he lay dying from a gunshot wound. Central City had been a rough and tough mountain town, and now tourists from Denver flock on weekends to drink, listen to music, go to the opera, and stare at the portrait of the beautiful long-haired woman in the Opera House bar, just down the street from the Glory Hole and the Gilded Garter.

Peter, Clark and I moved into an apartment above the Platte River, next to the big Bull Durham sign. The bathtub was in the kitchen, with a board over it to serve as a table when you weren't having a bath. Clark crawled and cooed, standing up and bouncing in his crib, longing to walk. By the time we moved back to Boulder in September he was taking his first steps.

I had earned enough money in my singing jobs that we could get out of the basement and move into a log house by a stream in Boulder. Peter was back in school and I was looking for work. Clark was toilet trained early, as though he had places to go and people to see and couldn't be bothered with diapers. He walked early, as I had, at nine months, and I had to run to keep up with his energy. He laughed at things, pointing to flowers, running their names around in his mouth, speaking in sentences by the time he was in his second year. Peter and I both read to Clark every chance we got, bedtime stories and, as my father had done with me, more advanced books. I remember reading E. B. White to Clark, the story of *Stuart Little*. We laughed together about the little mouse jumping into his father's pants leg and getting a ride to work, sometimes jumping off to take a pea pod boat down the drain in the street.

Clark grew and talked, walked and laughed and made our little log cabin by the river dance with his smile. We had a black and white husky named Kolya, who was growing into a mammoth dog, and he and Clark were buddies. Clark would throw a big ball in the yard and Kolya would run hard and retreive that ball and race back to Clark, who would take the wet ball out of the dog's mouth and do the whole thing again, both dog and baby boy enthalled with each other. There was a clanky piano in that house and I would play it, cursing the out-of-tune strings, and try to sing melodies to Clark. More often I wound up just singing with the guitar, or singing his lullaby a capella. He loved to sing along with his mommy in a voice as melodic and in tune as any I have heard in a child. Peter, I know, prayed his son would not be a singer.

That fall I worked at the Exodus, a new folk music club that had opened in Denver. I sang there many weeks during that winter, and also once again was hired to sing at Michael's Pub. Things were going well and Peter and I were happy. Peter was in school, finishing his senior year at the University of Colorado, getting his degree in English literature.

In March the following spring, on a ski trip to Winter Park, I had a very bad double spiral fracture in my right leg as the result of a skiing accident. I was in the hospital in Denver for a week after the surgery. Mom took care of Clark and when I returned home to our house by the river, I was in a plaster cast from my ankle to my hip and was told I would have to be in it for six months. It was awkward but I got around on my crutches, and as soon as I got a walking cast I was singing again at Michael's Pub. No one thought anything of it, since in Colorado everyone skis and, from time to time, has injuries from the slopes. It seemed perfectly normal to me to jump around on one leg doing housework, with Clark under one arm and a mop in the other. I performed in the same manner, slinging the guitar around easily in spite of the cast.

I was the breadwinner in the family, and the show had to go on.

That spring, Peter won a Guggenheim fellowship teaching at the University of Connecticut and I was offered a job singing at the Gate of Horn in Chicago, the folk club where Peter and I had heard Cynthia Gooding perform a few years before. We were also offered a job doing the fire watch on Twin Sisters' Peaks in Rocky Mountain National Park. It was a difficult decision, for we loved the mountains and wanted to stay in Colorado for the summer. On the other hand, the job at the Gate of Horn was a great opportunity. And of course, we would go to Connecticut, that was never a question.

As we usually did when we had to make difficult decisions, Peter and I and the baby went to the mountains. We sat on a high hill where we could see the great Continental Divide, white and pristine and majestic. We talked it over and over while Clark toddled among the wildflowers on the hill. Finally we decided that as long as we were headed for Connecticut, we might as well go by way of Chicago.

It was a decision that was to change our lives. I like to think that if we had stayed in Colorado I might have worked for the Park Service for the next thirty years, singing for my friends, but that is an illusion. I was meant to make music, to have a career in music, and it was beckoning to me. I had to follow its call.

After Peter got his teaching fellowship my mother-in-law, Margaret, told me that she thought it was time for me to quit my "job." I remember we were in her big Detroit-built car and she was driving as I sat in the passenger seat. Clark was in the baby seat in the back of the car. Without looking over at Margaret, I answered her.

"I don't want to quit singing. Singing is not a job. Singing is my life."

It was a moment I will never forget, nor will I forget the look on

Margaret's face as she continued to stare straight ahead, jaw firm, mouth tight. Early on I had suspected Margaret had hoped for at least a Denver debutante. I was not only not a debutante, I had also had crossed an invisible and delicate line.

In the summer of 1960, Peter, Clark and I rented a spacious apartment on the South Side of Chicago. Bill Berry and his wife Betsy were neighbors and became our closest friends. Bill was the head of the Chicago Urban League. He and his wife were easygoing, generous people. Betsy's mother baby-sat for Clark sometimes, and in the big, light apartment near Hyde Park and the university, we spread out, made ourselves comfortable, and adjusted to Chicago. It was a big city, more sophisticated than Denver, more varied, more cosmopolitan.

At the Gate of Horn I was the opening act for Hamilton Camp and Bob Gibson. Hamilton and Bob had a good following and had both made records. They sang traditional and original material and the three of us got along well. It had been Bob Gibson who had brought a tape of my singing to the owner of the Gate of Horn, Alan Ribback, who had hired me.

I was still in a cast from my ski accident in March, and when I walked in for my first night of singing and hoisted myself up onto the stage on my crutches, the only thing Alan said was "You didn't tell me you were in a cast!" I replied that it didn't interfere with my singing, and that I thought that my singing was the reason I had been hired. As long as I would sing "Great Selchie of Shule Skerry," the song on the tape that had enticed him to hire me, Alan seemed to forget about the cast. Every once in a while he would look at it in exasperation, but Alan and I were to become good friends.

Peter, Clark and I explored the city during the days, visiting the Art Museum and the Museum of Science and Industry. Peter would carry Clark on his shoulders, wanting his son to experience the wonders of science even at the tender age of one and a half. Six nights a week, for six weeks of that summer, I sang at the club while Peter studied Blake. Clark was happy. I found children for him to play with during the day. The summer was a transition from Colorado to the East, one that we were enjoying.

At the end of that summer Peter loaded up the Chevy Carryall and headed for Connecticut, where his job would be to find a wonderful house in the countryside. With my job, singing in clubs, we could afford not to stay in the tight quarters provided by the university to its fellowship teachers. We would be able to afford a country house in the florid, rich greenery of Connecticut which I had seen only once on my visit to Stamford in 1957. I headed back to Denver to get the rest of our gear, to return in a Volkswagen Bug that belonged to my sister-in-law, Hadley, with Clark in my arms.

❧

When we arrived in Connecticut at the end of the summer, Peter had found a two-story, red farmhouse with a peaked roof on Brown's road. There was a pond set amidst a flock of late summer fireflies that greeted us on our arrival in the light of the August evening. Our landlords, Jan and Vic Scottron, cooked dinner for us that first night and we settled into our new home.

The fireflies danced in the evening light among the long tall grass, sparkling like tiny angels as Clark called out to them, chasing their lights in the soft sunset, mesmerized by their magic. Peter and I would sit under the big tree, holding hands and memorizing the figure under the tree, the dancing lights, our happy thoughts, the tranquillity of the moment. At night Peter studied the poems of Blake, searching through those bright angels. In front of a dancing fire, Clark in bed upstairs while I learned new songs, there were golden moments.

There were cows on the farm, up in the pastures on the hill, and Clark learned to say "black and white." "Angus." "Firefly." "Light." "Mommy has to go to work and sing." I remembered my own childhood, riding in the backseat of the old Buick, telling my father that when it rained, the windshield wipers said "Daddy works, Daddy works." Now I, too, was on the road, as my father had been, fulfilling my dreams, perhaps fulfilling his. "Mommy works, Mommy works."

Peter was settled into his teaching fellowship at the university. We had a group of friends in the community. Some of them had children, too, and Clark had friends to play with.

I had more work since my exposure at a big-city club in Chicago. Many more offers to sing were coming in. Leaving the tranquillity of our home on the green hills to "bring home the bacon," as my father always put it, I traveled to Ontario, Boston, New York, Denver, Omaha, Buffalo, Washington. The coffee shops and bars where I sang were the centers of the folk movement where, a troubadour with my guitar and my stories, I was pedaling my wares, supporting my family: the Gate of Horn, the Purple Onion, the Gilded Garter, Gerde's Folk City, the Gaslight, the Exodus, the Laughing Buddha. I sang three shows a night including, sometimes, a last show with three people watching. I continued learning my craft, always struggling to improve. I wanted to make magic. I yearned to transport my audiences. Often I felt my love of lyrics and melody made people happy, gave them joy, lifted them out of their own sorrows.

And I paid the rent. And the bills. Clothes for baby. Money for the baby-sitter.

In Chicago, at the Gate, Odetta and I became friendly. She had a big, smooth-as-honey voice and a warm heart. When she sang "Sometimes I feel like a motherless child," she made me understand what the song was about. I remember once I had arrived in Chicago the night before my two weeks at the Gate started, and I went to her show. The lights darkened, the announcer said her name, the applause started. She seemed to flow into the room and onto the stage. She was wearing a long, floor-length emerald-green silk dress that rustled as she passed and a perfume, some exotic scent that was the prelude to her entrance and lingered as she moved through the crowd. I thought it was amazing. She not only sang great, but looked great— and smelled great!

One night she introduced me to her husband, a charming man named Danny Gordon. Over drinks after the last show, Danny said he liked my work and thought I needed a manager to help me with my career, and was offering his services. Danny was very convincing. He proposed he would be able to get me better bookings and hinted at concerts as well and other timely additions to my club appearances.

I talked it over with Peter, and it seemed like a good idea. Over the next few months Danny took over my bookings and did increase my business.

One night in Toledo, in his hotel room over drinks after the last show at a club he had booked for me, Danny asked me point-blank why he had been unsuccessful in establishing a more personal—meaning a sexual—relationship with me. There was a very attractive woman friend of his sitting in the room. Those were the days of intimate discussions in the company of nearly total strangers. I told Danny that although he was very attractive, I wasn't in the least interested in sex.

The woman, an Irish gal from Toledo, laughed. "That's one of the best lines I've ever heard," she said.

"It's true," I said. And, it was true.

Danny was manipulative and very smooth, but his knowledge of the folk clubs was the extent of his expertise, and I had already been doing that on my own for two years. Although he got me more work, there was no rise into a more lucrative nor a more visible stature in the world of what my brother Denver likes to call the "folk scare.'" I was making my way, and people knew about me, but I didn't feel that Danny was making much of a difference. My reputation, I believed, was traveling by word of mouth.

I thanked Danny and told him I would go along on my own.

I hadn't ever considered making a record. Peter and I didn't ever talk about it, as I recall. I didn't think of myself as a singer, really, but as a storyteller. Records were for learning songs from! All that was going to change, dramatically, in the winter of 1961.

꧁ Easter again, white lilies and the promise of new life. After Clark's death I had a dream of him so vivid and real that I said to a friend it was more like a visitation, less like a dream. In this dream, my son said, "Mother, why are you crying?" In church the other day the bishop told the story of the celestial beings who came to Mary after Jesus had disappeared from the tomb. "Why are you crying?" they asked her. Jesus said the same thing to Mary when he appeared to her; "Why are you crying? I am with God."

When I told this to my friend Jim Morton, the Dean at St. John the Divine, he shook his head and said, "If all of this isn't true, we're in big trouble!" He is a gentle and kind man who embraces spirituality and healing wherever it comes.

I thought of my own death on this day of the Resurrection. What will I say to those I leave? I will say, "Why are you crying?" That is what my son is doing, sending his spirit, his power, his prayers, to help me through this vale of tears.

I pray to understand that my son is out of his pain and that my tears must be of joy and of surrender. His own pain is over now, and that is something I can celebrate. My son is at peace.

5

Child of Flowers

*M*y recording career began on an overcast, chilly Sunday afternoon in Greenwich Village in the winter of 1961. The invitation to sing at a television show broadcast from the Village Gate had come the previous week, and that winter morning I awakened in our farmhouse on the side of the hill, got Clark up and dressed, and had breakfast with Peter and the baby. The mild gaze of grazing cows and the call of birds followed me down the hill in the big Chevy van as I headed for New York, rolling three hours along the Merritt and Saw Mill River parkways to the West Side Highway, and on down to Greenwich Village. I snagged a lucky parking space across from the Village Gate.

The air was damp with approaching rain, and clouds hunkered down over the low brick buildings along Bleecker Street. I was glad for the job that Sunday afternoon. It meant I could stay home for a month or so with my son. I hurried, afraid I would be late. Like Alice, I was about to slip into another world, through a looking glass into a magical, wondrous, undreamed of land.

I hustled my guitar and suitcase through the door and down the stairs of the club, where a bank of television cameras and lights were set up. Art D'Lugoff, the bearded, round-faced, gregarious owner of the Gate welcomed me with his merry eyes. The Clancy Brothers and Tommy Makem were already well into their rehearsal. Art showed me where to change my clothes and stash my guitar case. When I returned I was introduced and came out into the bright lights. I threw my head back and began to sing, my eyes tightly closed, my guitar clutched to my breast, my songs pouring out into the room.

I sang "Maid of Constant Sorrow," the "Greenland Whale Fisheries," "I Know Where I'm Going," and "The Rising of the Moon." As I finished my set, stepping off the stage into the pool of blackness, out of the bright lights, an attractive man strode across the dark room and stood beside me. He stuck his hand out and looked me in the eye.

"I'm Jac Holzman," he said. I took his extended hand. "Dear, you're ready to make a record."

It was not a question.

That was my introduction to Jac, to Elektra Records and to the magical world that would enfold me; the new world I would help create. In those days, Elektra's symbol was the moth, but I called it the butterfly. I already had the wings. Elektra would give me the sky and let me fly.

In a funny twist of fate, a week later John Hammond called me to ask me if I would make a record for Columbia. John had signed Billie Holiday to the company and would soon sign Bob Dylan as well as Bruce Springsteen and many other artists. He also said I was ready to record. If these men, who knew the recording business, said I was ready, I thought I must be. I knew and liked John a great deal, but had to tell him that I had promised Jac Holzman I would record for Elektra. He said it was his loss, and wished me luck. John was to remain a friend until his death, a true gentleman and connoisseur of music.

If I had been smart about money in those days I would have auctioned myself, as Harry Chapin did when both Columbia and Elektra wanted him to sign, to the highest bidder. But I had no clue about money or business, only about singing, and wanting to tell stories.

Jac Holzman called me in Connecticut soon after our meeting and arranged for me to come to New York for an afternoon and sing all the songs I knew for my first album, *Maid of Constant Sorrow*. It was to be the first of nineteen albums I was to make for Elektra Records between 1961 and 1984. Jac booked time at Fine Sound studio in Manhattan. I drove into town in my Chevy Carryall, parked near the studio on 57th Street, went in and started singing. It took about five hours. Erik Darling and Freddy Hellerman, both of whom had spent time in the Weavers, played on the album; Eric played banjo, Freddy played guitar. I played too, of course. *Maid of Constant Sorrow* included the "Ballad of Tim Evans," a song by Ewan MacColl and Peggy Seeger about capital punishment. There were also two songs about the Irish troubles. "The Rising of the Moon" and the "Bold Fenian Men" seemed as fresh as they were when they were first sung, in the days of Michael Collins. There were songs about love, politics, loss and relationships. It became a blueprint of how I would approach all my records. The songs must be about serious personal things, about war and love and death and the heart. I had a love affair with each and every song I sang. Making that first record was simple and easy. The first day, I was back home in Connecticut for a late dinner with Peter. The baby was asleep, and we congratulated each other on having taken another step in my career. Peter was supportive, helpful, and always eager to see me do new things.

Peter was continuing with his teaching fellowship at the University of Connecticut. We were part of a community of students and teachers who all protested against the growing American presence in Indochina. We were quite sure that everyone, when they knew the facts, would think as we did.

The audiences who came to listen to me were primarily college students. Rebellion preoccupied our thoughts. Some of us were rebelling from our parents' values, music and political policies. I was an exception in that I thought my parents were as comfortable with what I was doing as were my peers. We sang about social issues, about freedom, about peace. A lot of my friends were in a whirlwind as I was; many of us were beginning to use drugs and take acid trips, trying to find a new reality on the outside, one that matched our inner reality. Many of us would soon be drafted and some of us would die in a war we believed was wrong. The peace we were searching for seemed to hover on the horizon. Drugs were a way of rebelling, acid trips were popular in part because they dissolved the walls that divided us because of our upbringing and put distance between ourselves and our parents and other "adults." Sexual freedom and the urge to try everything were also a sign that the times, as Dylan would put it, they were a-changin'. We were young and convinced we could make a difference, convinced we could have it all, family, work, hopes. It was time of prelude, a time of innocence.

I would return from my trips, driving home at late hours to collapse and be sustained in the arms of my husband and the green rolling hills of Connecticut and the smiles and first words, then sentences, then paragraphs, of my baby. When I was home I was happy. I cooked and cleaned and rocked my son to sleep singing to him. I listened to records and tapes of singers, looking for new material. The Scottrons up the hill invited us to dinner often. Jan Scottron taught me how to make New England clam chowder with bacon and onions, which she sizzled in a frying pan until the bacon curled up; then she added cubed potatoes, clams and canned, condensed cream and simmered, did not boil, for about an hour till the potatoes were done. Jan always added lots of salt and pepper and butter to finish off the smooth, rich chowder. She showed me how to make autumn wreaths of pinecones, milkweed pods and dried flowers which she and I collected in the woods around our farmhouse. Clark would accompany us on these occasions, playing happily with blocks and spoons and pots in Jan's kitchen or toddling with us through the woods, talking happily to himself, singing, and helping Mommy carry home our bounty. I would buy clothes for Clark in Storrs and Willimantic, snowsuits we called bunny suits in which he looked like a little bunny; little shoes, mittens and gloves, jammies and stuffed animals.

Clark had been a happy baby and he was a happy little boy and growing fast. Peter was fulfilled and pleased with his decision to become a teacher. The closer he was to getting his master's degree, the happier he seemed. Still, I was a bit of an oddball in our college community in Storrs. Most students wives had to work to support their husbands. But none of them traveled to the extent that I did. There was always some strain when I came home. I had to explain what I was doing in Oklahoma City, Boston and Denver.

My best friend in Storrs was Mary Twining, the wife of one of Peter's fellow teachers. A singer of folk songs herself, as well as a scholar, Mary had a baby and a two-year-old named Tom who often played with Clark. At Mary's house, or at our farmhouse, we would talk and talk, about life, about music, about my singing in clubs around the country, about Mary's marriage, which would later break up, and mine, which would do the same. We weathered the Connecticut winters, including a big blizzard in 1961 that brought everything to a stop, with recipes for soup and bread and dinners with the kids and our husbands and phone calls and a reassuring, tender kind of friendship that I will always treasure. She made it all right—with her eccentricities and fragile beauty and her own passion for folk music and for being independent—for me to be living the kind of life I was living. She gave me a kind of permission to be different. She understood that I had been called to the profession of music, that I had a gift and that there was a price for that gift. Mary came by her unique qualities honestly. Her mother once papered the walls of her house in Greenwich, Connecticut, with maps from around the world. With Mary as a friend, I didn't feel so out of step.

Not that I would have changed what I was doing. I knew what I wanted by then, although it was lonely out on the road. I was leading the seemingly glamorous life of a troubadour, going from town to town, from club to club, doing what I did best. The life was isolated, but sometimes I was able to spend time with wonderful singers who shared billing with me. I was learning from great talents like Josh White, the African-American folk singer whose version of the "St. James Infirmary Blues" still gives me chills. When Josh would break a string on stage he would put his guitar behind his back and sing "Summertime" a cappella while he restrung his guitar, finishing up with a great flourish as he brought the guitar around to its proper place. It never failed to bring down the house. He and I would drink and talk together between sets. His hearty, deep laughter lessened my loneliness. I also got to know Will Holt and his wife Dolly Jonah. They introduced me to the songs of Kurt Weill and Bertolt Brecht and taught me the "Golden Apples of the Sun." Sometimes I would be on a bill with Ramblin' Jack Elliot of the ever-present cowboy hat and cowboy songs and handsome smile. He had a ridged, angled face, and smoke curled up around his nose from his ever-present cigarette. He would narrow his eyes as he sang a sweet and sorrowful cowboy lament or a raunchy drinking song. Sonny Terry and Brownie McGhee, the great blues duo, would often perform at the Gate of Horn on the bill with me. I did a few engagements with the Chad Mitchell Trio and worked with Arlo Guthrie and Tom Paxton over the years. The Tarriers were on the bill with me often at the Exodus in Denver and in New York. I opened for Lynn

Gold at Gerde's in the Village. So many great artists. There was camaraderie in those long evenings, and many times we would swap songs and share each other's troubles for a week, or two weeks. Then it would be on to the next city, or home.

In between were the late nights of drinking too much, though I never drank in the daytime then, for I learned early that I couldn't drink too much or I would lose my voice. There was time to fantasize, and to yearn to be home with my son and my husband.

Even in the rough times of isolation on the road, there was a trade-off for the loneliness and the separation from my family. I was making something of my own, something no one, not my in-laws, not my husband, could take from me. Perhaps I was losing something I didn't even know, couldn't even think about. Yet I knew I was providing for my son, and for myself, and for my husband. I would never have to depend on anyone else for support. The promise I had made my father at five would be true forever: that at twenty-five, I would be independent.

In early 1961 I became aware of the fact that, in spite of the dreamy Connecticut countryside, having a beautiful son and the satisfaction of being a working mother with a fulfilling job, my relationship with my husband was not going well. Sexual freedom was part of the sixties revolution. Open marriage, alternate lifestyles, and doing things differently from our elders were all part of that equation. On the road in towns like Topeka and Tulsa, Denver and Duluth, I wasn't looking to have an affair; I was in love with my husband. I just wanted some excitement and, in the lonely nights on the road, some sweet company. Someone somewhere to help me make it through the night.

For my second album, *Golden Apples of the Sun,* I worked again with Mark Abramson, a gifted and bright man Holzman had brought in to help me on the first album and who was to become a close friend and coproduce many of my albums with me in the years to come. A producer is someone who makes suggestions, helps me find material, often helps structure arrangements of songs, adding to my own ideas or enhancing what I have already decided to do. A producer usually mixes the albums as well, although I fiercely keep control of the sound of my voice and have had to struggle to do so from the very first. Often it has been difficult, particularly when working with men who think they know better than you what you sound like. Today I produce most of my own albums. I do not give up control, particularly of the sound of my voice, to anyone.

Mark recommended that I work with Walter Raim, a gifted guitarist and arranger. I liked him immediately, and soon found myself attracted to him. Walter was an unlikely Romeo. He was quiet and mild mannered. He probably wanted an affair as much as he wanted another hole in the head. He spent a lot of time with me talking about material. Before either of us knew what had happened we were involved in something neither one of us wanted.

Walter taught me Yiddish phrases and Jewish songs and many things about New York. Walter was divorced from his first wife, Ethel, when we met. Although my affair with Walter didn't last very long, I was to become friendly with Ethel and, in later years, I would produce an album with her for Women Strike for Peace. I got to know Walter's second wife, Susan Hamilton, who wrote and produced with me, David Buskin and Robin Batteau a song on my *Fires of Eden* album in 1989. Walter's current wife, Marty Raim, taught my granddaughter Hollis at Marymount School in New York a few years ago. Small world.

Walter and I spent a few weeks making the new album. Walter's mother, who lived in Brooklyn, taught me how to make kreplach—the real thing, from scratch, starting with a chicken! I came home with a new recipe. Walter also aroused my sensuality. I felt things stir in me that had never been awakened. I was, in a word, in trouble.

I wasn't happy about this new turn of events. I hated the idea of having an affair because it made me dishonest. I didn't want to betray Peter with this man, or hurt my marriage. I thought Walter might be like a dream when I returned home. Unfortunately the dream did not vanish.

I tried to put the whole thing out of my mind. I had told Walter there was no hope that I would leave my husband. I began to drink more.

When I traveled, Clark was taken care of by sitters. When I was home, Peter and I began getting into arguments more often. I was tired from my traveling gypsy life and desperately wanted off the hook and off the road. I wanted the security of my family, my home in the country. I wanted to spend more time with Clark, who was growing fast.

My soul, I decided, was in jeopardy along with my marriage.

If I could get off the road, I thought, I could get back my life. I could rediscover the good qualities in my marriage. I was worn out trying to figure out what was right, and exhausted after months of working. At home, all of this might just go away; the affair, and the pain. At home, I could get back my soul.

❧◦❧

In the spring of 1962 I suggested to Peter that I stop touring. I thought that might solve our problems, which were more than problems of the heart. I was exhausted. I had a bronchial problem that made breathing difficult. I thought I had a particularly persistent flu but it had been going on for months. Peter and I sat down with a little black book between us, a ledger in which I recorded all our expenses: rent, food, books, utilities, clothes, furniture, gas for the car, whiskey, babysitters. I still have that little black book. I was making enough, combined with Peter's fellowship income from the University, to cover every expense. In the shade of the big elm, not far from the lowing of the milk cows and the dancing of the fireflies and the running feet of my son, I made calculations. In those days, I was meticulous about finances.

Peter and I calculated that my getting off the road would mean giving up a lot, including our farmhouse. We would have to move into university housing. Peter didn't want to do that, and neither, frankly, did I. It would mean leaving our farmhouse to live in the university digs where student teachers, their wives and children crowded together.

I didn't tell Peter all of my reasons for wanting to get off the road. My brief plea for stability ended in surrender. I saw that I would have to keep working, and after a month or so of resting, I was ready to begin again to rock and roll on those airplanes, in those trains. I realized that to get any peace back into my life, I would have to end the affair.

Sadly, that spring, I found myself pregnant and, alone and frightened, chose to terminate. At home that summer I spent more time with Clark, cooking, cleaning, playing with my son. Things with Peter didn't improve. Occasionally I would see Walter in New York or some other city.

That summer a friend of ours gave Peter and me a magic mushroom. We didn't take drugs as a rule, but there was said to be a mystic quality to this mushroom. It was supposed to help you see clearly. One night we drank magic mushroom tea and got into our big Chevy station wagon and went to Willimantic to the drive-in. The movie was *Breakfast at Tiffany's*. On the drive home we were both still very high. Suddenly in the middle of the road, a rabbit appeared, frozen in the headlights. Peter swerved hard and I heard the thump of the rabbit's body against the underside of the Chevy and my heart broke in two. I started sobbing and by the time we were home, I was in hysterics. I told Peter I was having an affair, but I wouldn't tell him who it was. I said I wanted to leave our marriage, that things had not worked out the way I thought they might. I told him I was miserable. Audrey Hepburn and the rabbit and the magic mushroom had forced me to break the chains of the lie I was living.

My marriage to Peter had been made in another time, by a girl with no illusions. Now I had many illusions. The life I led was hard, it was not filled with glamour, it was not the zesty sixties image portrayed in the media. Life hurt, and yet this was my life, seeing my son less than I wanted, working to support us all and having an affair I couldn't keep the lid on anymore. Peter was a good man. He was kind and loving to our son. It was just that I didn't want our life together anymore. I agonized over leaving my marriage. For months I chewed on the problem like a dog with a bone, trying to be fair, trying to think my way out of the turmoil in which I was living. I concluded that if my marriage had been good, I wouldn't have needed anything, or anyone, else. Peter and I muddled through the summer as best we could, frequently arguing. The problems with my lungs did not improve, but I shrugged them off.

I thought I was invincible.

In early September Theodore Bikel invited me to be his guest in his annual Carnegie Hall concert in October. I put concerns about the future on hold. Peter and I practiced not seeing the road ahead or the problems. I prepared for Carnegie Hall, bought material for a dress and found a dressmaker in Willimantic to put in the hem and take in the seams. I went to the dentist to have another root canal and took Clark in for his annual checkup. I read to Clark at night and Peter studied. I baked cookies and made bread and ironed clothes and listened to the Cuban Missile Crisis on the radio, cheering President Kennedy. The ice formed on the pond, Clark grew another size and I bought him a new snowsuit. I made a skirt from material I bought at Filene's Basement in Boston. We ate dinner with Jan and Vic and watched the colors change in the great woods of Eastern Connecticut, went to potluck suppers with university students and had heated arguments with nonbelievers about the military advisors in Vietnam. We prayed we wouldn't have to face the music.

Our van broke down and Walter loaned me the money for a new Volvo.

My parents came out from Colorado to be with me for the concert at Carnegie. Peter and I drove to the airport to pick them up, keeping up a good front, not talking about our troubles, although my mother had guessed from our conversations. She didn't know the details, just that I was miserable. We all checked into the Lincoln Hotel. It was a high time for my father, the coming true of many of his dreams for me. My mother was proud, as Daddy was, and she had on the new dress she had bought for the city.

The night of my debut at Carnegie Hall was bittersweet. I stood on that stage of magical history, where in years to come I would sing dozens of concerts and see so many artists perform; my head was thrown back as I belted out the "Greenland Whale Fisheries" with Theo Bikel. After our duet I sang a group of my own songs. It was thrilling, and the concert was a success. Theo brought me out for many bows and everyone around me was very happy. But I knew when the singing stopped, the trouble would start.

Peter's family and his brother's family, the Goodmans, were all there, sitting down in front. There was a lovely dinner after the concert at the Russian Tea Room and then all of us went up to the penthouse of Bergdorf Goodman, where everyone drank too much and we all looked out over the lights of New York City, oohing and aahing. I was in agony. It was as if I sensed the end of the world coming, and didn't know what to do, how to stop it.

My brother-in-law pulled me into one of the lovely, gilded rooms of the penthouse and told me with no ceremony that I would never, if I left my marriage, get custody of my son. Peter had told him I was having an affair, and said he would do everything in his power to prevent me from having Clark. But I knew they could not take my son away. I was sure no judge would take a child from his mother.

At the hotel the fighting started. Once again my husband and I were at it, and this time he became physical, trying to choke me. I left the room in tears, staying in my sister-in-law's room for the rest of the night.

I always pushed people to their limits when I was drinking. If there was a wall, I went up against it. If there were rules, I broke them. My rebellious spirit, combined with alcohol, made me think I was right about everything. The anger Peter felt in response to my behavior was what anyone might have felt, and we both had hot tempers and said and did things we would live to regret. But there was no going back now, the die had been cast. The next day Peter and I put on our proper faces and drove my parents up to our wonderful farmhouse. Mother was going to stay with Clark for the next few days while I was traveling.

I didn't know it would be my last visit to our country home.

The following Monday I got on the plane for Tucson, where I had a job. I kissed and hugged my son and my mother and father and Peter. I was unaccountably sad at having to leave Clark. I left feeling physically ill as well, aware of the coughing I had been ignoring, something I had been referring to as my bronchial problem.

In Tucson, the young people who owned the club at which I was singing happened to be medical technicians in their day jobs, and got me to see a doctor the next morning. I was diagnosed with tuberculosis and promptly hospitalized. The doctor queried me about the bruises on my neck.

This hospitalization came just in time. I was running fast and afraid. I didn't know what I wanted, and drank to cover up all the confusion I was feeling. Tuberculosis rescued me, in a strange way. I was put on a lot of drugs, my lungs drained, and I listened to the doctors tell me I would have to be in the hospital at least four or five months. I watched blood-red and violet sunsets fall over the red and golden sand of the Tucson desert. I wrote in my journals, missing my son. From Tucson I was transferred to the National Jewish Hospital in Denver, a hospital that specialized in TB and lung disease. Theodore Bikel helped me get a bed at National Jewish. I had no money and will be eternally grateful to Theo.

Soon after I got to Denver, Peter sent Clark out to be with me. Clark lived with Mom and I was able to be with him every day. That was like a gift from heaven. I began to make plans, and I began to think about where I might live, about getting an apartment big enough for my son and me. I knew I had some time, because I would be in Denver at the hospital for three more months. I would have to borrow money from my record company to start out, but that would be all right. *We* would be all right. It wasn't perfect, but it would give me time to think. And to plan.

I had a roommate in the hospital, a gentle, beautiful young woman named Pho Tuit Lan, a South Vietnamese in her early twenties. Her name, translated into English, meant Snow Flower. She and I did not agree about the war, but we talked of other things. I told her of wanting to leave my marriage. She sang me Vietnamese songs and taught me to knit and came to my mom's house and made bean thread soup, a Vietnamese delicacy, and told us about her life. She was from a wealthy Vietnamese family with French connections and told us she agreed completely that the Americans belonged in Saigon as military advisers.

Peter and I were talking regularly, but I was determined to leave. Still, I was grieving the marriage even before it was over, wondering if I was doing the right thing or not. My head said no, my heart said yes. Walter and I talked on the phone, and he was as confused as I was.

I was allowed out of the hospital in the afternoon and would go to pick Clark up from play school and bring him home to Mom's, where we played and talked and had dinner together and I read him a bedtime story and kissed him good night before I had to be back at the hospital. I was no longer contagious, the doctors said, and just needed the drugs and the rest.

At Christmas Peter came out to Colorado and we talked, promising each other to be understanding. But as soon as he was gone I was more than sure my marriage wasn't going to work. I called my lawyers and asked them to go ahead as quickly as possible with the divorce. I knew by then I would never go back to the dream we had shared on the farm on Brown's Road. I would stay in Denver to complete my recovery from TB, get my divorce and sue for custody. I had total confidence that custody would be mine.

Two days later, Mother called me frantically at the hospital. She had let Peter's mother, Margaret, and his stepfather, Hal, have Clark for a visit. He wasn't back, and when she talked to Margaret, my mother-in-law told her that Clark was gone. Margaret wouldn't say where. Mother was frantic.

My son had disappeared.

❧

As my suspicions of Hal and Margaret's role in Clark's disappearance mounted, the phone rang. It was my husband.

"I have Clark, I'm in Chicago, on the way back to Connecticut. You can't get him back, so don't try," he said.

Hysterical, I called the district attorney in Denver. I told a calm-sounding male voice what had happened. He told me that because I didn't have a separation agreement, there was nothing he could do. Peter was Clark's father. I asked the doctors if I could leave and was told I wouldn't be allowed out of the hospital to try to get my son back. My treatment was not complete, and I was, in a way, under house arrest. I felt I had been dealt a blow, and could think only of moving as quickly as possible to get my son back, to get my divorce.

Tuberculosis in 1963 was still considered a dangerous disease. It had not been many years since treatment for the kind of TB I had would have been a year's stay in a sanatorium, but now, with strong drugs, the treatment had shortened. At the hospital I knew many people who had been pulled off of immigration lines and put on the plane for Denver, severed from their families, with no time even to think about what was happening to them. They had TB, and that was enough to land them in the Denver Sanitarium, no questions asked. The medical issues with TB were serious, nothing to fool around with, and a little boy spirited away from his mother wasn't going to stop the wheels of medical procedure and science.

I called my lawyers in New York and asked them to hurry with the separation agreement so that I might have custody of my son as soon as I was released from the hospital. I didn't know then that you can't hurry lawyers along. The law, like the great glaciers, moves at its own slow and ponderous pace. Time in the hospital in Denver, like the glaciers themselves, seemed to stand still.

When I called Clark on the phone, he sounded happy to hear me, and asked when I was coming home. I could only tell him Mommy was sick and would be with him as soon as she got well, as soon as she could.

The next few weeks seemed to drag by. I often sat on the bed in my hospital room playing the guitar. Other patients would come in to listen and sometimes to join in the songs. Jac came to visit. I played the records he brought, songs of Jacques Brel and Bob Dylan. I was smoking and went with other patients to lectures about TB held in the big auditorium. The air was always filled with cigarette smoke, as no one had yet proven there was a connection between smoking and lung disease. One of the women patients from Russia took a look at my face and decided I needed a facial. Under her skilled hands, smelling the faint perfume of lilac and rosemary creams, I relaxed while she told me that she, too, had lost a child—in Russia, because of immigration problems. I saw my family regularly, visiting at least a few times a week. Holly was eight by then, Denver twelve, David fifteen and Michael nineteen. My father was broadcasting on the radio and everyone at the hospital knew the voice of *Chuck Collins Calling*.

I realize now that I was fortunate to be in the bosom of my family during this time. My mother always made special meals when I came for dinner and the smells of garlic and roast lamb and sweet potatoes and fresh-baking pies and bread always filled the house. I would sit at the Baldwin, playing Rachmaninoff and the old Chopin ballades I knew so well. And our neighbors knew so well! They used to come to the house and tell my mother how good it was to have Judy home again, playing the piano. The music comforted me.

Jac Holzman called me just before I was due to be let out of the hospital. I had been talking to him all along, telling him what was going on. He told me he would help me in any way he could. He said he wanted to talk about my next record, assuring me that I would have work, and an income. He also told me that B'Nai B'rith was going to award President Kennedy the Humanitarian Award and that I was invited to come to Washington to sing for the president of the United States.

૪⊃૮ૡ

It was a great honor to be invited. I admired Kennedy and knew that, given the time, he would do the right thing in Indochina and pull back our military initiative. How could it be otherwise? All the causes I had worked for were things I felt this president understood and would fight for. He was sophisticated and surrounded by advisers who, I was sure, would tell him it was wrong to have a military presence in Vietnam. Peter and I and all our college friends and my singer friends had voted for him. We considered his victory over Nixon to be cause for celebration and I was thrilled that I would be able to sing to him; perhaps I would even be able to tell him how happy I was that he was our president. Two months had gone by since Clark had been taken back to Connecticut by his father. The doctors said I could travel, and I packed my meager bag and my guitar, and headed for Washington, D.C.

The dinner was at the Shoreham hotel. The Anti-Defamation League presented Kennedy with the Medal of Freedom. The evening was televised by NBC and today can be seen at the Museum of Radio and Television. I watched the show recently with my mother and my stepfather Robert. I was dressed in a little short printed dress, a sash around my waist, singing sea chanteys and "Tis the Gift to Be Simple," a Quaker hymn for the first Catholic president. The show was hosted by actor Robert Preston, and told, in a generally accurate script, the story of American history through its folk ballads. I was joined by Josh White, my old friend from our years of shows together at the Exodus in Denver and the Gate of Horn in Chicago; Lynn Gold, who then had a voice like rich, pure silk; Will Holt, with his lilting tenor and lovely intelligence; and the Clancy Brothers and Tommy Makem, bold and handsome in their white knit cables, all of them accustomed, it seemed, to singing to presidents of all kinds, with hearty chanteys and Irish jigs.

The president seemed to enjoy our warbling folk history, laughing at the Clancys' jokes, his attention focused on us, even as Bobby slipped behind him, the camera catching him, on some errand or other, perhaps going off to call George Wallace or shake up Herbert Hoover. Perhaps to make sure Marilyn was all right. Shaking the president's hand at the end of the show, I remember feeling the bolt of electricity move through me; he was, after all, the president, and he was powerful, forceful, and charismatic.

At the time, I was naturally aware of other feelings; anger at my husband and at my lawyers, who were, I thought, not moving quickly enough on the divorce.

᯼

I returned to Denver for a few more weeks, then I borrowed money from Jac and headed for New York. Any friends other than my family were there. Jac and Elektra Records was there, Walter was there. In New York I would be only three hours from Storrs, so I could go and get my boy as soon as the court told me he was mine again.

With little else but my guitar and a sparse-looking suitcase, I flew from Denver to New York's Greenwich Village. I moved in with Walter while I looked for an apartment. I brought Clark to New York for a visit and soon found a light, spacious, fifth-floor one-bedroom apartment in an old prewar building overlooking the traffic rolling north above the corner of Hudson and Tenth. The streets were cobbled and the sidewalks lined with storefronts selling antique lamps and secondhand furniture. There were quaint shops where I could buy fresh bread and homemade cheeses and salami, a leather shop and the White Horse Tavern, a block or two uptown. Sheridan Square was close by.

My relationship with Walter was cooling. It occurred to me that he had only been a catalyst for my leaving, and that there were deep troubles with my marriage that had nothing to do with Walter. He was drifting out of the picture. He was always kind, and we remained friends, but the romance was over.

I brought Clark to New York whenever I could. We would wander the twisting streets of the Village, make trips to the Statue of Liberty, the Museum of Natural History, the Empire State Building and the Circle Line, the great tour of the rivers around New York. Clark loved the Circle Line. We would eat hot dogs and put our faces to the wind and breathe in the clean air pouring in from the Atlantic through the canyons of skyscrapers in the greatest city in the world. We loved our time together.

Sometimes, when I could get Clark for a few weeks at a stretch, we would go to Colorado and be with my family. My divorce came through but the custody issue remained in limbo. The court ruled that Peter and I would have to work out visitation until custody was settled.

During the next two years I continued to seek a legal settlement of custody in my favor. I spent my money on lawyers who assured me I could not lose; they said no mother ever loses custody.

In the fall of 1963 a social worker from the family court came down from Connecticut to interview me. I bought a new dark-blue suit for her visit. Her raised eyebrows said everything. The suit didn't do a thing. As I rocked in my wooden rocker and she sat, tight-lipped and straight-backed in a wicker-caned chair, I knew she did not approve of me or of Greenwich Village.

I felt vulnerable and small and guilty and less-than, sitting next to my rented grand piano. I could hear the traffic rolling by below the windows of my beautiful apartment, perfect for me and my son. I saw that the woman before me was not in the least impressed. I needed more space, and vowed to move immediately to a grander, bigger home in the city. I swore I would impress "them" with the kind of space they were looking for.

Until settle of the custody issue my lawyers were advising me to go along with Peter's suggestions for my visits with Clark and his schooling. They said the court would see my cooperation as a stabilizing factor for Clark.

Within weeks I had found an apartment on the Upper West Side of Manhattan and moved in. It had plenty of room for my son and for me. During our visits, Clark would often say, "Mom, why can't I stay here with you half the time and stay with my dad the other half? Or just stay with you? Why do I have to go back?" I had to explain that it was just a matter of time, and we would be together for good.

❧

In contrast to the difficulties I was experiencing in getting custody of my son, in the world of music, it was a rich and wondrous time. I met singers and roamed the streets of the Village, looking for songs, often running into friends, staying up half the night listening to music at the clubs in the Village, drinking at the Lion's Head and the White Horse Tavern, where I once saw Dylan Thomas, nearly as drunk as I was. But it must have been his ghost, as he had been dead many years by then. I was drinking, a lot, and part of me was dead as well—maybe that was why I could see Dylan Thomas's ghost so easily.

Recently I was being given an award by Peace Action for my work with UNICEF. Peace Action is a reconfiguration of a number of groups who in past years worked in the antiwar movement and for nuclear test bans. Jane Alexander, the actor and former head of the National Endowment for Arts, and William Sloane Coffin, minister at Riverside Church in New York, both of whom I have known for years, were hosting the evening. A woman I remembered from the early days took me aside to congratulate me on my award.

"I remember you in the early sixties, you did every fund-raiser there was!" she told me. "Every time I turned around, at an antiwar rally, a fund-raiser for the freedom workers in Mississippi, a benefit for women's rights, you were there, singing your heart out."

I wanted to sing, I wanted to help people, I wanted to do the thing I had been raised up to do: make a difference, or at least try to.

I was by now being managed by Harold Leventhal, who had given up his lingerie business in the thirties to manage Pete Seeger and the Weavers.

Harold used to say that Pete accepted as many benefits as were offered to him, even if they were all on the same night in different cities. Pete continues to be a big influence on me. I admire him and respect his politics and his music. His life has been a flow of songs and good works. I remember going to Harold's office one morning and seeing Pete stretched out behind the couch in the office, fast asleep, exhausted after having come in from one of those multiple fund-raiser nights.

When I moved to New York I knew I needed professional help and I applied to the William Alanson White Institute of Psychiatry at New York University, where I was given an extensive questionnaire to fill out. I was put on a waiting list for a doctor who would be available to take on a patient who didn't have the money to pay full price for therapy.

During this time Walter asked me to sing in a group called the Homesteaders. We made a record. The other singers included Ronnie Gilbert, of the Weavers, and a wonderful bass named Bob Harter. Bob and I got to know each other and Walter happened to mention to me that Bob was in therapy with someone who had helped him with his drinking and his depression. Within a week I had my first visit with Harter's therapist, Ralph Klein. Ralph was a member of a therapy community that called themselves the Sullivanians. Now my appearances started to come in waves and, as if by magic, I had the money to pay for therapy. Ralph suggested I see him three times a week and I was to do so, with him, or with another Sullivanian, for the next fifteen years.

Ralph Klein was an important influence in my life. He was extremely smart and I am sure being in therapy with him saved my sanity, though I would later realize he did me few favors in other areas, even, perhaps, damage. It was a dark time of hurt, guilt and depression. But being able to see Ralph probably saved me from another suicide attempt. Now, I had some kind of stability in my life, someone to talk to about how I felt. I was able for the first time to see the possibilities instead of only the dark side. I was able to talk, to admit what I wanted.

I told Ralph that I thought I had a problem with alcohol. Ralph, to my relief at the time and my horror later on, did not agree. He said we would work on the underlying trouble, and not to worry about my drinking. In our sessions, I was able to begin a process of healing that assured I would keep growing and find some joy.

☙ℂ☙

In New York I roamed the cobbled streets of Greenwich Village, listening to my peers sing songs in the Gaslight, Gerde's, the Village Vanguard and the Cafe Wha? My music seemed to have a pulse of its own. The next year was to be a continuation of the career for which I had been destined.

Jac Holzman and his wife, Nina, had become my friends. Nina loved to cook and used to throw great parties for the artists on Elektra. She later started a catering company, and I remember her having a terrible time getting the Yellow Pages to put it in their book because the name of the company was Pure Pleasure. She once had a great party after my third album at a loft in Soho, another at the Holzman apartment where everyone got very stoned on pot that had been measured out carefully by Jac according to the weight of the various guests, and served as dessert in cookies. I got paranoid on grass. Drinking was not very popular in the Village. If you drank, you probably had a problem. If you used drugs, you were just cool. So when in certain company I tried to disguise myself as a pothead, and Al Kooper from the Blues Project even called me "the viper." But still, I preferred to drink.

I would often see Dave Van Ronk, with his whiskey voice full of character. Dave's wife Terry cooked dinner for us sometimes and we sat around singing the night away with Jim Friedman, Chad Mitchell, Joan Baez, Mimi Baez and in later years, Leonard Cohen, Dave Blue, Eric Andersen and whoever was around in the clubs at the moment. I had a special bond with Van Ronk, strengthened by the two weeks we spent one bitter winter in Oklahoma City when we worked on the same bill at a club called the Laughing Buddha. The owners of the club put us up in a little house nearby in which there was a stove that burned barely warm enough to keep one person comfortable. After our last show at the club, we would head to the house and Dave and I would sit around the warm glow of that stove as the wind howled and the snow blew outside. He sang me songs and told me stories and we passed around a whiskey bottle until we were warm enough and sleepy enough to go to bed, me in the bed near the stove, he in the room upstairs where he shivered, I am sure, with cold. He is a good man, a fine writer, and a great singer, but I will always remember him most fondly for giving up the warm bed by the stove to a girl folk singer during one cold winter in Oklahoma.

Peter Yarrow was a sincere, earnest and deeply moving singer and guitar player who would bend his head over his guitar and take you to another world with his beautiful, lyric voice. It was before the historic marriage of Peter, Paul, and Mary, and we used to see each other a lot at Gerde's, the Italian restaurant turned club in the East Village, where on many nights after the last show we would find ourselves in earnest conversation about politics and music and the soul. It was Peter to whom I opened my heart about my broken marriage and my efforts to gain custody of Clark, and he was generous with his friendship and his time, once taking me home with him to his mother's house when I was desperately unhappy. His mother later returned my pajamas and told me she had found me in the morning sleeping on the couch like the vagabond that I was.

Tom Paxton is a blue-eyed, handsome singer with a sweet twang in his voice. His songs were good then and they still are now. He wrote a biting song about the riots at Attica prison called "The Hostage," which I recorded in the late sixties. When I got to the Village he was already married to the woman who is still his wife. Midge had a brother in Storrs, Connecticut, so we knew Tom very early and I used to see him at music festivals and then get together with him in the city. I recorded "The Last Thing on My Mind," "Bottle of Wine" and "Ramblin Boy." We would often work together at some club in the Village or see one another at folk festivals, and I was always asking him what he was writing and would he play it for me. Tom has done a lot of children's material for television and records in the last few years and sometimes works with Odetta and Janis Ian. He continues to be a vital and growing artist, which is a pleasure to see.

I used to hear Eric Andersen and Tim Buckley in the Village. Once I told Eric I wanted to hear any songs he had. On the way down West Fourth

Street to visit me, he later told me he wrote the last verse to "Thirsty Boots," which I recorded. Tim Buckley wore rough boots and had shaggy hair and a smile like sunshine and sang these sweet, bitter songs. He later died later of a drug overdose, but in those days he was like a ray of sunshine.

Song hunting had become a passion. I learned from my father that snaring the right song is like falling in love, and the feeling of taking in a song and making it my own is an alchemy that has as much to do with faith as with music. The fit has to be like a glove and there is no way to bottle it or to make a prescription out of that process. It is magical. There are songs I may like but that I know do not belong to me, just as there are songs I sing that belong to no one else. I believe the process of finding songs is as mysterious, unpredictable and magical as the art of songwriting itself.

Elektra was a small, boutique label at this time, but Jac Holzman was to become a major player in the folk boom, taking my records to multigold and platinum sales and signing the Doors, Harry Chapin, Bread, Carly Simon and many other fine artists to the label. Jac was and still is a particular, organized, type A personality. His desk was always neat as a pin, even in the sixties, when messiness was a sign of political correctness. He was always thinking about business as well as art, which accounts for his great success and, I believe, mine at the label. But in those days I thought only about the art, never about the business.

Jac was my friend, a friend with whom I shared my joys and sorrows. With him I had the rare opportunity to go through so many things that at times it seemed we were a married couple, with all but the sexual part of a partnership. He was wonderful to me, he was an asset in a difficult business, a solace when I needed a shoulder to cry on, a social companion who loved music as passionately as I did. He and I had a plan, even from those very first records. I would sing what I loved, and he would support whatever I did. He had opinions, but though we sometimes had heated arguments, he never really gave me a hard time about doing what I wanted to do. He was on the hunt for songs for me as well. In the first few years we made records together, I was one of the few singers in the Village who didn't write my own songs. There were songs "longing to be sung by you," he would say, just waiting out there, and he would help me find them. Sometimes he would take me to a Tom Paxton or Tom Rush or Dylan concert and say, after a song was finished, "You've got to sing that!" He first introduced me to Jacques Brel and unusual folk recordings from Europe and America.

Before I became ill with tuberculosis, Albert Grossman and I had almost become client and manager when he asked me to be one third of a girl's trio after he had put together Peter, Paul, and Mary. He facetiously said he would get me brown contact lenses because the other two women were brown-eyed. Instead, I had signed a contract with Harold Leventhal shortly after moving from the hospital in Denver to New York. Harold was a rock of solidity for me in the next eleven years, standing beside me through all the years of turmoil with Peter about my son, and helping me to create a foundation for a career that would weather the emotional and physical storms of being on the road, being a musician, and being a woman in what was essentially a man's business.

By the time I recorded my third album, *Judy Collins #3*, singer-songwriters had become a flourishing group in America as well as in England and Canada. Work, love, political passions, spiritual fervor, even betrayal could be lyrical. "Anathea" is about a woman who sleeps with a judge in order to save her brother from hanging, and then hears the gallows creak at dawn as she wakes in the betrayer's arms. "Turn! Turn! Turn!" "Bells of Rhymney," and "Deportee" were on this album. I first heard Dylan sing "Masters of War" at Carnegie Hall that year and knew I had to sing it. I recorded Shell Silverstein and Jim Friedman's "Hey, Nelly, Nelly." These city writers were creating a new sort of popular song that told a story of politics and people, of raw emotion, with well-constructed lyrics.

There were strong women singers both singing in the clubs and making records at that time. And then there was the indomitable Mary Travers, of Peter, Paul, and Mary, who had grown up in an activist family in the Village and was all I and so many young women longed to be: beautiful, brilliant, with her long blond hair and her incredible lean body, and her Lauren Bacall voice and her singing companions, who later set her off as though she were a smoky diamond. Peter, Paul, and Mary were destined to take the experience of the Village and that small community to the world with their recordings.

I was not writing my own songs yet. Most women singers were not. Buffy Sainte-Marie wrote her own songs, but Carolyn Hester, Judy Henske, Mary Travers, and Joan Baez, when she started to record, didn't write that I know of.

Jim McGuinn played banjo and guitar on my third album. He was a friend of Walter's and had been working for Bobby Darin in Las Vegas, where I first heard him play. Jim later was to change his name to Roger. He and I did the arrangements of "Turn! Turn! Turn!" and our collaboration is the basis of the version of it that he did when he started the Byrds. Jim had terrible teeth, as I do, and I have a vivid memory of Jim's constant trips to the dentist, as well as his gifted guitar and banjo playing, as we worked during the summer of 1964.

We recorded "In the Hills of Shiloh," a song by Freddy Hellerman, who had once been a Weaver, along with Pete Seeger, Lee Hays, Ronnie Gilbert and Eric Darling. The Weavers came together during the early labor movement and sang at many fund-raisers and rallies, later making records and becoming enormously popular. The Weavers were the beginning, and if they had not started recording, I probably wouldn't be making records now.

❧

On November 22, 1963, a few months after meeting John F. Kennedy, I was on a bus to La Guardia with my guitar and my suitcase, headed for Washington, D.C., where I was going to work at a club called the Shadows. The radio in the bus suddenly announced that the president had been wounded by a gunshot in Dallas, Texas. I remember my first thought was, I hope to God it isn't somebody black. There were riots in the South, Wallace was fighting integration of schools in Alabama, and racial tension was high everywhere in the country. If the shooter had been black, the country would have been in for more riots, and terrible trouble, and the integration movement would have suffered a large setback. For an hour or so, I never doubted the president would recover from whatever wounds he had sustained.

At the airport a cop got on the bus and told us the president was dead.

There were screams, sobs, and people sat in stunned silence. One man put his head in his hands and wept. I walked in a daze, making my way to the gate. I got on my plane. I couldn't think of anything else to do. I landed in Washington and called the Shadows. Of course, the shows had been canceled; the country, perhaps the world, had come to a standstill. I caught a cab driven by a stunned driver and gave him the Silbersteins' address in Georgetown.

Beverly and Lee Silberstein ran an art gallery in Georgetown and had been my friends in Washington since my first singing engagements at the Shadows. For three days, as we mourned with the world, I stayed in their darkened brownstone, drinking tea and watching the black-and-white tragedy unfold on television. We didn't venture out of Georgetown, fearing riots and crowds, and so I, along with most of the world, watched the riderless horse, the carriage hearse, little John waving his flag and saluting, on television. A great dream had died, and the world would never be the same.

Back in the Village, I had begun to make some friends. I felt at home in New York. Sometimes I would run into Dylan at Gerde's or one of the other Village clubs. Dylan had made it more fashionable to write songs, bringing with him an entire generation of new writers to follow in the footsteps of Woody and Pete Seeger. One night Scott McKenzie, a singer with a magnificent tenor voice, who was in John Phillips's first group, the Journeymen, asked me if I knew where 57th and Fifth Avenue was. When I said I didn't, he took me on the subway to show me Tiffany and Bergdorf's, which I remembered from my night at Carnegie Hall. I had forgotten that part of town, as though the night of my debut with Theo had vanished in some bad dream, along with the memory of the fight with my husband and my sad return to Connecticut and the trip out to Tucson, from which I had never, in a way, returned.

In the summer of 1964, along with many students, lawyers, singers and other professionals, I went to Mississippi to help register black voters. I wanted to be a part the revolutionary summer. I traveled to Jackson, Mississippi, to join Barbara Dane and a group from Chicago called the Gateway Singers. We traveled in a beat-up Volkswagen bus through Ruleville, Jackson, Drew and Hattiesburg, Mississippi. The Southern whites were, it seemed to me, universally furious at the intrusion of this assembly of visitors from the North. We knew murder was in the air, and there were beatings and jailings and threats to our physical health. I trembled at every truck with a gun rack coming down the road, not knowing whether to be more frightened if the gun rack was full or empty. In each town we would be welcomed by the local groups that were registering voters. We often stayed with black families and socialized both with workers from the North and local members of the Student Nonviolent Coordinating Committee and local families who worked in the movement. Fanny Lou Hamer joined the cavalcade in our VW bus and for a few days I rode from town to town with that great woman, taking courage from her all-embracing spirit. We would gather in the afternoon light around a cluster of houses, in a park or in the city square. Fanny would sing "This Little Light of Mine"; I would sing "It Isn't Nice," a song by Malvina Reynolds, and "Turn! Turn! Turn!" or "Twelve Gates to the City." Then we would all join hands and sing together, encouraging our audiences, mostly black, to register and to vote. This was dangerous for them in many parts of the state. We left, to go on to another town, but they had to stay, often to face the hostile hoses of the police, driven from the polling booths, frightened, intimidated. Their bravery succeeded, and during that summer, hundreds of thousands of voters were registered.

During the weeks I was there, three young men became martyrs for the cause of integration: Andrew Goodman, James Chaney, and Michael Schwerner were abducted in Meridian, Mississippi, and all over the country, and even the world, people feared for these young men's lives. They were later found murdered, their bodies buried in the red earth of a dam nearby. All of the country, all of the world was shocked to see the evil and deep, paralyzing prejudice. It was a disgrace to the ideals and the hope of the efforts to move ahead in our search for equality. Tears fell everywhere for those boys. The South, it seemed, was at war with children, and with those who would banish racism forever.

I returned from Mississippi with more experience but fewer illusions. I would go to Connecticut, or Clark would come to New York, and I longed for the time we could be together for good. My family was rooting for me, and supporting me. Much of the pain of the early sixties, historically viewed as the product of the war in Vietnam and the changing social structure, was also pain over the separation from my son.

In the late summer of 1964, my divorce came through. Peter remarried the day after the divorce papers were final. I awaited the custody decision.

I was still sure, as were my lawyers, that I couldn't lose.

❧

In 1964 I sang at the Newport Folk Festival on the big stage, staying up half the night listening to Mississippi John Hurt and Carolyn Hester, Dick Fariña and the Jug Band from Boston. The Charles River Valley Boys were there that year, and my friendship with Dick Fariña continued to grow.

I performed on the same stage with the Chambers Brothers, Maria and Geoff Muldaur of the Jug Band, Koerner, Ray and Glover, the Blues Trio, Joan Baez and Pete Seeger. Sometimes there were big finales where we all sang together. That was the year I was asked to be on the board of directors of the festival, and for the next few years I attended the meetings at George Wein's house in New York, where the shape of the festival was laid out and changes were fought out between very determined factors from both the traditional side and those more favorable to opening the festival up to new music.

I also hosted a live radio show that year on WBAI in New York, and brought singer-songwriters on to the show. I would put a bottle of whiskey and a few glasses out on the table, and, for an uninterrupted hour, let the songs and the conversation flow. The McPeak family from Ireland were my guests, as were the Pennywhistlers, the group led by Walter's ex-wife Ethel. They sang Eastern European folk songs in polyphonic harmonies that were elegant and stirring. Some of my other guests were Tom Paxton, Koerner, Ray and Glover, Dick Fariña and Mimi. It was a great experience. I was back on the radio, doing what I had seen my father do for so many years.

So much music, so many lyrics, told of what was moving college students away from the values of their parents. We would surely make a new world, we thought. The world would change, the dark times would evaporate, good would conquer evil. I kept singing, carrying an ever-deepening vision of what my music could do for others and where I wanted it to take me. I knew I wanted to be better, to become more than I was. I was searching, studying singing with my teacher, Max Margulis, working hard in therapy to understand myself. I was sure if I worked hard enough, everything would work out. I sang songs that spoke out against war, songs of the brokenhearted, songs that told of the casualties of battlefields and the casualties of the heart.

Dylan went electric on the stage at Newport in 1965, defying every standard, changing every rule. He sang "I was so much older then, I'm younger than that now," and the children of flowers and wildfire concurred. "The Lonesome Death of Hattie Carroll" and "Masters of War" and Guthrie's ballad "Deportee" were songs on people's lips. The country was waking up, but it was also being torn apart. I believed that the music I loved and sang could help it rip, and also help it heal.

The court date was finally set for my custody hearing. My lawyers had been assuring me for months I could not lose; my therapist told me it was always customary for the mother to get custody, and from what I knew to be true, I was confident that finally, I would have my boy back with me. I had moved into a larger apartment, with plenty of room for both of us. Clark had friends in New York by now whom he would see on his visits I was looking at schools, thinking about spending less time on the road. I was confident, positive.

On a day in late May 1965, I drove to Rockland County Courthouse in another suit purchased specially for the occasion. In the car with me was my therapist, Ralph Klein; my manager, Harold Leventhal; and my lawyer. My husband and his family were gathered together on one side of the room, I and my supporters on the other. The judge pounded the gavel to begin the proceedings. I answered questions, feeling totally confident, sure of the outcome. The day seemed to go well, and driving back to New York, my lawyer once again told me he knew I would win. I relaxed.

Ten days later, the court in Tolland County, Connecticut, granted full custody to my husband.

I had lost my son.

ℬℭℰ Gray day, a day of winds and wet, sudden showers of rain pattering against the window. On my desk is an African violet, purple and delicate, casting its beribboned color into the dark room.

I want so much to change what is, change the weather, say what has happened isn't so. Sometimes I am so weary of keeping up a good front, of being positive, of feeling the pain and surrendering to it and then praying for courage. I can't change what is, I can only change what I do about it. There is nothing I could have done to make your death not happen. I did the best I could.

Now, knowing in my heart that the only way out is in, I must write, and work and try to think of something positive, try to absorb color and life, even from the little African violet, braving the dark day, blooming for me. I can't rail against this gray weather, but I can change the weather in my soul.

I pray for the courage to change, and for acceptance of things I cannot change. There is one thing I know in my life, and that is that the weather will change, maybe not this afternoon, but soon. The weather will change and the sun will shine again.

I pray for the courage to get through this rough weather, for the serenity to know the sun is shining somewhere.

6

Child of the Sixtiest

*W*hen I heard the news of the judge's decision to give custody of Clark to my husband, at first I didn't believe I had heard correctly. It couldn't be so. When my lawyer repeated the decision, I fell apart. I called my mother and cried until I couldn't think. I drank until I couldn't walk or speak. Sober, I tried to understand what had happened, why the whole reason for my existence, it seemed, had been taken from me.

I later learned that the judge had told my lawyer he had decided against me because I was in therapy. The vision of the woman from social services sitting in the straight-backed chair, her lips in a tight line, kept floating before me. She knew.

My separation from my son came at a time when we needed more than ever to be together. Whatever the problems might have been, we should have been allowed to have our life together. The decision made it difficult for everyone. I believe the court betrayed us both.

In the weeks that followed, I was unable to shake the rage I felt. I was in a daze, confused. I felt I was a danger to myself. I called emergency wards and talked to Ralph in the middle of the night suggesting I should be hospitalized. I drank, numbing the pain. Although not a proponent of sedatives, Ralph was quite comfortable recommending alcohol for anxiety. I took his advice with no qualms.

I had been asked to go to the Soviet Union and Poland that summer for concerts and would have taken Clark with me. When the decision against me came down, I told Harold Leventhal that I was going to cancel the trip.

Harold talked to me for hours, insisting that the best thing I could do would be to keep to my plans. It would help me keep my sanity, he said.

I called my mother, who was in shock over the court's decision too. Now, she agreed I should not cancel my Russian and Polish tour, but said Holly could go along with me on the trip. God bless my mom. My beloved sister traveled with me during this hard summer of loss. She was eleven, Clark was six, and she was very close to Clark, who was like her little brother. She made it possible for me not to check myself into a mental institution somewhere. Instead, I worked, and embraced the presence of my beloved sister.

My sister is the confidante I could always tell everything, often the plumb line of my emotions. The sound of her voice resonates with the sounds of our lives, of our children, our hopes, our history.

❧

Our trip to the Soviet Union included a layover in Paris, my first visit to the city. We went to the church at Montmartre and lit candles for Edith Piaf and for each other, as Edith and her sister had done. The trip included a visit with Joan Baez's mother, Big Joan, who was saddened to hear that I had lost custody of Clark. She knew Clark and the story of my struggle to have my son with me, and she and Al, her husband, were very comforting to us. We went out to a restaurant on the Île de la Cité and drank wine in the candlelight and talked till nearly dawn. Holly and I had rooms in a small pension near the Arc de Triomphe and watched the skyline of the city brighten with the sunrise.

Then it was on to Poland, where we toured for three weeks on a minibus and I sang concerts with the Tarriers, a group that included my friends Al Dana, Eric Weissberg and Clarence Cooper. We were told about the black market dealings in the Polish currency, the zloty, and the American dollar, following with our eyes the man with the black briefcase hurrying down the street, who had been identified by our tour guide as a black marketeer. We imagined ourselves to be in a spy movie. I got a few bottles of strong Polish vodka, the color of good bourbon, and found the Polish to be hospitable and great audiences. I had spent the six months before the trip at the New School studying Russian so that I might be able to write and speak a little Cyrillic. Our tour manager was generous and taught us more phrases and Holly and I ordered cheese and eggs and tea and said "good morning" and "thank you" in Russian. I wrote a note to my Russian teacher at the New School and sang a song in Russian. The Russians laughed and clapped all during the song, and I thought they hated it. But when I finished, they clapped and stamped their feet, demanding an encore. They loved it, and were amused as Americans are when they hear Russians singing "Its a Long Way to Tipperary" in English. I sang in Moscow at the Opera House, in Odessa at the big outdoor concert hall; in Yalta and Krasnodar and in a resort on the Black Sea. Mom and Harold were right. I was at peace, traveling with my sister. We loved being together, learning Russian phrases, meeting wonderful people, singing to these amazing Russians. I wouldn't have been able to do that trip without her.

On our return from Russia, I was able to have an almost month-long visit with Clark. He came to stay with Holly and me at a house I rented in Amagansett on Long Island. We ran on the beach, swam in the surf, laughed and talked. I read stories to Clark and sang songs to him. He was six, a freckle-faced kid. We were glad to be together, even for a little while.

Peter moved to Vancouver that fall, where he started teaching at the University and it was nearly impossible for Clark and me to have regular visits. Dick Fariña, in conspiratorial tones, often suggested I kidnap my son. We talked about it with certain people who thought I should do it, but I didn't have the heart. It would have been a terrible thing to do to Clark.

Clark's father was certainly responsible, certainly stable, and if I were to take Clark from his father, there might be more trouble for Clark in the end.

But responsibility isn't everything. Stability isn't everything. Sometimes I am still sorry I didn't take Fariña's advice and spirit my son away.

The judge had cited my being in therapy as reason for denying me custody, but I suspected it was also because I had a career. I went to therapy religiously, and I worked constantly, trying to improve my singing, trying to find joy in songs and audiences that I could find nowhere else. The music was in my blood, and it was driving me. I was beginning to understand that it always had and always would. Work had to be my salvation.

As the months went by, I began to have some acceptance of the situation and a certain amount of peace about it. I would see Clark when I could. There was no way to reverse the situation. I would have to make the best of it, for my son, and for myself.

In 1965 I recorded my first solo concert in New York at Town Hall: *The Judy Collins Concert.* The musicians were Eric Weissberg, the self-proclaimed "banjophanist," and Steve Mason. Both were wonderful guitar, banjo and mandolin players. Chuck Isreals was on bass and Bob Sylvester played the cello. On the live album were songs by Billy Ed Wheeler, a fine writer from North Carolina who wrote "Red-Winged Blackbird," "Coal Tattoo," and "Winter Sky." I had become friends with John Phillips, with whom I had taken my first acid trip and who, with his wife Michelle, Cass Elliot and Denny Doherty, would put together the Mamas & the Papas. I recorded John's great song, "Me and My Uncle," and the Dylan song, "The Lonesome Death of Hattie Carroll," about a Baltimore swell who strikes and kills a black maid.

The cello on this album was my first conscious departure from the folk sound that had characterized my previous albums, and, moreover, a departure in feeling from my first three recordings.

But in 1965, as I had done when I was fourteen, I jumped the track, changing course. At fourteen I had moved from Mozart and Beethoven to folk music. Now, it was from folk music to a unique combination of songs from many different genres. Raised on Broadway songs, I had learned Mozart, Beethoven, traditional songs, Woody Guthrie, Pete Seeger and the other writers of the city. Now, I was moving into new territory. Each rebellion, each change of course, each discovery, was necessary to finding my own voice.

In the following year I spent a lot more time with Dick and Mimi Fariña. They were writing great songs and singing and playing them on the guitar and dulcimer, a lovely and unusual combination. Dick was working on his first novel. I recorded their song "Pack Up Your Sorrows" on my fifth album. Mimi played guitar and Dick played dulcimer.

I adored Dick. He was the buddy I had never had before, a pal I could tell anything. I needed his friendship. That spring he wrote a poem for me in which he compared my voice to amethysts; but his friendship was the true jewel.

In 1966, on the eve of the publication of his novel, Dick died in a motorcycle accident in Carmel. I flew West to be with Mimi. Dick's loss was devastating to all who loved him and knew his charismatic, bright presence. A light had gone out in my life, for I treasured him as a rare friend with whom I could cry and laugh and make music, and I mourned his tragic and too-young death. I had looked forward to being able to laugh with him for the next fifty years, at least. I was learning it doesn't always work out that way.

Dick often said that there is nothing to do with some grief but sing it. Today, I know even more that what he said is true.

I was doing many concerts in the States, and, in 1966 I went to Australia. I had originally met the Limeliters at the Limelight in Aspen during the first winter I was working, in 1959. They also recorded for Elektra and were on that trip with me—Alex Hassileff, Glen Yarborough and Lou Gottlieb. Alex was a friend of Harold's and had found a place for me to stay in Los Angeles when I had first worked at the Troubadour in 1964. Glen Yarborough had a silky tenor voice.

One day in the airport in Sydney en route to Brisbane, we were all drinking shandies, a favorite Australian drink made with lime juice and beer. I was throwing them back one after another.

"You should watch your drinking, dear," Lou said, "because you might have a problem." I watched my drinking after that, but only with Lou.

A few months after Dick's funeral I traveled to Japan to perform with Mimi and our friends Bruce Langhorn and Arlo Guthrie. We played in Hiroshima and Tokyo, Osaka and Nagasaki. It was an extraordinary trip. We soaked in hot baths and stayed in the Frank Lloyd Wright Hotel in Tokyo, the Imperial, and a Frank Lloyd Wright house in Osaka. An Osaka art dealer named David Kidd brought out his collection of antique Chinese clothing and let us dress up as Chinese princes and princesses. We met the younger brother of the Dalai Lama in a Japanese garden. He was peaceful and tranquil in spite of the fact that he could not go back to Tibet and that the Chinese were destroying his homeland. His serenity impressed me a great deal.

In most of the cities in which we played, the audiences did not clap very much. The Japanese do not show their enthusiasm with applause. It threw us for the first few times, as it always throws American performers, until we got accustomed to it. At the University in Tokyo, however, the student audience was just as enthusiastic as the audiences we were used to in the States.

On the way home from Japan I had promised Mimi I would stop over in Hawaii. For a few days there I walked the beaches and swam in the blue water, let the Pacific run over my body and wrote in my journals. I prayed for a way to begin writing songs. It was a momentous experience, like discovering sex. Something happened there on the beach in Hawaii that would move things around and set me on the road to a new universe. I began to heal.

ও৫৪

Back home, I started playing the piano again, which I hadn't done seriously for years. I got to Vancouver whenever possible to see Clark. Our pattern of having summer vacations continued, whenever I could get him.

But things were not going well for Clark. He started to have problems in school in Canada and his father began sending him to a psychotherapist. I could do nothing to help. I was far away and Peter was doing the best he could.

ও৫৪

I went to England in 1966. My records were doing well there and I sang in Manchester, Birmingham and London. Then I went to Brussels and on to Paris, where I sang at the Olympia. Back in London, I fell in love. Except for

Walter and an occasional lover, I hadn't been with anyone steadily since the breakup of my marriage. Michael Thomas, my new beau, was a Welshman and a writer, charming, brilliant, and endearing. He came to New York after I returned home and we continued our love affair.

Ralph Klein did not think people should be in monogamous relationships or live with anyone exclusively. He, and the rest of the Sullivanians, believed in the sexual revolution. They viewed monogamy as the seed of annihilation of personal freedom. It wasn't that they cared one way or another about sex, per se. They were interested in the continuous development of the creative individual. They encouraged groups: painting groups, social groups, artists' groups, anything to break down the isolation they thought people acquire in a one-on-one relationship in which each partner becomes dependent on the other for everything.

Michael had been a part of a very similar group living in Australia. There were many such philosophies evident during this time as, I imagine, there have been during every time in history. Sex, marriage, and every traditional living situation were being examined by an entire culture of young people in a search for more meaning, more contact, more creativity. More reality. It was a time before AIDS, and before we had an understanding of consequences. In my case, it was before I had any idea that alcohol played such a part in any of the choices I made.

Under the tie-dye and the alcohol I was quite conventional. I wanted a relationship with one person, one male person. My therapists also tried to end avenues of communication with my family, which failed totally. I was always enchanted with my family, engrossed by them. I spend as much time as I possibly can in their company, traveling to Colorado, making the effort to see them, talk to them, and have loving times with them. I only listened to some of what my therapist said.

Michael had a gypsy soul, he was often as flighty as a rare bird, and was as likely to go off on a trip around the world, bringing me back a sitar five months later, as he was to settle down for a year. Certainly I had a serious love affair with him, as serious as I had had with anyone since leaving my husband. But there was no question of our time together being permanent.

Permanence was a thing of the old regime, and we were of the new breed. We could come and go as we pleased. Or so we thought.

Michael was a breath of fresh air. We got along very well. He was good for my soul. He made me laugh. He encouraged me to write. He knew how to say things in a way that made me lighten up, and he appreciated my work, as many other men in my life had done, including my father and my husband and Jac Holzman. He also acknowledged the price of artistry and the value of letting things go. He encouraged me to make the best of the situation with Clark, to enjoy who he was without worrying so much about what might have been or what should have been. Michael brought back some of the light into my life.

He wrote articles for newspapers in Australia and England, and was working on a novel. He later was to make movies, including a wonderful film about the Profumo scandal in England called *Scandal*. Michael was very smart about music. I listened to what he said. I admired his brain and wanted his ideas about new material and singers and songs. Michael believed in breaking the rules and encouraged me to do the same.

Michael got to know Clark on our visits in Colorado and Clark's trips to New York. The two of them got on famously. They had similar senses of humor, finding joy in odd things, in everyday things. My siblings and my parents got to know Michael over these years. He endeared himself to all of them.

One wonderful summer in Colorado in 1966, I rented a house in Allens park, near Estes. John Denver came for a visit. I had met John when we sang together at the Exodus in Denver. He had changed his name from Henry John Deutschendorf to John Denver after coming to Colorado and falling in love with the state. During John's stay with me that summer, he and I would sing for hours upon end. He taught Clark songs and joined in the cooking and the horseback riding. My brother Denver John was in his teens by then. He couldn't quite figure out the name thing—why he was Denver John and John was John Denver.

I started going to the theater, I searched through my own records and my friends' records. I tried to remember what had intrigued me when I was younger, what I had heard that I wanted to explore further. I listened to a lot more jazz and to Miles Davis's *Sketches of Spain.* (I remember first hearing *Sketches,* with Victor Mamudes, Dylan's first road manager, and Albert Grossman.) I was trying to develop another ear for hearing, a kind of sensor that would seek out another wavelength, another form of music that appealed to me, that I could sink my teeth and my soul into.

The Beatles had stormed the country. I loved their song "In My Life." Why not sing it. What could I lose? My fans? My following? Everyone thought music had gone crazy after Dylan went electric at Newport, although electrified instruments quickly became the norm. I started to think of drums on the road. I played around with rhythms.

My searches were interrupted by having hepatitis and mono, and I was in the hospital for two weeks. Except for the fact that I had to stop drinking for three months, the hospitalization didn't slow me down. I wrote a letter to Mimi Fariña from Lenox Hill Hospital describing my room—"Map of the world on wall; Balloons—Jimmy Dean button, Japanese chimes, etc," as well as a description of the doctor, who had told me I couldn't drink for three months.

My friend Mary Martin, who worked for Warner Brothers, kept telling me about her friend Leonard Cohen. They were both from Canada and she wanted to bring Cohen to New York to meet me. She said he had written two novels and a few books of poetry and that he had just started to write songs.

I think of great songwriters as gods and goddesses, bringing me gifts, as surely tagged with my name as though they had been written especially for me. Hunting for the right song, searching for the best, sometimes I get lucky.

When Leonard walked in the door of my Upper West Side apartment I decided I didn't care if he wrote songs or not. He was gloriously handsome. One of the things I am grateful for is that I never fell in love with Leonard, though I love him dearly. He seems to me like the kind of man who could drop through your heart like a sharp weapon, leaving blood behind. It would be delicious. And dangerous.

The first night we didn't do any singing. We hung out, got to know each other. Later, we went to dinner with an Australian friend of Michael's who had arrived in town. The next night, Leonard visited again. He was staying at the Chelsea Hotel and I lived on the Upper West Side. He played me "Suzanne" and "Dress Rehearsal Rag." The songs were stunning. I recorded both on *In My Life.*

Leonard, a published poet and novelist, was very shy and nervous about singing in public. He had a quiet, tucked-in voice. He said he wasn't a singer, but behind his shy manner, I knew he was. That fall I persuaded him to go onstage at a benefit for radio station WBAI. Onstage he began to sing "Suzanne," stopped in the middle, looked out at the audience, and walked into the wings. I got him to return, with me, and we sang the song together. Leonard has become in these later years one of the great performers, an intelligent, poignant artist. I am always honored that I was there to sing his songs first. Altogether in the Elektra years I recorded ten songs of Leonard's, among them "Priests," "Sisters of Mercy" and "Blue Raincoat."

My producer on *In My Life* was Mark Abramson, who had been working with me since my first album. Mark became my creative partner in many ways and we worked together for many years. We talked each record over, every piece of material. We argued, we did research, we often fought about what was the right direction. He was important in my forming the ideas of what I would do. I value the contribution he made to my process, the ever-evolving search for the next record. Along with Jac, who was the executive producer on my albums, we tried to create magic, wanting to make memorable, unique albums that would last forever.

The *Marat/Sade,* Peter Brook's great theater piece with music by Richard Peaslee, came to New York that year. I put together a suite of the music from the play and asked Peaslee to do the orchestration. Mark suggested we bring in Josh Rifkin, who was making records of early Renaissance and medieval music for Nonesuch, Elektra's new classical label, to write other orchestrations. Mark and I went to England to record the music from the *Marat/Sade* with an orchestra and choir. "Pirate Jenny," by Brecht and Kurt Weilh; an early Renaissance song, "Sunny Goodge Street"; "Tom Thumb's Blues" in a chamber orchestration by Rifkin with woodwinds and strings; "In My Life"; Fariña's "Hard Lovin' Loser"; Randy Newman's "I Think It's

Going to Rain Today"; "Liverpool Lullaby"; and "La Colombe," the Brel song about the pain of war, with a translation done by the English poet Alistayre Clayre, were added to the album. The material in *In My Life* was different and unusual, which was what I had wanted.

It was this period—with encouragement from Michael, meeting Leonard, and stretching musically—that sparked my yearning to write songs. I needed help, and I drove to White Plains to visit Bruce Langhorn, with whom I had been on tour in Japan, and who was gifted musically and a friend. I told him of my desire to write songs.

It was simple, Bruce said. "Go home and write five songs about a relationship; the beginning, middle and end."

I wrote my first song on the piano. It was "Since You Asked." It was the spring of '67. I wrote the song in about thirty minutes. I was so surprised, and stunned that it had been so easy. That's the way they hook you. Some of my later songs took as long as five years, but I couldn't know that, and anyway it wouldn't have made any difference.

There was much of the mountains in 'Since You Asked," the inspiration in part a trip I had made with Clark, my sister Holly, Michael Thomas, John Clark and the Fletchers up to Thunder Lake, in Colorado, one of the most beautiful hikes in Rocky Mountain National Park. I still see my son's shining face when I sing it, and remember the long, exhaultant hike, my small son striding up the mountain trail, putting his feet into the mountain streams, hiking with his mother and his aunt Holly. It was a special trip.

⁂

In the years we had been working together Jac, who had started Elektra on a shoestring, working out of offices downtown with three or four people on staff, had built a successful and, according to any standards, important, label. In the late sixties he added Nonesuch to the Elektra family. It was run by Teresa Sterne, the first woman to run a major record company. Tracy, as we called her, did an incredible job for Jac, taking his original vision and adding to it. Jac established offices in Los Angeles and built a studio there, spending a lot of time on the West Coast. I felt abandoned. (Like lovers, Jac and I could fight like cats and dogs, but always made up more devoted to one another.) He meant so much to me, and I feared I was losing him, losing the center of my sanity and stability. I didn't like Los Angeles. It always made me feel uncomfortable and a little sad. I would be startled by the warmth and the ocean air and the nostalgia of watching the green grass go by, remembering my childhood. People seemed to know more and have more and do more of everything from drugs to big houses in Los Angeles. On the other hand, they seemed to fall asleep on some level, and I was terrified that if I went there, I would permanently fall asleep, into some dulled slumber from which I would never wake. I thought everyone felt that way, but most people seemed to be able to hide it. I never could. I found Los Angeles intimidating and could not hope to keep up.

I knew Jac had done a wise thing professionally and that it could only mean more success with what I was doing. I had Jac's blessings. Because I also wanted his input and his companionship, in the coming years I often went to Los Angeles to record in the studio on La Cienega, which was, I must admit, very comfortable.

I began to like L.A. I would find myself seduced when I stayed a few weeks, working on a record. I would come home to New York, land at La Guardia or Kennedy, cab in to the Upper West Side through the dirty streets past the buildings with no swimming pools in their yards, and think, I must be crazy to live here when I could live there.

But home was always the rough, real streets of New York. I said New York kept me honest. It also kept me moving, working, exploring.

I had begun to hear of Joni Mitchell by then. She had a good following in the Village and in Canada and many cities in the States. She didn't have a recording contract at the time, and one night one of her ardent fans (I remember it being Tom Rush, but he always denies it) called me up at three A. M. and had Joni play me "Both Sides Now." I immediately began to weep. I said I had to record it, she said she wanted me to, as she didn't have a contract at that time, and was eager for her songs to get out to the public.

One night I went to Joni's little apartment in Manhattan, where we ate a delicious dinner and then sat, over glasses of wine, while she sang me more of her songs. Each one made me weep. I sobbed over their beauty, their luminous lyric strength. She played me "Michael from Mountains" that night as the candles flickered against stained glass and ruby wineglasses. We talked about our lives, about our children. Joni told me about her heartache of having a child she gave away when she was a teenager. Each of us had a sorrow to bear. (Joni has recently been reunited with her child, a miracle of time, patience and love.)

I was still on the board of directors of the Newport Festival, along with Peter Yarrow, Pete Seeger, Harold Leventhal and George Wein, the founder of both the Newport Jazz and Folk festivals. I worked to get a singer-songwriter concert in the festival. Dylan was always on the big show, as were most of us who were professionally "successful," but often the lesser-known writers didn't fit into any of the daytime workshops. I finally convinced the board to have an afternoon concert that turned out to be historic—Leonard Cohen, Joni Mitchell, Janis Ian, David Blue, Mike Settle, Tom Paxton, Eric Andersen, all together on the stage in Newport.

Wildflowers, my next record, was the first to have my own songs on it; "Since You Asked," "Sky Fell" and "Albatross." "Albatross" is a song written on a big canvas, like a painting, spilling over into prose-poetry, with the kind of drama that would be a part of the songs I would write in the next years— songs like "Ché," "Houses," "Nightingale" and "The Blizzard." Writing gave me an inner strength, a foundation in my life that had to do with my feelings about myself as well as my professional journey in the next years of records and concerts.

I told Josh Rifkin I wanted to do some unusual songs on *Wildflowers* and he found me a thirteenth-century piece called "A Ballata" by Francesco Landini. And finally I recorded the Jacques Brel song that had haunted me for all the years since Jac Holzman had sent me my first record of Brel in 1963 when I was in the hospital in Denver. When I heard the half-French, half-Flemish singer, he won my heart. Now was the time to sing his love song about old lovers:

Oh mon amour, mon doux, mon tendre,
mon merveilleux amour,
De l'aube claire jusque le fin du jour,
Je t'aime encore, tu sais, je t'aime.

Oh my love, my soft, my tender,
my marvelous love,
From the clear dawn until the end of the day,
I love you, you know I love you.

The song belonged with these others, these songs of love, of tender passion. I think I was finally grown up enough to sing them. I had by then had the first great heartbreak.

In all my records I have been involved in every aspect, every nuance, from the choosing of the material to the arrangements—which always had the form of my likes and dislikes even when I worked with an arranger or an orchestrator, right through to the overdubs, vocals, mixing, and final mix. I ache with each phrase, each nuance. It all matters so very much. I am like a lover hovering over every phrase, and every moment of each song has to be right. I was fortunate in the people I worked with, great engineers and great producers—Mark, Arif Mardin, Phil Ramone—and, in later years, Alan Silverman, with whom I have worked now for nearly twelve years. I learned from the best. But I rarely could turn over any part of the process. It all had to be right. The hours and hours on end in the studio paid off. The mixing time, the days when none of us saw the sun, the nights when the magic happened and it was as though the light was shining only in that studio, in all the world—these made it all worth it. There is no feeling like making music with a group of gifted musicians in an orchestra or a band and hearing the take, the one you all love, the one that sends chills up and down your spine. But it was the meticulous hours hovering just behind the mix board, watching every move of my engineers and telling them when I didn't hear what I wanted that taught me about music. And about patience.

Josh Rifkin, Mark Abramson and I went to Los Angeles and lived at the Sunset Marquis while we were recording *Wildflowers*. Every day I hovered over Josh as he scribbled, asking him if he needed anything—tea, lunch, a back rub—trying to get him to finish the arrangements on time and making my own comments as he went along. I had played him what I wanted on the piano, sorting out the arrangement for each song, and now I was praying that he would make the orchestrations do what my arrangements of them called for. He did, and added to their luster. He was extraordinary and the musicians played like angels. We completed most of the orchestral recording and vocals in California and then we came back to New York to record Joni's song, "Both Sides Now." Josh did something amazingly daring. He put a harpsichord on "Both Sides"; it is a very distinctive sound. We had by then become accustomed to hearing orchestral arrangements—the Beatles had used a string quartet on "Eleanor Rigby" and other songs. But I think the harpsichord really appealed to people.

Wildflowers was a terribly important record, a departure, and had I known how groundbreaking the approach was, I would have been terrified. There was not a guitar in evidence. I had gone all the way with my belief in Rifkin, the sounds of the orchestrations, the texture of the instruments. I was no longer a girl with only a guitar. I felt as comfortable as though I had been making heavily orchestrated records this way all my life. In a way, I suppose, I had, ever since playing Mozart with Brico's orchestra.

After the album was out, it took many months for "Both Sides Now" to become a hit. But Jac believed in the song and asked David Anderle, the head of the offices of Elektra in Los Angeles and a wonderful producer who now works for A and M with artists like Sheryl Crow, to remix the song. Elektra reissued "Both Sides" as a single, and soon I had my first major hit single.

It is funny what happens when you have your first real success in the eyes of the world. My life had been going very well professionally. In seven years I had made seven albums. I worked in concerts, I had toured in the Soviet Union and Poland in 1965, had gone to Japan, Australia and New Zealand in 1966, been to England and France, sung all over the United States. I did big concerts each year at Carnegie Hall in New York, sang in

Boston at Symphony Hall. I had been to the Newport Festival, been on television. But now I had a single, playing on the radio. People began to return my phone calls.

I had begun to have some financial success that year and for Christmas in 1967 gave my parents tickets to Hawaii, all expenses paid. They made the trip in March and while they were there, my father became ill. He was in the hospital in Hawaii, but doctors could find nothing wrong with him. Back home in Denver, he was hospitalized for tests and then sent home again, then back to the hospital. I spoke frequently to the doctors, asking them if my father's illness was serious, as I had commitments in England for concerts in May. They assured me that he was not in any danger, and I went ahead with my plans for the English trip, knowing I would be in Denver a few weeks after returning.

Wildflowers came out in April. That same month I sat down and wrote "My Father." I was excited about the song and planned to sing it to Daddy when I went to see him after my trip to England. My brother Denver came to England with me, and it was there that we had the terrible news that Daddy had died of a spinal aneurysm. I canceled my concert at the Albert Hall and Denver and I flew back to Colorado and the family to mourn my father's passing. He was so very young, fifty-seven.

He never heard "My Father."

Clark didn't come to his grandfather's funeral. He was in Vancouver, in school. Clark had loved his grandfather. Daddy had been wonderful to my son, caring and loving. I wrestled with grief over my father's death, which seemed to have come out of the blue like a thunderclap. Today, medical techniques are available to find aneurysms on MRIs, but in those days there was no way to detect their presence.

That summer, trying to soothe the pain of my father's death and find time to talk about Grandpa Chuck and be together, Clark and I went on a wonderful vacation to a ranch east of the Canadian Rockies, that mysterious desertlike land where the sky has dropped all its water on the Western slope and the earth is golden and red and mountains rise from the earth in bizarre and beautiful shapes. We rode hoseback and talked and laughed and I read

Clark stories and sang him songs. It was always so sweet, the time I spent with my son.

I knew that things were not going well for Clark in Vancouver, and that my son was troubled and unhappy. It would not be until the end of the following year that I learned the extent of the difficulties.

I was recording my next album, *Who Knows Where the Time Goes,* that summer. After our desert-mountain trip, Clark came to be with me in Los Angeles. I rented a house on Mulholland Drive with a swimming pool Clark and I splashed around in. He had grown so tall in the recent months, and his sweetness was more evident than ever. I took him everywhere with me. During that summer he had to have surgery, rather minor. His father and I had talked about it and agreed Clark would have the surgery while he was with me. He was such a good boy about it, so brave.

He was always excited to be around the musicians I had brought from New York, some of whom he had known for many years. David Anderle became my producer and added some new players to the record. I met Stephen Stills, Buddy Emmons, the pedal steel player from Nashville, and a wonderful drummer named Jimmy Gordon.

One day Stephen and I began singing "Some Day Soon" in the car driving to the sessions and recorded the great song by Ian and Sylvia Tyson. It became my second top-ten single and I could often hear it playing on the radio. It was country, but more funky than usual country, and was considered a crossover song.

That summer Robert F. Kennedy was assassinated. My friend John Cooke stayed over the night at my house the night we heard the news, too distraught to go home alone.

John Cooke is a tall, good-humored, very talented musician who played the banjo and sang with the Charles River Valley Boys. He and I became friends when I worked in Boston at the Unicorn and the Golden Vanity in the early sixties. John is the son of Alistair Cooke and always used to quote his father's introduction to the television shows he hosted; "I'm Alastair Cooke. And you're not." He was friends with Mimi and Dick and we had a comfortable, easygoing friendship. I took my second acid trip with John and

Michael Thomas, out at John's family's compound on Long Island. It was the winter of 1967; the frost covered everything with diamonds; it was cold. I heard the birds preach, a little sparrow sitting in a tree appearing to me to be the angel Gabriel; but at the end of that trip, as had happened the first time I took acid, I was curled up in a ball, moaning and praying I could come down. We drove out to Orient Point to look at the sunset and lost the keys to the car on the beach. We had to walk all the way back to John's house. It was a gift, because the walk sobered me up in a very short time. Next morning we made the trip out to the beach and found the keys, and I swore I would never take acid again, and didn't.

John later became a road manager for Janis Joplin and was, sadly, the one to discover Janis's body at the Sunset Marquis. Janice died of a drug overdose. I knew it could have been me, drinking too much, taking some kind of pill, so very easily, on any night of excess in any town, in any of the those years.

Sometimes I took Clark to the studio when I was recording *Who Knows Where the Time Goes* and the guys would teach him songs on the piano, the drums and the guitar. Stephen made a tape of a song Clark wrote, called 'I'm Flying." Clark adored Stephen. Later Stephen bought Clark his first guitar. He loved to be in the studio and his singing, soulful and sweet, was already good.

The new album had a slow, back-beat country feel that rolled right along. Sometimes the songs were bittersweet, like my song, "My Father." There was a song by Robin Williamson called "First Boy I Loved" over which I had struggled for ages, working to get the notes into my guitar playing. Leonard's writing appeared once more in my rendition of "Bird on the Wire," done slow and funky.

One day David Anderle said, "I have a tape to play for you," and put on Sandy Denny's great song, "Who Knows Where the Time Goes." I fell head over heels in love with the song and used it as the title song of the album.

Sandy Denny sang with the Fairport Convention, an English group that had a lot of success. She was a great writer and I came to know and hang out with her later in England when Anthea Joseph, a red-haired fireball who worked for Polygram in England, introduced us. Sandy was pretty and blond, with a voice that could cut through a concrete wall or lull a baby to sleep. Her solos with the Fairport Convention are still hauntingly beautiful. On a visit to New York she once came to my apartment and we swapped songs. She sang me a great song called "Solo," which I would someday like to record. And she gave me a little porcelain vase of lavender and white glass flowers that sits on a table in my studio to this day, a remembrance of her visit. Sandy fell down a flight of stairs at a party in London one night, and two days later dropped dead as the result of an unsuspected concussion.

(As I write this, our friend Anthea from England has just died. Two women who were my friends, gone, like the time goes.)

That year, while staying in Los Angeles finishing my record, I was at a party at my producer's house when some guy came around with a handful of pills, smiling and offering a taste of drugs to anyone who wanted. I didn't even like drugs. Alcohol was my thing. But everyone else was taking advantage of this guy's generosity, and I took a pill. Moments later I was in the bathroom trying to throw it up. I was already pretty drunk and knew there could be repercussions if I had taken a strong depressant. I spent the next eight hours curled up in a ball on the floor, literally paralyzed. No one called a hospital or even thought it particularly strange that I couldn't move. When I came out of it, I had a lot of trouble swallowing. I could so easily have been an overdose, and I didn't even do drugs! The insanity of the times, the promiscuity of the times. No wonder the world thought we were mad. We were.

By the time the record was finished Stephen and I were in love. I was crazy about him; about his sweet, agonizingly beautiful voice, his genius on the guitar. When he played for me I melted, when he sang with me I usually cried. The first night we met we stayed up all night singing to each other. He could touch the guitar, sing a note, and turn my world around. It is a good thing to work with someone so gifted. It brings out the best in you, whoever you are. He and I made good music together.

Back in New York, I broke the news to Michael that there was "someone else," and we parted. Stephen didn't want anything to do with New York, and hated shrinks. I wanted New York, I needed shrinks. Stephen had developed a pretty good relationship with Clark. They were alike in some way, both wiry and bright and tormented by their own perfectionism and their own talent. I do not doubt that Stephen loved me and loved Clark.

Nineteen sixty-eight was a year of change for me and for the world. My beloved, baffling father was dead. Robert Kennedy and Martin Luther King were both murdered. It would take me years to unravel the grief I felt over all of these losses. While the war in Vietnam went on, and I marched and protested with millions of others, this particular phase of my own war was soon to be over, though I didn't know it.

The rock musical *Hair* was on Broadway, and I started wearing miniskirts. The Democratic convention in Chicago in the summer had been a setback to everything we all believed in. It had been violent, it had been chaotic. The Chicago Seven were imprisoned after the convention and William Kunstler asked me, during the following year, to testify at their trial in the spring of '69. Called on by Kunstler, I would be asked where I had been during the press conference to announce the formation of the Yippies. In answer, I began singing "Where Have All the Flowers Gone," getting out enough to identify the song before the court officer placed his hand over my mouth and escorted me from the courtroom on the order of Judge Sirica.

The war in Vietnam went on and on. The idealism we had felt in the early sixties was evaporating in tragedy: Johnson's policies in Vietnam spurred the antiwar movement and the marches and rallies against the war continued to pit parents against children, friend against friend. United States forces in Vietnam would peak that year to over a half million troops. The war was killing the country.

People were looking for something peaceful, some way to heal the pain. An Indian influence had begun to be felt in music. The Beatles went to Indian gurus and I went to hear Ravi Shankar at Riverside Church and in Aspen at the Music Festival. I heard the Maharaja speak at the Plaza Hotel, where I sat, staring at his orange robes, strewing flowers at his feet, listening to his calming voice, hoping he could help me, ease my pain, make up for my son's absence in my life. If only, I thought, it could be other than it was.

One night in December of 1968, I got a phone call from my husband.

"As you know, we have been talking about Clark coming to live with you."

I was bowled over. I knew nothing about this. As far as I knew, Clark was living with Peter and Sue and his stepsister, and there was no hope of Clark's coming to live with me, although I had prayed that he would.

I will never know exactly what happened to change Peter's mind about giving me custody. Clark, at nine, was a bright, cheerful and incredibly warm little boy. He was also hyperactive. I didn't have any idea he would prove, as he had for his father, a handful. Later, I learned that Clark's father had said to him, "It's your mother or military school."

I loved my son, wanted him with me, and he wanted to be with me. I rejoiced.

I sent an airline ticket to Canada and Peter put Clark on the plane. I picked up my son at the airport, thrilled to have him with me. The first day the courthouse was open I applied for permanent custody. There were no arguments from Peter. We found a good school and I settled into a much calmer concert schedule. I was with my boy, my life had purpose, my dream had come true.

୨୨Cଵ I see my son everywhere, in the glint of the diamonds on the snow, the songs of birds. I think of how he
would have appreciated a painting or seen the poignancy of
a life. His heart was gentle and I never heard him criticize
anyone. He didn't have a mean bone in his body.

I often find myself holding my own imperfections up
against his more forgiving nature. I tend to drive a hard
bargain with life and the people in it. I expect a lot, as my
father did. I often see the world as turf to be conquered.

My son was much more open to possibilities than I
am. Now, he will have to teach me, in that great capacity to
which he has graduated. He has become the teacher, I the
student; I am the child, he is the parent. I am the disciple, he
is the guide.

In the flutter of birds' wings at my window, I see my
son's spirit. In the ripple of the stream, the trumpets of
cacophony in the traffic in the streets, the light from the
windows at dawn, I feel his soul, his face, his laughter.

I will let him teach me how to be more loving, and
more gentle.

7

Child of Fire

$\mathcal{M}$y beautiful son was with me and my life was full, rich, and, at last, fulfilled. We settled into a routine of being together, Clark getting to know other kids in the neighborhood, choosing a school, getting comfortable together in our new life. He had play dates with the sons of a neighbor with whom we had become friends, Denny Demac, who lived with her children in our building on West 79th. I enrolled Clark in the Professional Children's School in Manhattan and got on the list for the school bus pickup. I outfitted Clark at Morris Brothers on Broadway, filling the drawers of his dresser with green and red and white and black socks, oxford shoes, tennis shoes, shirts of blue and white and bright canary yellow. We bought a bunk bed so that he could have sleepovers with his friends. We bought heavy winter jackets, thick sweaters of bright blue, fleecy wool. We went shopping for a karate outfit so Clark could take lessons in the nearby class on Riverside Drive on Saturday mornings.

Clark made friends easily, and seemed to adjust to his new home quickly. It was as though this had always been the way things were meant to be. I would put my son to bed at night, read him a story, kiss him, turn out the light. Sitting on the edge of his bed, I'd stare in the dark at my sleepy boy, watching his breath rise and fall, taking in his sweet and innocent face so free of worry. In silence, grateful for whatever had happened that had brought us back together, I would let the moments linger, relishing the happy ending, wondering how things would have been if he had been with me all these years. Joy would flood me, and I would kiss his forehead and whisper that I loved him before I tiptoed out of the room and closed the door.

I was a mother again, as I was supposed to be. I had my son with me.

In the morning I roused my sleepy boy, ruffled his red hair, smoothed his forehead, kissed him and helped him pick out what he was going to wear, and told him to get dressed. We ate breakfast in the kitchen together, laughing over little things, like the new kittens I had adopted—Jam, a little tortoise cat, and Moby, our Siamese, and Clyde, a big orange and white tabby; they sometimes walked on the counter and stepped in the milk bowl and Clark and I would laugh together over these small and wonderful things.

I hired a housekeeper named Dahlia Judson, a beautiful, soulful woman from Trinidad with a sweet, calm manner. She helped me with the laundry and the cooking and cleaning and soon established a warm relationship with my son and with me. She took care of both of us, and Michael, when he was around. She made what was soon Clark's favorite: the traditional West Indies dish, beans and rice. Dahlia took care of Clark when I went out to do concerts, arranging play dates, making dinners, getting my son off to school. I no longer had to work in clubs and was able to travel on an easier schedule to make a living. I was home much more of the month, then out only a few days at a time instead of weeks at a time. Clark and I were comfortable and happy together.

Dahlia cooked bacon and eggs (I was still eating bacon and eggs!) and the smells would filter through our two-bedroom apartment with the grand piano in the living room and the flowers in vases, the skates and parkas and Tinkertoys and Erector set and toy train in my son's bedroom.

At school, my son was eager to learn and open to every new experience. In the evening, if Clark didn't have homework, we might go to a movie or have dinner out together in one of the neighborhood restaurants, where one of my friends or Clark's might join us. There was homework and cleaning up Clark's room, for I wanted him to be responsible about his clothes and his toys, even though we had a housekeeper to help out.

Sometimes Clark had after-school activities, karate and gym. I got a potting wheel and a small kiln and Clark and I learned to throw pots and wedge clay, fire little bowls and cups. I decided I wanted to study the cello and my friend Robert Sylvester, a great cellist, began to give me lessons.

We were happy together.

I noticed Clark's hyperactivity, but at first I didn't think very much about it. He was high-strung and loved deeply and responded visibly to people. He could be emotional, but he was also very bright. It made sense to me.

But slowly over the months, it became clear that there was more than just a little more energy in Clark than in other children. If we were together, in a calm mood, he was fine, but he got overly excited about things and sometimes it might take time to smooth him out. I talked it over with my therapist, and we decided Clark should start therapy sessions with one of the Sullivanians.

By then I had been seeing Ralph Klein for seven years. I talked about everything to him and usually took his advice. He still encouraged my independence. "Thursdays and Saturdays," as Stephen's song, "Suite: Judy Blue Eyes," would later say.

The Sullivanians had taken their name from and loosely based their philosophy on Harry Stack Sullivan, whose book, *The Conditions of Human Growth,* served as a kind of Bible for the group. Their input about child rearing and their philosophy of interpersonal relationships were going to have a great impact on the way I handled the problems that later came up with Clark. They did not really believe that parents belonged with their children. If parent and child lived together, a lot of bonding with other adults was recommended for the child.

Later, the Sullivanians became quite obsessed with this notion of children being raised apart from their parents. Saul Newton, the leader of the group, an old warrior dog who could be irrational when angry, would be accused of illegal attempts to forcibly remove children from their parents. But Ralph, my therapist, was a good psychologist in the sense that he helped me solidify my process as an artist and overcome my isolation from people. For the troubles that Clark was to have—and for my increasing addiction to alcohol—there was not to be much help from the Sullivanians.

Today, many therapists will not see a patient who is abusing drugs and alcohol. They will, instead, insist that patients find a way to rid themselves of their substance of choice before they see them professionally.

What the Sullivanians did know about was isolation and its dangers. They encouraged me to make friends and by the time Clark came to live with me, I had many good friends in New York. By 1969 I had been studying with my singing teacher, Max Margulis, for five years, had started writing songs, was continuing to learn from my therapists about being a creative artist, and had a wonderful group of friends in New York. Some of us began to talk about living in a commune together. The group consisted of Nancy Bacal and Jafa Lerner, both of whom had been introduced to me by Leonard Cohen; my producer Mark Abramson and his wife, Janet, who was an actor; Arnie and Ruth Black, both gifted musicians; Irene Zaks, who at that time worked with Harold and had traveled with me to Japan; Al Brown, a violinist; and my friend Jim Friedman, a songwriter. We decided we needed to buy some land, put up some houses, and get out of the city. Our first meeting was to be held at my apartment on 79th Street.

One night a few days before the meeting was scheduled, I had dinner at the home of Thomas and Nancy Hoving. Hoving was president of the Metropolitan Museum and that night I was introduced to Candy Latson, an impressive black man and recovering addict who had worked at Synanon on the West Coast and had escaped; Synanon, a drug rehabilitation community, had a policy of not releasing people from their group. In New York, Candy had been hired to run encounter group sessions for Phoenix House, a drug rehabilitation center on the Upper West Side. "Encountering" was the new socializing and healing technique that was supposed to level egos, force people to get their problems out, face each other honestly and, in that manner, recover from their problems with drugs. Candy told me he believed the system worked for all problems of communication.

I explained what my friends and I were planning. Candy was very convincing in his belief that before any group of people considering living together would benefit from encountering one other. Impressed with his ideas, I invited him to the first meeting with my friends.

For the next two years, Candy led my friends and me in a series of emotional and intense encounter groups. The group grew, moved around the city; Candy brought in another Phoenix House facilitator, Sandy Jackson. We became so big we had to divide into two groups. Other friends joined, including Stacy Keach and Jac Holzman. The group was an important part of our lives for a time, teaching us how to relate to one another. But, eventually, some friendships in the group were torn apart in the name of honesty and mental health, the fashionable expression of the times. In the last few months the groups met, Elizabeth, one of the young women members and a secretary at Elektra records, was found dead, stabbed in her apartment. Her death became a cause célèbre of the loose, late sixties; it was never solved and was memorialized in Judith Rossner's book *Looking for Mr. Goodbar.*

Needless to say, my friends and I never bought the property of which we had dreamed.

Women's consciousness-raising groups were springing up too, during these years, and I went to some of the early meetings. One had been started by Gloria Steinem and I went to a few sessions with Gloria, Marlo Thomas and Flo Kennedy, among others. Gloria and I had already developed a friendship which has grown over the years. She has braved criticism and cynicism and shared her innumerable gifts as well as her intelligence with both women and men to help us all achieve our dreams.

The point of all these groups was the search for individual as well as shared power. We wanted to look into our sexually imposed patterns and find ways to break the bonds of society's and our parents' values. These groups helped me grow and flourish. One of the things the groups helped me see was that my parents had been there for me in ways that many of my peers' parents had not. They had stood beside me, they saluted what I did, they were proud that I stood against the Vietnam War, and they were happy that I could think independently and that I had chosen my particular path. Both of my parents belonged to this new, brave and challenged generation as they had to their own generation. If my father had stayed around, he would probably have taken hallucinogens with the best of them.

But there had been many casualties by this time: Jimi Hendrix, Janis Joplin, Dick Fariña, Martin Luther King, both Jack and Robert Kennedy. Many of our friends, certainly many of our illusions, were dead.

In the summer of 1969 I took a part in a production at the New York Shakespeare Festival in Central Park, directed by Jerry Freedman, produced by Joe Papp, with costumes by Theoni Aldredge. Stacy Keach played Peer Gynt. The music was composed by John Morris. I was cast as the long-suffering Solveig. After the first few weeks of rehearsal, Stacy and I began spending time together. Stephen was out in California, and we were not seeing much of each other, though the feelings were still there. Our stormy love affair lasted about a year but produced heat and fire in me, at least, for many years after that. But he didn't like therapists and we had dramatic phone calls, and in the coming year there was too much drama, there were too many sparks, most of them setting me on fire. Stephen wrote "Suite: Judy Blue Eyes" when we were splitting up. The song is the story of our time together.

Stacy Keach was already an accomplished actor by that time, with many roles to his credit. He had been trained at the London Academy of Music and Dramatic Arts. His father was a respected actor in Hollywood and Stacy had grown up in the world of theater and film. He was single-minded about his career, gifted and generous onstage, making way for both my character and for our blooming relationship. He came to dinner that first night wearing a leather jacket. He looked sane and steady, rock solid and lovable. I felt immediate relief. There might be a way to have it all, after all. After a few weeks of seeing him regularly, Stacy seemed to be exactly what I wanted. I couldn't take the fire I felt still burning for Stephen. Stacy lighted another fire which banked the one that was burning out of control.

It was a summer of art and friendship, music and learning. We all got on well. Stacy broke up with the woman he had been seeing, Stephen and I broke up, with painful scenes; Stacy bonded with Clark and got along with my family. The summer in New York, being in a musical instead of on the road, was good for me and good for Clark. Stacy introduced me to his parents, his brother Jim, whom I introduced to my sister. They later married and had a son, Kalen, my beloved nephew. I liked Stacy's theater friends in New York and we spent time socially with James Earl Jones and Rene Auberjonois, Harris Yulin and

Jane Alexander, Olympia Dukakis (who was also in *Peer Gynt*), Raul Julia and Diana Davilla. I felt more stable. I tried once again not to drink so much.

In the latter part of the summer Clark went to camp and, when I visited him, I found him freckled, happy and healthy.

One night backstage at the Delacorte Theater, Roger Payne, a marine biologist with the New York Zoological Society, gave me a tape of his first Bermuda recordings of the mournful, soulful singing of the humpback whales. I played the songs of the whales over and over, listening to their haunting calls.

Soon, *Whales and Nightingales,* my next album, fell into place. I sang "Farewell to Tarwathie," an old whaling song, over their mournful calling. I added all the songs that seemed to go with that ancient reverie of romance and murder. "Song for David" was Joan Baez's song for her husband, David Harris, in jail as a conscientious objector. I included "Sons of," written by Jacques Brel, about the trials of all men, boys, and souls who suffer; Pete Seeger's "Oh, I Had a Golden Thread"; and "Time Passes Slowly," by Bob Dylan. They all seemed to sum up the feeling in the country of waiting for the insanity to stop, as did "Prothalamium," a song of hope written by my friend Michael Sahl, who had played piano for me on the road and in the studio. I also sang "Marieke," by Brel, about a long train ride over the Flemish countryside between the cities of Bruges and Ghent, and "Nightingale," a song that I began about my affair with Stephen which turned into a lyric about the continuity of life, to assure myself that it was, in fact, continuous. I sang "Simple Gifts," a song of Shaker origin about beauty in simplicity.

One night at the encounter group we wanted to sing a song to end an evening that had been particularly touching to us all. The only song everyone knew all the words to was "Amazing Grace," and I led the singing, as I knew it well. Later, Mark, my producer, told me he thought we should record it. I thought it was a wonderful idea. I didn't know what else to do about the war in Vietnam. I had marched, I had voted, I had gone to jail on political actions and worked for the candidates I believed in. The war was still raging. There was nothing left to do, I thought, but to pray and sing hymns to life. Nothing left but to sing "Amazing Grace."

Mark and I found St. Paul's, a small chapel on the campus of Columbia University with perfect acoustics. I put together a group of singers consisting mostly of friends—Mark's wife Janet Young, my brother Denver, his girlfriend Abigail Lewis, Harris Yulin, Stacy Keach. When the record came out, "Amazing Grace" became an instantaneous hit. It was as though my fans had been waiting for it, waiting to embrace it. The song was a talisman against death, against the raging war.

Sometimes I went on location with Stacy in those years. I traveled to California for the shooting of *Fat City,* directed by John Huston. After I finished making *Whales and Nightingales,* Clark joined me in Spain to spend time with Stacy on the set of *Doc.* It was wonderful to have my son with me. We stayed in a villa near the set of the movie. There were some other kids on the set, and Clark had his friend Josh Klein, my therapist's son, to play with. Clark had the quality of curiosity, as well as the kindness that he had always shown. People of all ages liked him. The boys got along well and seemed to have much in common.

In *Doc,* Stacy played Wyatt Earp, Faye Dunaway was Kitty, Harris Yulin played Doc Holliday and I had convinced Frank Perry to read my brother Denver John for the part of the "kid." Denver got the part, and all of us spent a few weeks eating, drinking, and watching the movie being made in Almería, Spain.

At the time, Faye Dunaway was ending her affair with Jean-Paul Belmondo, who made a very dramatic visit to the set of the movie. After that visit, Faye appeared to be more relaxed. Stacy didn't like to have anyone around when he was doing a love scene but that day I watched the filming of a love scene with Faye. That night over l'angustino grilled on a charcoal fire at a local restaurant in Almería and washed down with gallons of Spanish beer, someone in the film crew whispered that Faye usually fell in love with her leading man, who in this film was Stacy, who was taken. But Faye fell in love with Harris, and they began to spend a lot of time together. After we all returned from Spain, they continued their love affair.

During our weeks in Spain I took a few days to join a new friend, Susan Crile, a painter from New York, for four days in Paris at the Matisse retrospective at the Grand Palais. Susie and I had met in our mutual therapist's office and hit it off immediately, and she had invited me when I was in Spain to join her in Paris. We ate, slept, and looked at Matisse, until we were surfeited with color and beauty and could take no more for the day, only to come back the next day and do it again. We stayed in a little pension where, when we woke in the morning, the sound of pounding hammers signaled the workmen getting started on the plumbing repairs; we only saw the early morning and our coffee in our little room, and then we wandered the boulevards of Paris together, talking endlessly, greedily. In those first few days together looking at Matisse, we began a friendship that has lasted for what has turned out to be the rest of our lives. Susan and I have shared triumphs, heartbreaks and, as the years have gone by, tragedies.

🙨🙦

Stacy and I had decided before the summer that we would try to live together. There was even talk of marriage. When I returned from Spain at the end of the summer of 1971, I put Clark in school. I had rented a much larger apartment, found a new housekeeper and hired a contractor to remodel the kitchen before leaving for Spain. Emily Isles, who was to stay with me for the next few years, was busily overseeing the work and unpacking boxes of books and clothes when I got home.

I got back into the swing of having Clark in school. I practiced the piano every day, started writing new songs, and prepared for my tour, which would begin in the middle of October. I was anxious for Stacy to return from Spain and I started, once again, seeing my therapist three times a week. I had moved from Ralph Klein to another Sullivanian, Julie Schneider, a pleasant, insightful woman therapist, feeling I needed a change.

Problems began to emerge almost as soon as Clark started back to school. The previous year had been pretty good, but now Clark began to behave in such a chaotic and unpredictable way that I felt I couldn't handle him by myself. He was having troubles at school, he was incredibly angry, and he had severe mood swings. He would get into trouble over seemingly meaningless situations. Only later would I understand that drugs and alcohol were playing a part in my son's behavior. At the time, I only became more and more hysterical.

Stacy returned from Spain, but our experiment of living together was difficult. I was looking good outside and dying inside, my drinking having taken a downward spiral. The fear and difficulty in my life were instrumental in my deciding to terminate another pregnancy.

The headmistress at Reece, the small private school to which Clark was now going, was at a loss with Clark's behavior. I had become close to Ellen Reece and I knew she had strong feelings for Clark and that she would have done anything in her power to help him. He continued to have troubles in school, problems with other children and difficulty doing his work. Even Ellen's calm was ruffled. Clark, by now, had been in therapy with Mildred Antonelli, another Sullivanian, whom he was seeing weekly.

Nothing seemed to help. At home we fought, and apart I worried. The day came when Clark and I had a terrible confrontation, he screaming at me, I screaming at him. We fought about his secrecy, what he was doing with his friends, why he appeared to be drunk, or stoned. He denied taking anything, but I knew he was using some kind of chemicals. I felt like checking both of us into the hospital, which would not, in retrospect, have been a bad idea. I turned to the people I trusted.

Mildred Antonelli asked me to see Dr. Saul Newton, the thorny leading therapist of the Sullivanians, for a consultation about Clark. I think she felt out of her depth, as did my own therapist. I knew Saul only to say hello to the rather intimidating, gray-haired doctor who had, I knew, fought against Franco in Spain and ruled his group of younger therapists with an iron fist. He pulled no punches when I told him of my confrontations with my son and the mounting tension, as well as the problems in school. He said that Clark needed to get away from me. He said I was the problem, and I needed to find a boarding school for Clark.

I resisted, saying Clark's behavior would surely calm down. Saul was more graphic.

"You have to send him away!" he told me. "Your son is at risk, there is too much drama between you. He needs to get away from you. You are the problem! If he doesn't get away, he may kill someone!" I would only learn later that Saul was subject to these dramatic proclamations, and in an article in the *New York Times* in the eighties, many of his former patients would accuse him of paranoid and even psychopathic tendencies, words he often used in references to patients, friends, and families.

But I knew none of this at that time, and Saul literally terrorized me into the decision to find a school away from New York, away from me. In retrospect I now know that Clark, even at that young age, belonged not in a hospital or a school but in a treatment center for drug addiction and alcoholism. Many years later, Clark would finally confide his drug use to me. I often wonder what might have been had I recognized Clark's illness for what it was.

Clark was not happy about my plan to send him away to school, but he had little choice. I was at my wit's end. We visited a number of schools and settled on one in Maryland. Stacy went with Clark and me, and Clark was impressed with the school in spite of himself. It was a lovely place in a great, natural setting in the country, where a group of healthy, happy-looking kids convinced us the school was right. In January 1971 I packed Clark off to what I thought was going to be a solution.

A few weeks after getting to the school in Maryland, Clark ran into a car on his sled and nearly died in the accident. I got the call in the middle of the night and rushed on the plane to Hagerstown, Maryland, where a fine surgeon had been able to operate on Clark. Still, the surgeon promised nothing, saying my son was still in grave danger. I sat with Clark in his hospital room for two weeks, as he hovered near death. Slowly over the course of the eleventh day, his color changed, his eyes opened, he looked at me and smiled, and I knew he was going to live.

"I made a decision not to die, " he told me later. He remembered that coming out of the near-death state he had been in a white light. He said he went to a place that is peaceful and full of beauty, but that he decided he must return.

After his recovery from the accident, there would be many schools for Clark, many therapists, many teachers, and many problems. I tried to keep centered on my work while trying to figure out what to do. Clark did not see much of his father in those years, and I remember feeling it was just Clark and me, and the chaos. It was a difficult time for him and I was at a loss to know what to do. But he and I kept trying.

❧

I kept working, doing concerts and writing, through these difficult times. In the spring of 1971 I recorded my concerts on tour, resulting in a live album called *Living*. In 1972 Jac put out another collection called *Colors of the Day*, with the best songs of the previous few albums. It had the hits on it, and bridged another gap of a year or so while I tried to decide what to do next.

I took some time off to write in 1972. I went out to Long Island and rented a house where I watched the ocean and wrote songs. Clark had found a new school in Vermont, a place he and his therapist had chosen. I was staying as far from his decisions as possible on the advice of Dr. Newton and Dr. Schneider. After his accident I had acknowledged that I was not able to handle these questions well. Mildred, and another friend of mine, Billy Green, who Clark trusted and liked, arranged for the school interviews, without my participation. I paid the bills: the advised distance from Clark was supposed to help him get through his problems. I took mine to Long Island. Clark and I talked on the phone but I didn't see him for a few weeks. According to the Sullivanians, this is what was needed—some separation.

The few months of total concentration on Long Island took me to a new place in writing. "Secret Gardens," "Holly Ann," and "Ché," my song about Ché Guevara, were gifts of that time. A friend of mine from Colorado, Mart Hoffman, killed himself in the spring of the year, and I wrote "Song for Martin." Soon I was longing to put some of these songs on record and started recording *True Stories and Other Dreams*. I was still with Stacy, though he had found another apartment and we weren't living together. Stephen's songs were in my head and I loved "So Begins the Task." I found "The Dealer," one of the best gambling songs I ever heard, by Bob Ruzicka. The Attica prison riots were in the news, prisoners taking hostages of guards. Tom Paxton, whom I had known since the early sixties in New York, captured the feel and the horror of it in "The Hostage." I started performing "The Hostage" in concert, and it riveted the audiences.

After *True Stories* came out, Jac called me the night before he was scheduled to have a press conference to announce that he was leaving Elektra. He had previously sold the company to Warners but had been acting president in the company. I was devastated. The next day Jac introduced me to David Geffen, who was taking over Elektra. Jac told me that David would take care of me and that he was passing the flame to the best.

I went to see Geffen a few weeks later and told him I was lost, that I didn't know what to do next. It was the summer of dance music. The sixties were over. My romance with Stacy was also fraying at the edges. We were both seeing other people. I didn't have a clue as to where I could go musically. David said, "Do what you love. Do what you are good at." It was the best advice, the only advice.

When Duke Ellington died I went to the open casket viewing of Ellington's body at a Harlem mortuary. After waiting in line with hundreds of other mourners, I was able to touch the hand of the man who had composed so much music in his life—more, it is said, than any other American composer. It seemed a magic touch to me. I went to Ellington's funeral with our mutual concert agent from Europe, Robert Patterson, who had been a great friend of Ellington's and arranged for me to have a conversation with Ellington on the phone from the hospital a few days before his death. I will never forget that conversation, or Ellington's great sensitivity and kindness to me. The funeral was a musical tribute at the Cathedral of St. John the Divine, where I would be married in another twenty years and where my son would experience his own epiphany. Billy Taylor played, Ella Fitzgerald and Sarah Vaughan sang, and Mercer Ellington conducted. It was a transforming experience after which I wrote "Song for Duke."

I asked Phil Ramone to engineer and Arif Mardin to produce my next album, *Judith*. Nancy Bacal and Ann Purtil, an A and R person at Elektra, both sent me "Send in the Clowns," Sondheim's great song from *A Little Night Music.* It was two years old and everyone in the business had recorded it, but I knew I had to as well. I recorded "I'll Be Seeing You," my father's favorite song;

"Houses," a song I wrote after a dream about Stephen Stills; Jimmy Webb's song "The Moon Is a Harsh Mistress"; Steve Goodman's "City of New Orleans"; Wendy Waldman's "Pirate Ships." The tapestry began to come together.

Along with the rest of the country, I felt a great weight lift as the last American troops came home from Vietnam in 1973. They were, in most places, unsung, unwelcomed, and unsaluted—one of the great blots on our history and a sign of the awful price we had paid for our adventures in Indochina.

Things on the surface looked good, I was happy. I had hit records, my concerts were going well, but I was drinking an enormous amount and on the inside, my life was full of holes. My son's life was in constant turmoil, as was mine, and there was little continuity in my life. I started to have real trouble with my voice.

The disease of alcoholism is clever: it lies in wait, like an undiagnosed cancer. For nearly twenty years, no one would have known I had a problem. I looked good, I worked hard, I was successful, I showed up, and I did what I had to do. I was responsible, I had a profession, I tried to be a good mother to my son, I loved him, and I searched for answers everywhere, sending him to therapy, going to therapy myself. I wanted a better life. I went to doctors, many of whom even today don't know much about alcoholism. I won many of life's battles, but I was losing the war.

The disease was there, like a time bomb, ticking away the years. I still didn't drink during the day, so I could use my denial when things were getting out of control. The steady, slow ingesting of alcohol was killing parts of me I couldn't even know about. There was beginning to be a slight haze over everything.

But there were good things in these years, too. I decided during this time that Saul Newton and my therapists were wrong about the need for distance with my son. I became very involved with his life again, with his choices of schools, and, in 1973, after another serious episode when he overdosed on drugs, together we found a school that I hoped would be a solution for him. We had more therapy together, and when he decided to live on his own, and then came back to go to high school, he and I got much closer and were able to communicate. We loved each other and I think Clark understood I was trying to help him in every way I could.

But in my own life I began to make choices of which I did not, in my sober moments, approve. They were tearing me apart. I was on the way down, the control was fading fast.

In the years from 1975 to 1978, I began to drink on a round-the-clock basis, often first thing in the morning. I couldn't wait, and I couldn't stop.

When drinking begins to destroy, it destroys the most important parts of a life. Alcohol first took away my inhibitions and then took away my pride and eventually took away my ability to sing. I think it also took away my ability, try as I might, to give the best help to my son.

⚮

Max Margulis was still my teacher and I worried with him about my voice troubles, and went to doctors, trying to figure out what was wrong. I had been studying with Max throughout the passing years, and the vocal chord trouble plagued me more and more. There were endless remedies, strong drugs to calm down the swelling capillaries in my throat which were causing the problem. I went on working, dependent on doctors now, and, at times, on various medications.

Working on *Judith* was difficult. Each song took weeks, because of the vocal problems I was having. Finally, however, it was finished, and in 1974, "Send in the Clowns" was being played on the radio all over the country and in England. That year, Nixon faced with Watergate and impeachment, was forced to resign. The following year, President Ford pardoned President Nixon.

For me the years were tinged with sorrows. My son was having more problems.

⚮

In 1974 I had begun an on-again, off-again relationship with a writer named Jerry Oster. Over the four years we were together, I thought I was actually having an adult relationship with Jerry, though I was incapable of having any kind of relationship with anyone. I was drunk on most days. I was falling into the four-year end game of the disease, hanging on to Jerry for stability.

In the midst of this turmoil, my ability to work continued at its own pace, as though it had a mind of its own, outside my body, outside my problems. Nothing I did seemed to completely slow it down.

Arif, Phil and I began to talk about my next album. As usual, I hunted for songs, searching as though for gold. After the death of her husband, Dick Fariña, Mimi Fariña, Joan Baez's younger sister, had started a nonprofit organization in San Francisco called Bread and Roses, to provide free entertainment for people in homes, jails and hospitals in the Bay Area. She wrote the "Bread and Roses" melody to a poem by James Oppenheim and I recorded it, using a choir of voices in a church in New York.

Victor Jara was a gifted Chilean songwriter murdered in the political massacres following Allende's arrest and murder in Santiago in 1973. I was introduced to Jara's widow, Joan, and she brought me the last song her husband had written, "Plegaria a un Labrador," prayer of a laborer, a song crying for democracy. "Lift up your eyes and look to the mountains, " it said, "source of your strength, your sustenance."

I recorded a song I had heard on an Ella Fitzgerald record, "I Didn't Know About You." Arif, my producer, brought in Hank Jones, the great jazz pianist, to play. I also sang another Leonard Cohen song, "Take This Longing"; a beautiful song written by Renaldo Hahn in 1918, "King David," about the healing sound of the nightingale in the garden of a sorrowful king; and "Love Hurts," by Andy Gold.

In the recording sessions with Arif and Phil, I was barely above water. I would go in, sing a bit, and then lunch would come. By now, I couldn't wait till the evening to drink, and after I drank I couldn't sing. Lunch for me would be wine, which meant there was no more singing for the day, we would wait till tomorrow. And tomorrow. And tomorrow.

Worse and worse, going down. I tried changing therapists, I tried going to physical therapists, tried acupuncture. I used to think that if I went to jail, maybe I wouldn't drink. If I were in a monastery or a nunnery, maybe I wouldn't drink. I would see the signs in the taxis: "Have a problem with your drinking? Call this number." Ashamed, I never called. I thought drinking was a moral issue. I thought I should be able to control it.

I tried everything but quitting drinking. That would have been impossible.

One morning that spring, Clark came into the kitchen where I was drinking vodka out of a coffee cup. It was eight A.M. and he was about to get on the train for school. My son looked at me, looked at my coffee cup, looked at the clock, and said, "Do you know what time it is, Mom?"

There had been a lot of humiliating times with my drinking, blackouts and cancellations of concerts because my voice was in such terrible shape from alcohol. There were friendships that went haywire, professional situations I botched, days, months, even years that were a blur. There was so much damage, but I didn't have a clue of how sick I really was. But it was that moment, and that look in my son's eyes, that finally broke my denial.

$\mathcal{D}\mathcal{C}$

In 1977 Elektra put out a fifteen-year collection of songs from all the Elektra albums I had made since the first, in 1961. I called the collection *So Early in the Spring*. On that album I included "Send in the Clowns," which became, for the second time, a big hit, actually going higher on the charts than it had the first time when it appeared on *Judith*.

I was very ill now, though somehow able to function. On the inside I was dying. I went over and over my will—what I would leave Clark, my siblings, my mother, my friends. I divided up my life, dreaming of death.

So Early in the Spring
Album Notes
June, 1977

My life sometimes had the qualities of a glacier. Movement was so slow as to be invisible, as though a ballet were being done under the water of a still lake. People about me walked and talked. They were festivals of activity. They appeared to have had a thaw in their glaciers, a flood that had cleared canyons where now vegetation thrived, thickets of scarlet and white flowers blossomed. I curled cautiously under water, daring to breathe as lit-

tle as possible, frantic in my plunges to the surface to gulp air, slide back
and resume a pose conducive to glacial progress and underwater breathing. I
surfaced through ice or through water. Sometimes crystals fell around my
shoulders or boats sank with the weight of jewels. I collected them with a
net, or with an ice pick. When I came up to breathe for an instant, or spiked
through the hard edge of ice, there might be a girl in a torn dress with blood
running into the ground from a sword wound; a figure of a man riding
away on horseback, his voice laughing from under a dusty Stetson; three
women with sapphire crowns moving through the arc of a dungeon's mouth
from black light into sunlight, their skirts billowing forward, and one Queen
remaining in the shadows behind, her face white and her wrists wrapped in
chains; one gypsy, who could dance as though on point, came whirling
through the forest into a clearing, and was followed by a woman with bare
feet who had thrown away her shoes and her infant and her fortune, and
wished only that all should remain as it was at this moment, in this clear-
ing; gale storms hit the cheeks of men on ships while the sails burst with
wind and water above their heads; virgins lost their hearts and had their
hair pinned to the ground by thieves in masks.

The thief was time. I was hitting bottom. The singing problems worsened. I became hoarse, my voice graveley and undependable. After never
missing a show, I began to have to cancel dates: first *The Muppet Show* in
early summer, which I was able to reschedule a few months later; then a
dozen or so concerts. My voice was faltering, holding up for a few dates, then
going hoarse. I would go on two-week courses of prednisone to take away the
swelling and the rough surface of the capillaries on my vocal chords. The
chords were actually irritated by the alcohol I was drinking. After the prednisone, I could go on for a few more dates before I collapsed once more.

I was sure I had cancer, or that I was losing my voice for good. My doctor told me we would eventually have to do laser surgery. I am fortunate my
problem and the laser occurred in the same decade. I went into the hospital
for the laser surgery in October 1977, registering under an assumed name and
spending the night before the surgery drinking with friends. I am lucky that

I didn't die of overmedication when they took me in at six A.M. to operate. I went home and spent a few days in medically advised silence, drinking more and more, terrified that I wouldn't be able to sing at all.

Quite the opposite happened. When I was recovered, my voice had gained upper as well as lower notes, and greater confidence and depth. I was able to sing things that had been impossible for years. I celebrated by drinking for a few more months, but reality was setting in. By the end of the year I had to admit I had a problem I couldn't lick alone. I had finally hit bottom.

They say, "Don't walk away until the miracle comes."

On March 2, 1978, Jerry Oster walked out of my life, without a backward glance. I sent him back his typewriter, on which he had been writing what I was sure would be the great American novel, and his bicycle. I sent him a white rose, but there was no luring him back. I hadn't been left till then, and I was licking my wounds, determined that I would live alone and not get involved.

Jerry's leaving had catapulted me into my last long painful drunk. In early April I went to see Dr. Stanley Gitlow, a doctor who knew what was wrong with me.

Gitlow is an expert in the diagnosis of acute alcoholism and drug abuse. He speaks and writes and travels all over the country, lecturing about the disease. I walked into Gitlow's office and knew the gig was up. He was clear and open when I told him my story. I didn't lie to him about the drinking. He said I had a disease. I somehow hadn't known that. I felt sudden and great relief. He told me I had three choices: I could check myself into an institution right now, where I would probably die. I could drink until I had a wet brain, or I could go into treatment. He recommended treatment and I made plans to fly to the Pennsylvania hills on April 19.

At the time, I didn't know where Clark was. He was nineteen. He had graduated from St. Anne's High School in Brooklyn, where he had stayed clean and sober, and then gone back to drugs and alcohol. I knew he was somewhere in the city, but we hadn't talked in weeks.

A few days later, my friend Jeanne Livingston told me that she had met a man she wanted me to meet, and could I see him, go out with him, have a blind date with him? Louis Nelson was his name. Wouldn't I just meet him for a drink?

Just what I needed, I told her, and no thanks.

She persisted. She told me she had done our astrological charts and that Louis and I had something very special in common: he was a Libra, I was a Taurus, and we both had moons in Venus. I gave up and said I would meet him.

The Ginger Man, a very good restaurant in the Lincoln Center area in New York, had changed its name for the ERA fund-raiser to the Ginger Person. Bella Abzug, Gloria Steinem, Stephen Sondheim, and other luminaries were there. In walked a handsome, interesting-looking Norwegian. My first impression was that he was too considerate, too kind, not my sort of man, too gentle, too mannered, too sweet, much too normal and natural. I liked him enormously and as he not only put me into a cab but accompanied me home, I was surprised. And interested.

The next day, I called him. After all, we had met at an ERA fund-raiser! I wanted to know this man. I told him I had just ended a relationship.

That was not really my problem. I was dying. He didn't know that. Neither did I.

I spoke evasively about some travel I was planning, and said I had to go away on a trip to see my sister. It was partly true. I was terrified of going down to Pennsylvania for treatment, still wondering if I might be able to do this alone. Holly and I talked about my coming to Los Angeles. Finally she said she would come to help me and arrived with Kalen, my nephew, who was then nine months old. I bought a high chair. Clark was in and out of the house, in his elusive period, doing a lot of drugs. I told Holly about this man I had met who was not my type. But I knew I would see Louis again.

Four days later, I went into treatment. I had my last drink—by the grace of God—eight ounces of vodka out of a jelly jar, in a stall in the ladies' room at the airport in Reading, Pennsylvania, at seven-thirty in the morning. I was already drunk, but that drink was necessary. I dumped the jelly jar into the trash bin, tried to put my face to rights in the mirror of the tiled bathroom, and staggered out to the lobby, where a nice-looking young man was waiting and poured me into the old station wagon that had been brought to meet me.

He lugged my suitcase full of books—I had thought I would do a lot of reading!—and my suitcase full of clothes, a swimsuit, jogging shoes, running shorts, all the clothing you might need for a high-class spa, which is where I thought I was going. Plus my typewriter. I didn't know the first thing about treatment centers except that Chit Chat (honestly, and what a name!) was one of the best, supposedly, in the country.

It was April of 1978 when I walked through the doors of the white farmhouse on the hill among the gloriously budding trees of the Pennsylvania countryside. I collapsed into the arms of people who knew what to do with people like me, people who are alcoholic. I made it just in time. It had been a long run and it was over. I was finished. I was whipped. I had nowhere else to go but to a drunk farm in the hills of Pennsylvania, a place that turned out to be heaven on earth. They told me to hand over the wheel, that they would drive for a while.

❧

Louis and I had our second date on July 10, 1978, and have been together ever since. We have been through everything together, the bad and the good. He is my soul mate.

❧

My life on this side of the darkness began. It was a new life, a rich life, a life of renewed energy and hope, of growth. I was to find joy and fulfillment, all the wonder of truly living free of chemicals.

If I had had a clue about how much I would have to change, I would never have had the courage to face my alcoholism and do something about it. Knowledge of how much pain it would take to grow would have scared me off. Instead, all I could do was not drink, a day at a time. I talked to people who had the same problem I had, and knew what to do and told me where to go, what to say, how to live. As I got better, I recovered my sense of humor and my health and my joy in living.

Clark was going down further each month. As I got better, I had to watch him getting worse. There was nothing I could do to help, though I tried, sending him to see Stanley Gitlow, telling him my story, much of which he knew. The damage was done, the line had been crossed, many years before. My son had inherited the disease, just as he had inherited his blue eyes and his singing voice. He would have to find his way out of the darkness, and I prayed each and every day that he would.

In sobriety I found I was stable and steady and able to be a good friend to myself. I knew what I wanted, and it had nothing to do with the flighty and obsessive life I had led when I was drinking. I wanted to love one man, have my dignity and lead a relatively simple life. In the following years Louis and I became more and more deeply committed to each other. I found in my lover and companion the things I had been looking for all my life. We were a team, I helping him and he, kind and supportive, helping me relearn how to perform, watching my shows, making notes, helping me find new strengths to add to the ones that were already there. Louis was supportive about Clark's problems, helping when he could. He formed a friendship with my son that I believe had a great deal to do with Clark's eventual decision to get his life together.

I had started to write songs again after getting sober, and in 1984 I started work on my autobiography, *Trust Your Heart*. By that time, after suffering terrible damage at the hands of the disease of alcoholism, Clark too had gone into treatment. The miracle had come to pass in both our lives. My son was sober and healthy, had a job and good friends, and he and I had a wonderful relationship. Both of us had recovered from a terrible and devastating disease.

Clark had met a young woman, and in 1987, a few months before the publication of my book, Clark and Alyson Lloyd celebrated their wedding in St. Paul, Minnesota. There were many blessings in our lives. We had all waited a long time, but somehow we had achieved that longed-for peace and serenity. For the moment, we were all right. Life was unquestionably beautiful.

Trust Your Heart ended with Clark's marriage, and the following words:

The years of struggle for Clark are in the past, the dark times and the heartbreak. Our paths have merged and paralleled. Today is a new beginning.

Amazing grace, how sweet the sound
That saved a wretch like me.
I once was lost, but now am found
Was blind, but now I see.

My beloved Clark, it has been a year today since you died, taking yourself from us, spinning your spirit into space, wandering into eternity, where gods and goddesses surely caught you in their threads of light and eased your soul as it sped toward heaven, showing you the way at last. They bore your pain away and brought it down to me.

Today, the anniversary of your death, the very hour, we gather at the church with the priest who christened you, along with your family and your friends. The light from the rose windows shudders and glints with the words that are spoken, and the thundering song of the bagpipes. The face of the bagpipe player, dressed in his clan MacLean kilts, is even younger, even smoother than yours.

The voices of your friends and your family bring you to life in the echoing shadows and flames of the candles: you as a child, you as a man, you as a lover, you as a son, you as a friend. You are here beside the flowers, white and amethyst, the glass, emerald and blue, the harp music in the air, here where you received baptism. You are with us, your brightness and your beauty and your courage around us. Like the wings of angels I feel your face against mine.

Though you are gone, yet you break the veil, the almond tree blossoms, you transcend time: my child, my son, my teacher.

8

Sweet Spirit Clark

*I*n 1986 I sent Clark the first draft of *Trust Your Heart*, wanting to know if it agreed with what he remembered of the story of our lives. He told me it was accurate to a point and wanted me to know some of the things he remembered about his growing up and his struggles, in his own words. The result was a long letter of confession, honesty and friendship.

"This is the way *I* remember it, Mom.

"I was born in Boulder, Colorado. When my parents later told me about this I imagined myself being brought to life under the shadow of a huge rock."

Clark remembered "watching my mother wash her hair in a bowl . . . in the farmhouse in Storrs, Connecticut, and sitting on my father's lap, watching him blow smoke rings." Childhood memories followed—catching fireflies together in a bottle under the big tree on the farm in Storrs, and all the cows in that pasture on the hill.

When I was about three I started to go to nursery school. My father drove the school bus, our white Chevy Van. I was already conscious of my mother's success in music and knew that not everybody's mother was a star. Going from living with my father to visiting with my mother was like living in two different worlds because when I saw her it was special and wonderful. She gave me presents and a lot of attention and took me into the recording studio and to performances. It all felt very special. . . . My mother would come and get me and we'd go to New York. I liked that. I remember going to Colorado in the summers with my mother. I learned how to ride horses and I remember being really proud when I rode a wild horse. . . . I got to know Aunt Holly and Uncle Denver well in those summers. I remember that John Denver was a friend of my mother's.

Rosalind [Clark's half-sister] was born and we moved to Vancouver because my father got a job at the University of British Columbia. I was unhappy in Vancouver. A strange town, a strange school. I got into a little bit of trouble there. Once I got caught for breaking beer bottles and Mr. Templeton (the same name as the rat in *Charlotte's Web*) hit my hand with a shaving strap. I hated school and was often asked to stay after school for talking and generally making trouble in class.

By this time my father had me going to a psychologist. . . . We'd make papier-mâché things. I think we made a puppet around a lightbulb and then broke out the lightbulb. I didn't like going to see this guy. I think I would rather go to the dentist. There was a big dramatic scene where my father and Sue [Clark's stepmother] and I were in this guy's office. In the middle of third grade I decided that I wanted to go live with my mother [Christmas of 1968]. My mother had always asked me to come and live with her. I was on a plane to New York within a week.

Life was a lot different living with my mother. I could let my hair grow. She got me a bunk bed so I could have my friends stay over . . . .

I had my first drug experiences when I was nine or ten. I wasn't fitting in at school very well. I went to a private school in Manhattan. I disrupted classes. I was sent out to sit in the hall quite a bit. I cried hysterically when a girl's brother was killed in Vietnam. A psychologist decided that I should go to a school for "gifted and special children."

Many troubles in school followed, Clark and I trying in these years to figure out how to live through his adolescence as well as our mutual alcoholism. In later years I would come to look at it as a time where we were trying to stay alive long enough to learn to live.

The school sent Clark to be tested by Dr. Jerry Brown, a psychiatrist. Brown recommended putting Clark on drugs for his hyperactivity. I refused. I suspected he was already using drugs—and knew more wouldn't help. I found a very good, small school called the Reece School, in which Clark flourished for two years. After Reece, when things got difficult with Clark, we tried a boarding school. The first try, at a school in Maryland, ended when Clark had the accident on his sled. After his recovery, the next stop for Clark was Glenrock, a nonstructured school in Vermont. Perhaps, Clark's therapist thought, he would do better there, where there was not so much pressure.

That year at the new, free, open school was another stop on the road to more trouble with drugs, more of the story of Clark's private hell, and more getting into trouble as he began dealing drugs. There were plenty of drugs, plenty of alcohol, and very few classes, and now, Clark started getting into trouble with the law. This began relationships with detectives to hunt him down when he disappeared, and therapists to talk to him when he would not talk at all. I began to experience the holy terror of losing him every month or so. That winter I went to Vermont to bail him out of jail, and we came home to lick our wounds and try to make a plan together. The Glenrock experiment, like so many others, had failed.

Clark's attitude about the trouble he got into and my attempts to help him was remorse and promises not to do these things again; he always made apologies. There were tears, hugs, resolve to change. He knew I loved him, he knew I was trying to help him. He wanted to help himself, but he didn't know how.

After the experience at Glenrock, Clark and I interviewed at a number of private schools, looking again for a safe haven. We met with Heinz Bonde, the headmaster of Windsor Mountain, nestled in the pines of the Berkshires, and were both encouraged by his openness about the problems of drugs. We felt the school, a stone structure with substance and history, would be good for Clark. He was excited about the chance for a new start.

But he was into drugs there as quickly as he unpacked his bags, and the experience resulted, a few months later, in Clark's first overdose. I drove to Lenox and found, waiting for me at the Pittsfield General Hospital, a shivering, thin, white-faced addict. Scared to death. Half-dead. In the backseat of the car, driving down from Pittsfield, Clark was like a lean, ephemeral ghost. It was the same look I was to see over and over again for the next ten years.

I got so I could almost hear that look, even when I wasn't with him. I was to see it so many times in the coming years. It was a look I was powerless over, which tore my heart out, rendered me helpless. I couldn't change that look, and I didn't know what was wrong with him—or with me. How could my son be this gaunt, dying person, this ghost who couldn't listen to me? How could he be someone who listened to the voice of the angel of death?

I am reminded of George McGovern's journey with his daughter, Terry, who died a few years ago, freezing in Minnesota after she passed out, drunk, during a heavy winter snowstorm. The story of her struggle, the valiant effort she made to overcome the disease, how she was in sixty-eight rehabs and still died of alcoholism, is a testimony to the fact that we are powerless over this disease. All of us.

I tucked Clark into bed and put hot food into his stomach and some clean clothes on him, and Clark and I settled into another healing mission, one of remorse and apologies, "Mom, I won't do this again." "Honey, maybe this time we'll do it all differently." Those discussions usually lasted all of a day. I would try, I thought, to keep him at home, even though the therapists thought this was a terrible idea. But love, tenderness, care, home-cooked meals—I believed all of these could change everything.

The next day my son vanished—gone like one of those silver fish that you think is on the line. He was out hunting for a fix, for a high, for a good time, for death.

I chased him, and the detective I had hired found him with the help of my brother, Denver John, and Stacy. They tracked him down at the home of a drug dealer in Brooklyn and brought him home. Clark was enraged. Thinner, even more gaunt, his eyes like saucers, unable to get any more booze, any more drugs. I was appalled at the way he looked, at his deterioration. I didn't yet know I was looking at alcoholism in progression. Neither did the hospital. They didn't know much. Not many medical hospitals did at that time.

Today, my friend Monica Wright is head of the treatment program at Gracie Square Hospital. If Clark's life had fallen apart from alcoholism a few years later, my son would most certainly have been put into a twenty-eight-day program. I often wonder, does that mean he would be alive today?

In the psychiatric hospital, Clark was put on a locked ward. Knowing his history by now of using, running and getting into trouble out on the street, the hospital felt Clark should remain there for two weeks. He was not happy about this, and neither was I. We looked for a safe place, not knowing one didn't exist. The psychiatrists told me Clark needed to be in a psychiatric hospital. If he were out of the hospital, they said, he would keep running: into the next drug deal, looking for the big one, in the sway of his disease. Clark stayed in a locked ward at Gracie Square while we searched for the "right" place, a place where he could get the help he needed.

It was 1973. Nobody was sending people to alcoholism rehabs in those days. Where could I send him? Saul Newton recommended Shepherd Pratt, in Baltimore. He knew the woman who had founded it. I talked to the admissions people, and they seemed very good, very professional. They had no "program," no "recovery," as we know it today, but these words were concepts still in our futures.

I drove Clark down to the lovely and safe-looking hospital near Baltimore, with elegant brick buildings full of craft rooms, plant rooms, classrooms, dining rooms, and kids who looked normal enough, running around in their untied tennis shoes and their down parkas.

I made the trip to Baltimore every month, taking the Amtrak ride from New York along the coast. For a year and a half, at ninety miles an hour, I filled yellow-lined pads with poetry and wrote in my journals. I would rent a room at a hotel and a car to drive to the hospital. There, in sessions with Clark and his therapist, we made some progress. My son and I, after yelling at each other and getting out our anger and frustration, started to laugh and appreciate each other. It was a good time for Clark. These sessions were healing and brought us closer. My mother and stepfather came out to visit Clark. My brothers and sister paid visits to my son during these months. He was getting better. I knew it, and he knew it.

"This was an important time for me," Clark says in his written story of his life.

> I wasn't happy to be there (at Shepherd Pratt), but I did some growing up. They made an attempt to educate me at the little Quaker school they had there. I learned a little math and biology. I did some work in English class in addition to the other reading I was doing. I read the *Autobiography of a Yogi*. I was asking basic questions about life and for a while I decided that I wanted to do yoga, renounce the material and become enlightened. I started playing guitar there. I began to develop a sense of identity. I began to grow and try to find myself.

> There were drugs available at Shepherd Pratt. Mostly pot. I tried to get high every day and usually succeeded. We even grew our own. I sometimes got high from inhaling Right Guard and furniture polish—even took apart the radiators because I knew the thermostat had freon in it. I was glad to hear recently that they now have a peer-group self-help-oriented chemical dependency program there.

Clark's therapist had planned a session with Peter, Clark and me. On a Monday in the spring of 1973 Peter was scheduled to fly from Vancouver.

It had been a long time since Clark and his father had spent any time together. The therapist felt there were problems between Clark and his father that could be resolved and might help Clark to get well.

The Sunday before this meeting was going to take place, I was in New York planning to get on the train the next morning in order to be at the hospital by eleven for our session. I got a call from the hospital telling me Clark had run. No one knew where.

It was the beginning of winter in our lives again.

About a week went by, and there was no word of Clark's whereabouts. The police were looking for him. I was frantic. After a week I had a message from one of his friends that I shouldn't worry, that he was all right. A few days later he called me himself to tell me he was living somewhere: "I'm not going to tell you where, Mom; but I'm all right. I don't want you to worry. I love you. I've got a job with a rock-and-roll band."

I wept, and called my mother, my sister and brothers. They consoled me, and they encourged me to put the pain in my songs. I sat at my piano in my studio and let the tears flow and my heart break and wrote "Born to the Breed." Later I learned that Clark had lived like a street person in Ocean City, Maryland, hand to mouth—freedom, he called it—sometimes cooking in a short-order restaurant, sometimes selling drugs. He started shooting heroin at that time. He was not even sixteen.

But Clark kept in touch, more and more. He started phoning me regularly, saying he missed his mom, he missed being in New York, and that he wanted to come home, live with me, and go to high school. It was 1976. I was relieved, but scared. We talked about this plan for weeks, and decided that we had a loving relationship together and agreed it would work if we both tried to make it work.

He came home, and it was so much the right thing. I was overjoyed to have him with me. He seemed to have grown so much, he was more loving, and even did his chores! He kept his room clean, he helped me with the dishes, we spent hours talking and laughing together. Together, we did things in the city and explored a number of schools in New York.

St. Anne's, a high school in Brooklyn, was Clark's choice, although there were schools that were closer to home. It was a long subway ride from the Upper West Side, and I was impressed with the way my son got up, got to school, did well, devoted himself to his classes, and made a good bond with his fellow students and teachers. He and I had our ups and downs that year but we learned to live together again. Clark settled down a lot. I watched his sweetness and his intelligence bloom. He seemed to have a reprieve from his terrible compulsion to use. He got his high school diploma and everything was better.

After graduating from St. Anne's, where he did well, making good grades and many friends, Clark seemed to slip back again into the kind of chaos that had been the pattern before. He pointed out my drinking while his own increased. After I got sober, he was erratic—not showing up for a large family reunion, going in and out of contact.

Then, Clark was accepted at Sarah Lawrence, a small liberal arts school in Bronxville. He started classes and met Amy Wagner, a young woman from New York. Clark brought Amy to meet Louis and me. She was tall and beautiful, with soulful brown eyes and brown long curly hair and a deep commitment to making the world better. She wanted to teach children, and she and Clark shared mutual ideals about helping other people. I liked Amy and was pleased Clark had found someone steady and "normal."

But soon, Clark was thrown out of the college. ("How," I asked him, "can you get thrown out of *Sarah Lawrence?*") Clark started dealing drugs again, living fast, pushing the envelope.

Now, I was not alone in watching my son go down the dark path. Louis and I were together. Louis gave me the courage to continue to try to help my son, and the loving understanding I needed to know that I couldn't do much of anything except love him.

Clark was nineteen when he and Amy moved to Providence, Rhode Island. Louis and I were sorry to see him move out of New York, but we both felt it might be just the thing he needed to bring him around.

I went to work for Manny Silver. Manny was an old carpenter who sort of taught me the Zen of carpentry. One of these very spiritual people that don't appear to make a conscious effort at it. He was a pleasure to work with and I still think of him often when I pick up a hammer.

My girlfriend didn't like me when I drank, and I really got nasty when she tried to stop me. One night I came home in a blackout and she told me that if I didn't stop drinking she'd leave me.

So I stopped. I continued to smoke pot for a while but my

mother told me it didn't make any difference what I used so I stopped using all together.

After a few months, Clark returned to New York and started using. I thought I had some power over what Clark did or didn't do with his life. Like most parents, I had trouble seeing my son's problems as an illness. I continued to give my son money. He was a dreadful and pathetic sight and my heart would tear to pieces each time I saw him. I wanted to save him and still thought I *could* save him. Nothing I did seemed to be enough, and as I was to learn, as long as the drugs and the alcohol were in control, I didn't stand a chance of helping. Maybe no one did, no one but Clark, and he wouldn't admit he had a problem.

God knows how, since he had been trown out of Sarah Lawrence, but once Clark was back in New York, he was accepted into Columbia. He was a mess, but he was a brilliant mess. He would stop delivery men on bicycles in the streets of Manhattan while on a drug run to speak to them in Chinese and talk about the Sung Dynasty. I had the bewitched faith of a mother, but finally when Clark was twenty-three and a half I told him I would not give him any more money for school as I knew he was using it for drugs. I said I would pay for rehab if he would go into treatment, and for whatever he wanted to do in his life that was positive. It was incredibly painful because I didn't want to let go. I didn't want to let him dangle out there, freaking with pain and unable to stop dancing with the gorilla.

He was furious when I told him I was going to cut off his money, telling me he knew plenty of blue collar workers who sent their children to Ivy League schools. I told him emotional blackmail wouldn't work and if he wanted to stay in Columbia he could get sober and could earn the money to pay for it. I would be glad to help him, but only if he were clean and sober.

᠀᠀᠀

It took Clark a year and a half longer to be ready for help. During those months we saw each other often. Sometimes he would be a bit better, more often sicker. He would sometimes ask me to take him to one of my groups, but he would say, "This is good for you, Mom, but I don't need it."

I started talking to some people who knew about alcoholism in families. I also continued my attendance at recovery groups for friends and spouses of alcoholics. The wisdom of these kind friends was what kept me going, bonded me to the hope that if I didn't interfere, my son might run his course with his disease and be ready for help.

Detachment is a difficult lesson for anyone who loves an addict. It is especially difficult for a parent. I was told that as long as I was in the middle, trying to fix my son, I was adding to the chances that he wouldn't get well. I learned that in spite of my son's illness, I could find joy in my own life, the gift of friends and fellowship, of work and of the light of creativity.

In not allowing my son to drag me down into his deep well of illness, I was told, I was not only helping myself, but helping him as well. And I wanted, with all my heart, to help my son. I always had, and always would.

✿

One young man, named Jesse, gave me hope. He was Clark's age and had been sober and doing well for a number of years. He told me that his parents gave him money and supported him for as long as he was ill, always coming to the rescue, bailing him out of jail, trying to fix him with money, ideas, doctors, solutions. He told me he believed that just so long as they did this, he was not willing to face the truth about himself and his illness. His parents had finally been worn out by the drama and the hysteria of their son's illness and let go of Jesse, allowing him to find his own bottom. They began to have their own lives and to recover themselves, and so did their son. Now, he said, he had a wonderful relationship with his family. He had been sober for four years.

I hung on to Jesse's promise for dear life. I focused on my friends, my family, my work, my life partner. I detached with love and I prayed for my son. I knew I could do nothing for him until he asked for help. I watched Clark go down to the bottom, this boy I loved with everything in me, this child who was growing into a frightened and trapped man.

In the last days of chasing his dragon Clark was having hallucinations; he would show up for family events thin as a rail, incredibly scary, his blue eyes like steel marbles in his thin face, his red hair long and stringy, gaunt limbs sticking out from shirts that were frayed, spindly legs clad in old Levi's he refused to wash or replace. He had a haunted, wistful look when he did show up. Often he wouldn't arrive. Often there were nights of waiting, days of calling the police and detectives to track him down, bring him back. There were weeks of mystery. My son was walking and talking with death, like any respectable junkie.

> I gradually started using again. . . . I really liked coke [cocaine] and when I got access to the next year's money from my mother I basically went completely out of control on cocaine and thought I was going to kill myself by trying to hang myself out a window. . . . I had rope burns on my neck for weeks.
>
> My mother had an idea of what was going on even though I was lying about it. But I couldn't stop. I quit my job and told my mother that I'd go into treatment if I couldn't stop using by going to meetings. . . . my ribs stuck out and I had nothing for an ass but bone. I weighed about a hundred thirty pounds . . . every few days my mother would call me and I'd say I was doing great, still lying. . . . I was at the critical point. I could either give up and get some help or continue to slip back into my active addiction. I realized that I couldn't predict whether I was going to get high or eat when I had ten dollars in my pocket. . . . Sitting on the steps of St. John the Divine Cathedral [on the morning of February 13, 1984] I decided I would give it up. On Sunday I called my mother and told her about my decision. . . . She said she would pay for treatment and Valentine's Day of 1984 found me at Hazelden Pioneer House in Plymouth, Minnesota.

The day before Valentine's Day in 1984 Clark rang my doorbell at seven-thirty in the morning. He knew I would be awake and having my coffee. He told me he had gotten down on his knees and surrendered himself to God and asked to be shown the way to recovery. The message he received, he said, from that God in whom he believed, was that he must go into treatment.

When he told me about his decision I wept. My prayers had been answered. My fragile son and I talked, and held each other. It was an hour I had been praying for for so many years. Now, as I watched him dial the phone number to Hazelden treatment center in Minneapolis, his long, thin fingers trembling, and make the arrangements to save his own life, lights were going off in his eyes, lights I hadn't seen for years.

I was scared and I didn't know what they were talking about when they asked how I felt but I was sure that I didn't want to use anymore and that I'd do what they said, go to any length to stay sober. I'd try to feel if that's what they wanted and I started praying and making my bed and trying to stay awake in the morning lecture and really listen. I got close to people and really opened up. I graduated and accepted the recommendation to go to a halfway house.

I've gotten back the trust of my family. And I'm lucky to have a lot of support from them. My mother is an inspiration to me.

In the third week of Clark's rehabilitation, Louis and I went to Minnesota to the Family Treatment Center of the rehab center Clark was attending. There were so many tears in those rooms, tears of confused and suffering people who were learning that they didn't cause the disease in their daughter, son, husband, wife, father, mother. In those rooms with other families of addicts and alcoholics who were recovering, learning about the disease of alcoholism, I found hope.

In the meetings with Clark and his counselor at the center, we cried together all over again; I was able to make amends once more for the dark years of my drinking, and now I was speaking to a clear-eyed young man who was listening with his heart and his brain. My son made amends to me for the years of lying, deceit, disease. He granted me the honor of sitting in on the session with his peer group. I listened to the story of his life, in his own words, told to the young, recovering people in the circle with us: he told of things I didn't know about, couldn't have guessed. He had been to the bottom and returned, like the prodigal son, like Lazarus from the dead. The light at the end of the tunnel was not, it seemed, just the train coming toward us, rushing through the darkness, whistle screaming; the light was an inner light of joy. We could barely believe our good fortune. We counted the days as they turned into years. We savored this new life, reveled in it, believing we had paid a high price for our seat on that train, moving out of the dark tunnel.

Those healthy years, together, over seven and a half of them, were the most beautiful years of our lives. Clark, Louis and I talked as we had never talked, laughed and shared, becoming friends. Louis supported Clark in all the things he was doing to make a healthy life. He made sure Clark knew he loved him and was there for him. He would call to talk to Clark, make trips out to Minnesota with me to see Clark and visit.

For those seven and a half years, next to Louis, my son was my best friend, my confidant.

In 1986 Clark wrote to me one of his infrequent letters:

Dear Mom,

When you become a Minnesotan one of the first things that you are expected to learn is that talking about the weather is not superficial, it is rather one of the highest and most meaningful forms of communication possible . . . the summer brings that kind of beautiful storm that we both love . . . big, dark, heavy sky, flash and crash. God's fireworks . . . I took to calling on the great spirit and watching the sky in hopeful anticipation of rain when I really should have been painting. (A second job Clark took while he was in school.) I love being able to share with you the weather report of the soul.

I have some of those dark clouds gathering but I believe the storm coming is meant to clean up the dirty winter snow and bring forth green shoots . . . I'm very grateful that you're my oldest friend.

Love, Clark.

Clark married Alyson, a young woman from New York whom he had met in St. Paul, in 1987. The miracles continued—Clark and Alyson had a beautiful baby girl and Clark finished his diploma in computers, got a good job, developed interests and made new friends.

At my sister's wedding in Wyoming the summer before Clark's death my whole family gathered. We square-danced and played the piano and told silly stories and watched the newborn billy goats struggle up onto tiny legs in the barnyard. Tom Chapin, [Harry's brother], and his family were there as well and Tom sang songs for us and we rode on horseback, long lines of us among the shaking aspen, shouting aloud to each other at a gallop on the tundra above the timber line, singing old cowboy songs, loping and cantering across the big meadows, whooping and hollering. On a ridge above the timberline we cantered under the big sky, sat around the fireside singing at night, looking long at the stars that blazed above, diamonds in the clear mountain air, dancing among the Northern Lights. Life was better than it had ever been. On the day of my sister's wedding Clark and Louis and my brothers built a bower of willows and wild roses. The wedding was a celebration of the heart. My sister Holly wore a dress of lace and a white lace hat with ribbons that trailed down her back, fluttering in the breeze. She was a beautiful bride, someone old and someone new under a shining western sky. Clark with his little girl, Hollis, my brothers, my mother and stepfather. Louis in his tux and top hat, my handsome lover, life partner, friend; Holly's wedding bouquet in her strong potter's and painter's hands, her smile I love so. The little honey-colored Shetland, her head nodding like a duenna, pulled Holly in the pony cart to the grassy patch in front of the willow bower, where the preacher met her and all the blue and brown eyes of our families turned once again to wish good things for a new marriage. Under the bower of willows and roses, my sister and her husband Harvey Kahn repeated their vows, and we all shed tears of joy.

With his three-year-old daughter at his side, Clark sang a song he wrote for my sister, Holly, and her husband, Harvey, a lovely, perfect song.

> Underneath an arch of willow branches
> you stand together
> Circled by the loving witness of your vows
> The winding river and the eagle high,
> The mountain flowers and the giant sky
> seem to say;
> Best wishes for your life together
> Good fortune and the finest weather
> As you build a family with your love.
> All the love you give to each other and those around you
> May you find returned,
> May the bountiful gifts astound you.

They say you can look back, but don't stare. Although I could never change the past, the present was different. After all the years of chaos, Clark's clarity was a miracle to behold, to me and to everyone around him. His using years, so full of pain and wreckage, were the typical story of devastation, and we could talk of the past with humor, with appreciation. We told each other war stories, shared the glimpses of things we had only suspected about each other, and sealed our friendship with the bond of the heart, mother and child, now mother and friend, son and friend.

We had finally made it home through the storm. For a while, we had it all.

> I've made my share of mistakes...but I'm doing better and
> better. . . . I've begun to find my values and I try to live by
> them. This is a day-by-day process that goes better some days
> than others but I'm making progress.
> I decided to go to school in electronics and get a job that I
> won't hate after two weeks. I've completed one quarter and

received an A and I still like school. I go to a lot of meetings and I work as a volunteer at my old halfway house which is a great way to stay in the mainstream of recovery. I pray every morning and night and I remember throughout the day that God is with me and that this good life is only mine through the grace of God and recovery.

I've got a future. This life is worth living even on the bad days. I can continue to bloom as God intended. I can work and play and dance and cry and laugh with real friends and life is beautiful as long as I continue to try to do God's will.

Clark Taylor

ᘒᘒ *A line of melody is never still, never over. It rings and soars, moves and dances, sounding its music even after the song finishes.*

Still, I would like to arrive at a perfect pitch, a perfect release, a perfect zone of peace, although I know there is no perfection, there is only continuity, perfect climbing.

I have come apart again in the last few days, my composure shattering and my tears falling suddenly, unexpectedly. My tuning is off, my pitch sour. My song feels interrupted. During the holidays, the first without my son, I was able to hold myself together, I felt normal from time to time, but now again I feel my whole inner being is raw.

Grief has no timetable, no system for beginning, middle and end. The shadow outlines of deeper meanings, the waves in this ocean of healing, come over me again and again.

I pray to accept the pattern of my grief as it comes. My music will soar again, and on both the beautiful days and the bitter days, I am healing.

9

Surviving the Blow

And then, suddenly, it was midnight on my watch, and it seemed the sun, moon and stars were blighted out. There were few signs with which to guide me and my family and Clark's friends on our perilous journey, and we held each other close.

Consoling friends called, wrote to me.

"What is the opposite of life?" one friend wrote. "Death? No, birth is the opposite of death. There is no opposite of life."

It helped me, that day.

To survive, I knew I had to go to the center, right to the very heart of the pain. That way, no matter where I turned, I would be healing from the inside out. How could I do that? How does *anyone* go on, knowing he or she will always be a suicide survivor?

I wanted to sleep and sometimes I wanted to die. I didn't want to drink, for if I drank I knew I would follow my son. But there were other ways: step into the traffic, jump out a window, take a gun to my head, to my heart. But I don't have a gun. I threw out the pills, anything I thought might be there for me in a weak moment when I reached into the medicine cabinet, in the middle of the night, in the middle of the day, in the middle of the morning, in the middle of the afternoon. I got all the booze I had kept for guests out of my house. I couldn't let myself complete my first suicide attempt. One of us had already done that.

I prayed all night and all day sometimes, and tried to eat three meals a day, tried to remember to breathe.

Some days I couldn't get out of bed.

A few days after I got back from Clark's funeral, Joan Rivers called me. She had been where I was. "There are no guilts in suicide," she said. "You couldn't have stopped it, even if you had been there."

She went on, in that familiar voice, my tears falling quietly on the other end of the telephone. "Don't cancel your life," she said. "Go out. See friends. Keep living."

I searched the shelves of bookstores, staring wide-eyed, dumbstruck, to learn that there were books for every other kind of recovery: books to get you in touch with your inner child, books on how to face childhood sexual abuse, books on how to lose weight, books on how to get fit; books on how to meditatate, on how to get along with your spouse, find a lover, keep a lover; books on how to sail a boat around the world. There were books on family dysfunction, on pills, on booze, on being the adult child of an alcoholic, on recovery from alcoholism. I already owned most of them. There were books on how to build a boat and a house and a business and books on the principles of successful people, those too.

There was practically nothing on suicide and suicide survival. The surrounding problems that face suicides—depression, drug addiction, alcoholism and chemical imbalance—make it hard to write about. Hard to think about. Survival meant having to face these difficult issues head-on.

I knew I had to.

A few books, sent to me by friends, were smuggled, it would appear, into my solitary emotional confinement: *Silent Grief* (Living in the Wake of Suicide) by Christopher Lukas and Henry M. Seiden, Ph.D. *The Savage God,* by A. Alvarez, and *In the Midst of Winter,* a wonderful collection of poetry and prose by Mary Jane Moffat. Eventually, through friends, I found Iris Bolton's wonderfully healing book, *My Son ... My Son.* Adina Wrobleski, a therapist from the St. Paul area, has written many books about suicide and about depression, which she feels is the primary cause of suicide. I devoured every word, and called her to talk on the telephone, which she did, generously, for an hour. Another hour I could make it through.

"Everyone has a skeleton in their closet," Stephen Levine quotes the father of a suicide in *Who Dies?,* "but the person who kills themselves leaves a skeleton in yours." When I read this I knew I had to break the bones of that skeleton, exhuming the remains, rifling my own life and my son's to find reasons, learning to heal and find enough peace to go on living.

A. Alvarez talks bluntly about suicide and alcoholism. Reading his book I was reminded of the story of one of my friends, a woman who is successful, beautiful and healthy, sober and very undepressed today. She often talks of the twenty-five times she tried to take her life when she was drinking. She was able to comfort me greatly, because she understood what I was feeling, but there were many people who were frightened to speak of Clark's death, frightened, I believe, by their own deep revulsion of suicide.

Society once took its misunderstanding of suicide out on its survivors, denying survivors spiritual and social healing resources, condemning the soul of the departed suicide to perpetual torment in hell; covering the suicide with denial. Centuries after St. Augustine first damned each and every suicide to perpetual purgatory, the Church has come to agree that God forgives all.

I heard a survivor say, "Sometimes I cannot separate the taboo of the loss from the loss itself. The sorrow brings me to my knees. The shame keeps me there."

Suicide is different from other, "natural deaths." Like murder, there is something in the very word for self-slaying that sends a chill to the heart, makes the breath come faster. Suicide is the last taboo, according to A. Alvarez in *The Savage God*. Rather cancer, brain tumor, high blood pressure, stroke, accident. These are deaths that are easier to explain, to accept.

Sometimes there appears to be no depression or alcoholism in a suicide's life. That can be even more terrible for the survivors, who continue to look for reasons.

"Don't die when you think the light has gone, don't give up," I tell myself, "don't abandon your ship." "I am going to live in spite of the fact that you decided not to," I tell Clark. A mantra to keep from dying.

Deborah Morris, whom I saw at Canyon Ranch for sessions which she called "Catastrophic grief," says: "Until there is creation in the face of loss there is no healing." I did the thing that has been my bell in every weather, I worked. I wrote songs about Clark, sitting at the piano, tears falling on the black and white keys. I made an album of Dylan songs, listening to all Dylan's music that Clark and I had heard together and loved and talked about. I completed writing my novel, *Shameless,* in which I created a character who is a rock-and-roll cocaine addict, a scrawny, gifted kid who makes a suicide attempt that is stopped by his friends and his mother, doing in fiction what I had been unable to do in life.

I recorded an album of all my own compositions which I called *Shameless* as well, releasing it at the same time as my novel. An album of my own compositions was a first, I had to push the limits, do things I had never done before, so that I could live my life as I had never done before. I wrote "Bard of My Heart," about Clark. I wrote "Song for Sarajevo," for the children of Bosnia who were torn by their own wars, and who were fighting desperately to live, not to die. I made my first Christmas album, *Come Rejoice,* and then my second, *Judy Collins Christmas at the Biltmore,* accompanied by a Christmas special on the A&E network. I put together a collection of all the songs I had recorded for Elektra, called *Forever,* which included three new songs of my own: "The Fallow Way," "Nothing Lasts Forever," and "Walls," which I wrote with Louis. I did watercolors, pouring out the colors on paper to still the frantic beating of my heart, to comfort myself.

And I wrote about Clark and my life, pouring my heart out onto paper, recapturing his personality, his humor and his beauty.

Every song I sang, every word I wrote, every painting I made, helped me to heal.

Clark understood so much, why could he not understand that he didn't have to die?

Alvarez says that suicide is "a terrible, but utterly natural reaction to the strained, narrow necessities we sometimes create for ourselves. And it is not for me."

In Clark's family script suicide may have always been the "wild card," the exit sign that would pull him out when things got rough, when he was lost in the rain, beat out by the clock, up against the wall.

A friend of Clark's said at his funeral, "Clark was so very vulnerable."

"Yes," another said, "and look where his vulnerability got him!"

Me and my young and
beautiful mother, Marjorie.

(Author's collection)

A fairy-tale day in Colorado,
with Peter, Clark, and Kolya, before our
move away from the magic mountains.
(Photo by Terry Williams)

Mike, Holly, me, Denver, and Dave—
skiing at Jackson Hole, Wyoming, in 1993.
Another family reunion. (Author's collection)

Jim Keach, my nephew Kalen, Clark, Denver, Mike,
David, and my nephew Matt at Denver's wedding
in Colorado in 1979, when the world was young.
(Photo by Allison Collins)

Other acts: with Stacy on the stage at the New York Shakespeare Festival in 1969, rehearsing for Peer Gynt. (Photo by Julie Snow)

From 1976: Leonard and me—birds on the wire! (Photo by Jon Randolph)

Short hair, it's me in each and every picture, circa 1964, give or take. I don't know what happened to that guitar, but the haircut is gone for sure. (Photo by Erich Locker)

Pete, me, Bill Lee (Spike's father) on bass, Arlo, Bob Dylan, Tom Paxton, Odetta, Richie Havens, Jack Elliot, and Will Geer at Carnegie Hall for the Woody Guthrie Tribute in 1968. (Photo by David Gahr)

LEFT

In 1977, Arthur Fiedler
conducted while I sang at
Symphony Hall in Boston with
the Boston Pops. Back to the
orchestras, where it all began.

(Photo by Stan Grossfeld/
The Boston Globe)

BOTTOM

Posing in 1998 for the movie
A Town Has Turned to Dust —
a remake of the Rod Serling
script about the Emmet Till case.

(Photo © Brett Colvin / The Sci-Fi Channel)

OPPOSITE TOP LEFT

My most recent photo with
Francesco Scavullo, in 1997.
Back to basics. Nothing to wear.

(Photo by Francesco Scavullo)

OPPOSITE TOP RIGHT

My first photo session with
Francesco Scavullo, in 1974,
for Judith.

(Photo by Francesco Scavullo)

OPPOSITE BOTTOM

The girl in the white dress—
that's me in 1998.
Older, wiser, perhaps.
Singing for all I'm worth.

(Photo by Claus Wickrath)

Clark Photos

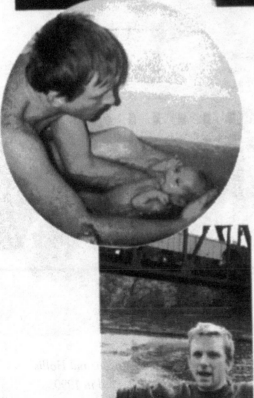

ABOVE

*Clark, shining at his wedding,
with his mom—me.*

(Photo by Louis Nelson)

CENTER

*"Hush little baby, don't say a
word, Papa's gonna buy you a
mocking bird."* Clark and Hollis
in November 1987.

(Photo by Alyson Taylor)

BELOW

*Clark, happy on the Mississippi
River in St. Paul in 1989.*

(Photo by Terry Williams)

Clark, Alyson, and Hollis
in St. Paul in 1990.

(Photo by Ann Marsden)

The Clintons

Louis, First Lady Hillary Rodham Clinton, me, and my friend President William Jefferson Clinton, in the Blue Room at the White House in 1996.

(Official White House Photo)

Jogging with the president.

(Official White House Photo)

Max and Brico

*Me and Antonia, backstage
at Boecher Hall in 1984.*

(Photo by Maria Pizzuro)

CENTER

*My great piano teacher,
Antonia Brico, in her prime.*

(Photo by Dr. Ralph Weizäcker)

BOTTOM

*Max—my voice teacher,
during his years with Blue
Note Records—with Pete
Johnson, recording* **Kansas
City Farewell.** *Pete (at
piano), Max, Abe Bolar
(on bass), Alfred W. Lion of
Blue Note, and Ulysses
Livingston (on guitar).
From* **Downbeat,**
February 15, 1940.

(Photo by Francis J. Wolf)

Hollis Taylor

Me and my beautiful girl,
Hollis, with curls.
(Photo by Louis Nelson)

UNICEF

ABOVE

With the children in the square
of Dubrovnik in 1994. Far away,
the shells are falling.

(Unicef/94-0639/Roger Lemoyne)

RIGHT

A clinic near Yen Bai, with a
beautiful Vietnamese boy and
his mother in 1997.

(Unicef/95-0046/Louis Nelson)

Wedding, 1996

"Uncle Louis in the rain forest with a girl."
Rowan Kahn, my three-year-old nephew, captioned this photo.
(Photo by Gayle Burns)

I had to acknowledge and accept before I could surrender, before the pain could be lifted. I had to find out as much as I could about suicide, and as much as I could about how people survive suicide. I had to talk and go to therapy, plow through it, blast through it. Sometimes I had to embrace it. Sometimes I put up my fists against it. Suicide, and the test of my own survival, was still there at the end of the round.

Sometimes I just wept, and remembered.

I was going through some old letters and discovered a note sent by two nuns who were Clark's neighbors in the years before his death.

Dear Judy,

I want to tell you a wonderful story about your son, Clark. During the mythical, magical Minnesota winter of 1988-89, we had a cold snap that literally froze our cars. At the time we lived in a duplex that backed up to the house in which Clark and his family were then living. We had not met them before. All during one very cold day we worked on trying to start the cars. Towing companies and even AAA were unable to get them running.

At about 3:30 in the afternoon, Clark came home from work, walked over to where our cars were parked, introduced himself and asked if he could help. He worked on those cars from 3:30 in the afternoon until he finally got one of them started at about 9:30 in the evening. He tried jumping them. He covered the hoods with blankets and old rags. He finally fished out an old electric space heater from his garage and placed it right under the engine of one of the cars, and then kept going out every fifteen minutes or so to give it another try. In the course of events, we baby-sat Hollis for a while and met Alyson, who came home later from work. Clark also brought the battery from the second car into the house to warm it up, and then returned the next morning to put it back in the car and get it started. We were very touched by his kindness to us. He is a wonderful young man. I am sure you are very proud of him.

When I think of Clark, I am reminded of these words: "Open the door and come on in; I'm so glad to see you my friend. You're like a rainbow coming around the bend." I know there are many neighbors in the Crocus Hill area who also find Clark a "rainbow coming around the bend."

Please know that.

The letter is signed Kathy Mclaughin and Kay Egan and was written on May 25, 1990.

I searched through letters, through journals. In a notebook from 1987, I found a dream from many years before Clark's death, written in a leather-bound journal:

February 16, 1987

I am on the surface of an iced-over river with Clark. He goes off, slipping into the water, over the edge, where the river tumbles. I dive in, and swim a long way. But he is not with the other swimmers. I say to them, "Where is my son?" They say, "He drowned. He didn't make it past the deep part." I turn, putting my head under water, to swim back. If I keep my eyes open, perhaps I may be able to find him, bring him to the surface, and save him.

"Suicide is a virtually unrecognized national public health problem," according to Dr. Lloyd Potter of the Centers for Disease Control. It is, according to Potter, a problem that isn't being addressed on national, state, or local levels.

Tendencies to suicide are more common than we think. Roughly thirty thousand people kill themselves every year. Many are teenagers. Perhaps as many as ten times that number make attempts. Often a person will make more than one attempt during any given year—a hundred thousand attempts is probably a conservative estimate.

Suicide is the third-leading cause of death among teenagers.

Each person who kills himself affects an average of ten people who suffer from the extreme emotional shock and physically debilitating distress of surviving the loss of a loved one through suicide.

Approximately three hundred thousand people a year become suicide survivors in the United States. That would mean that since 1950, 16 million people have suffered the loss of a family member or loved one through suicide.

Suicide survivors are on the wave of an epidemic.

I learned that there is no one who can help to heal the pain as much as another survivor, sharing his or her story.

"If you are laughing out loud in a restaurant," Joan Rivers told me, "and people look at you as though you were crazy, fuck 'em. They have no idea what you are going through."

Joan put me in touch with Iris Bolton, the author of *My Son . . . My Son,* who runs a family counseling group in Atlanta called The Link. Iris lost her son, Mitch, to suicide in 1978. Mitch was nineteen when he walked calmly to his bedroom after returning home from school one afternoon, shut the door quietly, and put a bullet through his brain. At the first sound of Iris's voice, three or four days after Clark's death, I knew I had connected with a woman who was to be a rock for me, to help save my life. Her book was essential to my recovery. She told the story, straight out, of the pain and the terror that a survivor feels. I felt warmed by Iris's voice, consoled by her experience; her story, one of a wounded healer who passes on her experience to others who have suffered the same as she, was a godsend to me and Louis and other members of my family.

"Call me in the middle of the night if you have to," she said. I did. She talked me through dark hours. "And don't be afraid of your anger," Iris said one night. "It is natural."

I read the suicide survivor's list of dos and don'ts from Iris's book over and over: Go on with your life, continue to do things that give you pleasure, see people you love, keep up your physical exercise, your walks in the park; if you don't have a pet, get one; meditate; don't use alcohol and drugs, they only make the survival more difficult.

Iris gave me permission to rage at my son, to feel the deep wound.

Louis, who was suffering from shock and grief as well, found in Iris' husband Jack Bolton the kind of help he had to have to get through this.

"They won't ask how you are," Jack said to Louis one night when they were talking about other people's reactions to the male survivor. "You have to tell them. And don't be afraid to say your heart is breaking."

She told me I couldn't have stopped him, even if I had been there.

"There was a woman in our group of survivors," she said, "who used to tell the story of her lover, and how he killed himself. We always asked her to tell it when people said they thought they could have done something to stop their loved one from pulling the trigger, jumping, taking the pills, slitting their wrists, from closing the garage door and turning on the ignition in the car.

"I was sitting on his bed," Sally would say, "saying, 'I love you, Jim. Don't do this. How can you do this?' I had my hand on his hand, my cheek on his cheek. He said excuse me, reached his other hand around, took the gun from under the pillow, and blew his head off. My face was inches from his."

"If somebody wants to kill themselves," Iris concludes, "there is nothing you or anyone else can do to stop them."

Suicide is only one of the disasters in the wake of depression and alcoholism. There are many, and guilt is one of the worst.

"Suicide is a permanent solution to a temporary problem." I find that quote from my sister Holly in a journal in the first days after my son's death. And another: "Every day I have to choose light, to put aside darkness. I cannot let the darkness destroy me. Or the shame."

❧

"The life of the suicide is, to an extraordinary degree, unforgiving," A. Alvarez says in *The Savage God*. "Nothing he achieves by his own efforts, or luck bestows, reconciles him to his injurious past . . . . Suicides always have a good reason to kill themselves." Resentments: Clark was angry about the problems in his marriage.

But many suicides also seem to be chemically connected. Statistics show that more than half of the suicides each year stem from alcohol and drug abuse accompanied by depression. Depression is said to be a chemical imbalance. Alcoholics sometimes kill themselves when they are drinking. Medicine is a mixed blessing in many people's lives. I know that as a recovering alcoholic, there are no mood-altering drugs I can take. There are no pretend beers or pretend wines I can safely drink. If alcoholism is a chemical allergy combined with physical obsession, I know and have to stay away from the triggers, the chemicals, in big or small amounts, that might set off my disease. I tell all my medical doctors I am an alcoholic and take only painkillers perscribed by a doctor, and preferably none at all.

I also believe that to some extent family history plays a part in the thread of suicide as a notion or a drive.

And I know I have lost the right, if I ever had it, to take my own life.

September 23, 1992, New York

 Magritte at the Metropolitan Museum of Art, eight months and eleven days after Clark's death. The message of a suicide survivor leaves a trail as distinct as the trail of a comet in the sky if you can read the sky.

 Magritte is a survivor. His mother drowned herself when Magritte was thirteen, by walking into the Sombre river. His mother's nightgown, when they found her many days later, was wrapped around her head, the suggestion of the paintings to come, the faces covered with what might be sheets, or silk, rendering the figure blind and mute, as though suffocating. There are candles by the sea in the painting "Meditation," twisted like snakes, three burning candles on the sand, dark of night, a vast sea in the background. The stone in the window, a parody of the great Matisse painting of the woman by the window, is the stone of suicide, the dark figure with her back turned to us, facing the sea, in place of Matisse's woman. Throughout the exhibition this death reverberates, suicide seeming to break open the logical points of view, suggesting the constant, ringing loss of the artist's mother by her own hand.

A large painting, intended for the exhibition in the thirties in Paris, is composed of panels: a naked woman with no head and no feet, the front of a house, ordinary looking, a blue sky filled with puffy white clouds, a forest of trees. In the foreground there is a fully rendered cannon, ready to fire and blow the tranquillity of the painting to bits, the life that is blasted apart by the suicide, a life that goes back again and again to the reasons, the feelings, the abandonment, the music of despair. Magritte repeats the image of a bell in some paintings, showing it in many ways; the stand of bells as a rendering of the human mind; a single bell rendered in bronze a foot and a half in diameter; the bells in the series around the "Cannon" painting. Bells ring through the show like a death knell. The dreamlike Magritte on the shore of the sea, the dreamer in his bowler hat, contrasts in the conformity and regularity of his outward appearance the shuddering reminders of death. "Meditation" was never shown at Magritte's Paris gallery because just before the show, the gallery went broke.

In 1950, at the age of fifty-two, Magritte painted a gun leaning against a wall, blood running onto the floor, and called it "Survivor." It was, according to the biography, a terrible year for him professionally.

The voice of Philippe de Montebello, the director of the Metropolitan, had ushered me and the other viewers through the show. (Never once were these images related to suicide by Montebello.) I wrote him a note:

Dear Philippe, the woman is not Mary, his wife, it is his mother. (He is obsessed with his mother's death; he is a suicide survivor.)

In "Youth Revisited" Magritte paints a road through a green field with a pond to the side. On the road is the white bust of a woman startling in the greenness of the painting; a lion (the essence of pride?) which to me signifies his father. The lion is repeated in a number of paintings, including one dramatic all-gray painting near the end of his life in which a drawing of a chasm and a ravine dominate the wall. The entire painting is gray, decaying, disintegrating. The father disintegrating. Pride disintegrating. In another late work, the artist is literally painting a woman out of thin air, making her appear as his partner in the room.

Oh, Clark, that I could see you clearly, not in dreams, but here before me, that I could paint you out of thin air, make you reappear in the room, in the world. Oh, that you were alive and working on computers and truth, even in Minnesota.

ജാ

In Sue Chance's book, *Leftover Life to Live,* she refers to her son's suicide as "lousy problem solving." The aftermath of her son's death caused, she writes, a "shit storm" in her life. Like Chance, every belief I had about myself, every myth and every reality, has had to be reexamined over and over. I awake to a universe that is devastated by this sudden loss, and I must rediscover all the reasons to live each day.

Suicide was not considered a sin until the early fourth century A.D. In many societies, taking your own life was once considered an honorable alternative, something perhaps even desirable in the furtherance of one's spiritual journey, and thought to be "noble." Suicide was often considered a preferable solution, rather than a problem.

In *The Savage God,* Alvarez describes suicide in the Greek tradition: those wishing to end their lives would be provided with poison for their self-annihilation. "If your existence is hateful to you, die; if you are overwhelmed by fate, drink the hemlock. If you are bowed with grief, abandon life. Let the unhappy man recount his misfortune, let the magistrate supply him with the remedy, and his wretchedness will come to an end." Even Montaigne put his seal of approval on suicide.

Mass suicides like the one in Jonestown, I learned, were common earlier in recorded history. To preserve religious beliefs, to save themselves from gods whose worship they considered blasphemy, people took their own lives willingly, knowing heaven was only a heartbeat, a sword thrust, or a poison drink away.

In *The Savage God,* Alvarez talks about warrior societies in which the gods of violence and ideals of bravery often encouraged suicide as a great good that could take a Viking to Valhalla, where only those who had died violently could enter the halls and partake of the banquet tables.

"The greatest honor and the surest qualification was death in battle," he says. "Next best was suicide. Those who died peacefully in their beds, of old age or disease, were excluded from Valhalla through all eternity."

Some say that without God suicide can be an answer to a world without meaning. Conversely, in early centuries, Christians who believed absolutely in God knew heaven was near enough to guarantee a quick entrance by self-inflicted death. They knew the god of their understanding would welcome them with open arms.

St. Augustine, who pointed out the sinful nature of suicide, was being pragmatic. A lot of Christians were killing themselves, offering themselves up to the lions, because life was no bargain and heaven beckoned with salvation to the martyr. St. Augustine's edict against suicide had a practical side as well, since suicides were draining the coffers of the church. His ideas set the tone for the next centuries. St. Augustine's condemnation replaced the previous centuries' tolerance, even encouragement, of suicide.

In medieval times terrible things were done to the surviving family of a suicide. If Clark had taken his own life in the fifteenth century, there most probably would not have been a funeral ceremony. A stake might have been driven through his heart before his poor remains were buried in unconsecrated ground. If I had tried and failed to take my own life in early times, I might have been executed for the attempt. Surviving family members were often denied a suicide's estate, which would go to the government or the Church. Burial in consecrated ground was routinely denied a suicide.

There are still deep taboos about suicide, and in such a climate, it is no wonder that car wrecks, overdoses that look like accidents, tumbling down flights of stairs, death as a result of wounds accumulated while in a drunken rage, banging one's head against the wall, provoking a violent spouse to murder—all are preferable to letting anyone know you actually meant to kill yourself.

The attitude of society has slowly changed over the past decade. Clark's home and his car and his belongings went to his widow; Clark was given a proper funeral. The insurance company honored his policy. There was insurance money for Clark's widow and child.

The fact that suicide is committed by great numbers of teenagers has begun attracting more attention; programs for survivors like Compassionate Friends and Survivors of Suicide are helping survivors. It is still hard for those who are reluctant to reach out on their own for help and stunned by the ancient taboos against talking about suicide, but there are more hot lines and more information available than there were ten years ago.

The real "problem" with suicide, beyond the question of the spiritual state of the suicide himself, of course, is the survivors. We survivors feel we have in some way caused the suicide of our loved one. It doesn't matter that we know on an intellectual level we couldn't have done anything. Even if we had been able to prevent the attempt we may not have been able to prevent another, perhaps fatal, future attempt.

As a suicide survivor I am now statistically at higher risk to commit suicide myself. I sometimes feel as though I am implicated in murder.

And I will always wonder: If I had known what I know today, could I have done anything to prevent my son's death? I believe Clark decided to kill himself long before he completed the act. One who commits suicide is trying to relieve the pain of life. Clark must have been in incredible pain.

On the other hand, I wonder if there really is a decision in the final act of a suicide. May it not be that the suicide has simply given up any decisions in the effort to grow, to live? To live, I have to make a decision to take on the day rather than the darkness, to do the thing that will take me out of pain. My son's decision *not* to reach out, *not* to call anyone, *not* to take an action that would change his mental state, cannot be my decision for today.

For today I must change my state, avert the gaze of my eyes from the waterfall of tears. That is discipline: to change habits, to ease the tension toward depression, to drive to a new emotional address. Discipline is something the disciples of Christ learned: they gave up everything, their families, their habits, their depression, even, to find God.

No matter how much I read, no matter how much I hurt, there is a time I have to let all of that go and come back to the gratitude in my heart for what I *have* been given.

Whether or not I liked it, I had to agree with a friend who says, "If you want to know what God's will for your life is, look around at what is." I must learn to live with this and to pass along what I have learned to others who are suffering.

A friend whose ex-husband killed himself wrote to me a few months after Clark's death:

James's daughter Pamela is suicidal. When she went to her therapist, he asked her whether, if she were serious about killing herself, she would like to write the suicide note, right there in his office. Pamela balked, said she felt like killing herself but didn't know what to say to her family, her friends, who she would leave behind. She told him she hadn't any idea what to say. The therapist wrote something on a scrap of paper and handed it to her.

"What about something like this?" he asked. Pamela opened the note.

"Fuck you," it said.

I couldn't feel the anger until lately.

Though I loved you, I couldn't save you. Can you forgive me?

୨୬୧

My friend Lee, who lives in San Francisco, lost her son at about the same time Clark died.

"They don't tell you about the yearning," she said. Sometimes I wake in the middle of the night and think about Clark's goodness, his sweetness. He had so much compassion for other people, including for me.

This part of the dance he did not understand, the suffering we have *all* experienced for the step he took. He simply had no idea what his death would do, could do, to me, to his family, to his friends.

I pray for the courage to dance, the energy, the joy, the commitment to live. The dance will be over soon enough. I pray that I may enjoy the music, the movement, the loveliness of the dance, even its sorrow.

Louis and I can laugh now, sometimes, without the mourning coming into our eyes.

God knows our every experience. God heals us. So do others who have suffered great loss.

The other night I met a teacher who had taught Clark in one of his high school classes.

"I haven't seen Clark lately," he said. "How is he doing?" I had to tell him that my boy was dead. Of suicide. Such a look of pain and sadness came over his face.

"I lost my mother to suicide," he said, "I know what you are going through." I knew from the look in his eyes that he did. The people around us disappeared, the noise of talking quieted, and there we were, at a public party, in a suddenly silent place, two people talking a language of loss that made them the same.

He is a man and I am a woman, we come from completely different backgrounds, I am a singer and he is a teacher, I am a Democrat, he might be a Republican, but at once our differences fall away, what we might think of this or that, one person or another, one cause or another. In loss, we are the same. When someone really knows where it hurts, when someone knows that nothing can really ever heal that place of hurt again, when someone knows the wound that opened up in your heart when the person you love the most decided to leave you, a wounded one can heal you. Only someone who has been down the same path can teach you how to walk down that path.

I was asked to speak to a woman named Cynthia who has just lost her husband to suicide. A little over a month ago, he hanged himself in the hallway of her apartment. She is in shock, can't work. She managed go out and get some food today, things that are already prepared. Cynthia asks me what to do: I tell her to eat, walk, pray, make a phone call, get a massage. And know that this is the most devastating thing that can happen to you, ever. I tell her what I was told by Deborah Morris a few weeks after Clark's death, that I would come out on the other side of this catastrophe if I were courageous and went to the very darkest place; that within the tragedy there was a gift, if I could look for it and be open to it.

I tell Cynthia what I know to be true: that out of this deep, dark, terrible place, no matter how many times I may look at my son's face and say this cannot be happening, there is a gift. A gift of such beauty and light and grace that to have come through the horror and be on this side of it is something that cannot be given; it must be won. The inner peace after the struggle, the brightness of the sun, the gratitude, the energy that has come to me, the forgiveness, the glimmers of understanding that have turned into illuminating joy—these are gifts that tragedy has given, and that no human power can take away. No one wants them, and yet they are more valuable than jewels, and the cost is staggering, impossible.

We need each other, in life, and in surviving death. When tragedy comes, we know the fight for each moment, each breath, each day, each week, each new plateau of recovery. There will always be the death of the loved one: the death, the wound, the inheritance, the blow, the surprise; the destination, the miracle, the gift. We, as well as the loved one who is lost to us, are swept out of this place into another, into something else, some other, some mystical place where we are unblemished by pain, unleashed from perfection. For a time we are in a timeless place and in and out of that timeless place is the path of recovery.

Every inch is hard won and sometimes I don't know if I am going to make it through the day.

Sometimes I don't know if I am going to make it through the hour.

In October of 1991 Clark and I were sitting in Clark's living room in St. Paul, he sprawled in a chair, guitar in his beautiful long-fingered hands, the freckles scattered on his thumbs, his knuckles, the backs of those broad hands I loved. Alyson was in the kitchen preparing dinner. The baby was asleep in her stroller.

"My latest song, Mom," he said, and sang me the words, softly, playing softly.

I didn't know, you never told me
What you really felt about me.

The wind came, the trees turned red,
Tires in the rain, my mind felt dead:

We can't get it back and do it over,
What's done is done.
We can't go back and do it over,
What's done is done.
We can't change the toss of the coins,
The roll of the dice, the wind or the tide.
We can only hold on to what we have today
Flow with the moment, seize the day.

Some men kill in the heat of a moment.
They spend their whole lives in jail
Thinking it over
If I'd only walked away, turned around,
I'd be a free man today.

The wind came, the trees turned red,
Tires in the rain, my mind felt dead.
We can't go back and do it over,
What's done is done.
We can't go back and do it over,
What's done is done.

As Shakespeare says in *Much Ado About Nothing*: "Everyone can master a grief but he that has it." I have to learn anew each day how to soar, how to fly free. Grieving is messy, there are no correct ways to do it. The questions come and the tears come, without warning, and I am going to have to talk about my loss until I don't have to talk about it anymore.

I know there is danger in secrecy. If I let the wound fester, close it up and hope it will go away, the infection will kill me, I won't be able to let the sunlight of the spirit shine on my own life and on the lives of my family. Maybe if I stay awake I can let light into dark rooms of fear and self-destruction, and perhaps we—Clark's friends and family, his cousins,—can break the spell and cast out some of these devils. If I don't talk about my son's suicide, grieve over his death and the death of all my dreams for him and for myself as his mother, something in me will die. I must pass on what I have learned and what I had not yet learned when my beloved son died.

Suicide survivors are like other people who have survived the traumatic death of parents, of children, only more so.

"When do I get to mourn my ex-husband's death?" one survivor asked me. "I have to deal with the will, the hurt feelings of the family, the consequences of unresolved issues left between my ex-husband and our stepchildren as well as our own children—the matters of money. All these things stand in the way of my own grief. When do I get to mourn him, for himself?"

My son was doing the best he could. He didn't mean to cause pain. Sometimes I think suicide was the only way Clark could figure out a peace that was going to last. Surviving continues for a lifetime, resonating through every holiday, every season. Recovery is a secret place, a place that must be survived, again and again. The questions I am asking are not only about Clark, they are about myself. Surviving Clark's death means sorting out the skeletons, searching for reasons, for serenity, for acceptance. Living through the tragedy. Learning something about failure. About success. About free will.

About forgiveness.

❦

I dreamed of my son three nights ago. He came to me at the age of twelve or thirteen, red-haired, sweet-faced, innocent. He was on his way to camp, all the name tags sewn onto his clothes, his bags packed, the schedule for his trip arranged. "When will I get to see you?" I said, as I kissed his freckled nose, his smooth cheeks. "Mom," he said, wrinkling his nose and smiling at my overindulgence, but with sympathy, "they really don't like the parents hanging around camp." So saying, he was off, the summer like a world of wonders laid out before him, parent's week circled on my calendar.

When I talk about my son's suicide, my blood stops. I go into shock again. I can be talking, and suddenly, I am white as a sheet emotionally. My breath comes in shorter takes. I am in it again.

"When the anger and bewilderment of first grief subside," Mary Jane Moffat says in *In the Midst of Winter,* "the true labor of mourning begins. This period of depression may set in after a few weeks or months, or even years later, if grief has been repressed. This is the phase of searching for the dead person."

I have to do more than survive; I have to transcend. The person I was when I first tried to kill myself at fourteen is not the person I am today. If she were, I would die of this grief. In order not to die, I must change.

January 15, 1993

    I have lived through the first year of my son's death. This
morning, rain, falling, falling on the city, this is real, the rain is
all I see, the rain, too, like a dark nightmare. Out of the fire of
pain in the past year, pouring into the rest of my life, I hope I
can survive. There must be another way, a way to find solace, to
live past midnight.

    One night a few months ago I went to a dinner party and
heard someone laughing, bright, hearty, beautiful laughter, like
the ringing of a bell in a room of strangers and friends. I looked
around to see who was there, laughing with such deep enjoy-
ment, such pleasure, such abandon.

    It was me, laughing.

I live on one side of the vail: he lives on the other. He is with my father and all the others who have gone on. We are living in a forever time, I touch that forever in dreams, in music, in the fullness that throbs in my heart when day breaks, when the sun shines on the snow, when the candles are extinguished, and when the light of his spirit shines in my darkened room.

I live in eternity's light with all those I love, bound by the laws of heaven, the laws of Karma, the sense and beating of the heart. Thank God for the here and the hereafter; I am part of them both.

"If we are not forgiving, we can never truly laugh," I have heard. If we are not forgiving, we can never truly cry either. I am learning that.

❧❧

In Colorado this past winter, I was on a skiing trip with my family. Whenever we gather—nephews, nieces, cousins, sister, brothers, granddaughter—I think if I just turn around at the right moment, I will see my son, he will appear out of the next room, laughing that bright laugh like no time has passed, like nothing bad has happened. When my family and I are together, I know my son is not far away.

We were skiing and celebrating my mother's eightieth birthday with a party in Denver and a trip to Winter Park, my brothers and sister and Louis and I spending days riding lifts, talking of everything and nothing. One cold day my brother David, Louis and I came down the mountain in a whiteout and stopped to get our breath by old pines on a run carved out of the hillside near where I first learned to ski. It was blowing cold and I stood with my brother Dave and heard that sound that is not a sound but a song, not a song but a note tuned and blown by the wind—a soft stuttering whisper in tall, old lodge pole pines, the wind going through their tops so quiet they don't even bend. The call is like the sound of a deep train whistle far off, like moving water down a deep mountain cut. It sounded to my bones. I could hear comfort in that song, and I could feel my son near me. The sound took me over, molded me, folded me. I stood there on the side of the mountain, snow sticking to my face and my parka, head bent to listen, till my brother David shifted on his skis and asked me if I was all right. Yes, I said, and skied on down behind him, reluctantly leaving the still, whispering, gigantic sound singing to itself in the trees above the whiteout, above the mountain, gathering all my sorrow, gathering all my love.

Near this mountain I fell in love with Clark's father, on the summit of

Berthoud Pass: one winter, three years ago, my nephew Matt rolled his truck on black ice and walked away, swearing it had been his cousin Clark who saved his life. Once Matt met a man on this summit who knew his name, spoke of his family, and looked like Clark.

Clark is here, in these trees, on this mountain, in this tree-spoken silence that comes when the wind sings through the old pines, the sound that can reach down into my heart and scoop out that loss and heal me, singing to me, comforting me.

The other healing sound is music, and it is healing for me to sing, healing in body, healing in mind, healing in spirit. The music I make and the music to which I listen—and the silences between the words, in which I hear the truth when my friends' lips are still—they heal me. When I think of my son's leaving and the first aching, shuddering words over my son's face, dead and cold, the first kiss placed on his face, and the last, the silence embraces me, saves me.

As the time passes, the dark becomes lighter, yet there is darkness still. I write in journals—prose, poetry, thoughts, notes, anything to get me through the moment, get me through the night. I hold on to God, for only a God in whom I trust completely could get me through this grief. From the ground up, from the heart in, from the soul out, from the outside to the core, I must learn to trust God as I understand Him, more than life and its disappointments, more than death and its illusions, more than any promises I will ever make, to myself or to anyone else.

Sometimes the pain comes, telling me I could have prevented my son's death. There were so many years when I could not help myself and could not help him. But I know I did the best I could do. I have no regrets for the recent years when we celebrated, hurdling, as a friend says, with joy. But sometimes the pain comes, the ache in my heart for the things I didn't do, the things I couldn't do when it might have helped, the things I will never be able to do now.

At times, in the middle of the night, I must hold my faith before the phantom like a cross of gleaming silver. I glare back at the phantom. I dare her: she has done her worst, and she can do no more. I fear her not.

On the surface everything is mending, the grieving has progressed. I am getting over it, as they say. Of course, they forget to tell you it is something you never get over. My son loved poetry and music, the flutelike song of the meadowlark, the beauty of winter, the flash of the sun on the water as he stood fly-fishing in the upper Mississippi River. He would understand the bittersweet poetry of having to go on living when you want to die of grief. I pray he understands my going on, into another season, without him. I must live my life. And his.

Each day I thank God for having given me the healthy years with my son Clark, the years in which we had light and joy. Those years were a gift. Life will never be the same, but I am recovering, and life can still be, as other friends have promised, even in the lingering sorrow, beautiful. Exciting. Thrilling. Is that a betrayal? Sometimes I hear a quiet voice, the voice of my sorrow, my nemesis, my pain, tell me it is. That voice would have me bury myself in sorrow and never venture forward. I must turn my back on that voice and live. I drown, yet I have learned to breathe and I laugh, and love comes and success and failure, the pillars by which we see time pass. I have to learn every day to live without that bright, shining beauty that was the best of my life. His death teaches me how to live.

Those who tell us the pain of the suicide of our beloved will go away with time are wrong. The pain of suicide never goes away. The pain must be transcended.

How do we survive? How does anyone?

A day at a time, like everything.

I dream of Clark, once more engaged in the dialogue about why he doesn't have to kill himself. There are so many other solutions, I say to him, looking into his blue eyes, so glad to see him, his beauty so vibrant, so near me. We speak on and on of life, of what it means. He says to me in many of these dreams that it isn't a big deal.

"Death is only part of the dance, Mother."

December 9, 1992

The fifth anniversary of my son's death is in a few
days, and his birthday, yesterday, crept by like a solemn
chant. I try only to remember the lightness of his laugh, the
loveliness of his spirit. I keep my head down and wait for
the day to pass, writing postcards, burning candles, once
again writing meditations to keep from losing my mind.

The skin over the wound is never completely healed,
though there will be no callus, no scar that shows on the
outside. Often, I wear my today face, hold my body guarded
like a warrior who knows what thrusts to avoid. Then a
word, a look, some music finds its way behind my eyes,
starlight reaches the place where the wound begins and the
tears fall. I must seek peace and sometimes it is difficult to
find that inward place, thinking on spiritual things, quieting
the wild and rushing feelings that surge around my heart.
The trick is to find the center of light, a center of peace in
the very place where raged the winds of trouble and loss,
each and every day, a place where I can move from tumult,
crises, anxiety, into hope.

Thank you, God, for what You have given me; thank
you for what You have taken away; thank you for what You
have left me.

10

The Black Dog:
Drinking and Depression

They say you must be careful of getting rid of all your monsters; some of them may inspire your angels.

Tonight, under a sky full of stars, the clouds drifting, the wind blowing in the palm and fig trees, soft on my face, the black dog of depression is far from my life. He hunted me down for many years. But here under starlight I feel my heart opening, melting, far from his fangs, far from his howling cry.

Tonight Louis and I sit on the roof of our vacation cottage in the American Virgin Islands. Orion is clear, crystal, the Pleiades dancing, Sirius the Dog Star like a clarion call of light, clusters of light swarming down the Milky Way, speaking to me as they have to all of us from the beginning of time, whenever people lifted their eyes to the sky, asking, praying, seeking answers. A shooting star flies into the milky cloud of light, finding its way to the center of the shining galaxy, a bright comet.

Nights, the wind blows, tossing palm and sea grape trees. Days, in the water there are blue and yellow fish, French angelfish and blue tang, rock beauties and shy hamlets, parrot and damsel fish with their electric blue dots and elegant faces. The parrot fish can change from female into male, at will—from a red-and-black dotted, rather unattractive fish, to a wildly green, blue, brilliant yellow fish. Like me. I am going to metamorphose into something bright and beautiful, this dull, stripped costume of mine shed like the skin of a snake. Striped sergeant majors guard a violet patch of eggs on a brain coral, chasing off the bigger fish as I swim by, a snorkel mask my viewer. A queen trigger fish finds her stately way from under a rock where a moray is feeling out the current, bobbing his elongated, striped black-and-white face out to peer at me—in my pink-and-black mask and my pink-and-black bodysuit and my pink and black fins— then it disappears.

For eighteen years, two weeks each year, Louis and I have come to this paradise in the Caribbean, departing the freezing streets of New York as Christmas trees are stripped and left abandoned by service entrances in the alleys and side streets of hotels and apartment buildings, tinsel dangling like fingers in the cold winds. We bundle up in heavy winter coats and leave the icy winds behind, loaded with current fiction and history and watercolor paper and paints, bathing suits and floppy shoes, silk shirts and snorkel gear, fatigue on our faces and the white, winter camouflage of city dwellers on our skin.

Coming to the islands is a pilgrimage, a gift. As pink clouds rise along the skyline at dawn, fading to blue across the Atlantic coast, Louis and I take an early plane down the coast from Kennedy Airport to the island of St. Thomas in the Caribbean. The light here is blue and green and you can feel the warmth even through the windows of the 757, even before the door opens.

Familiar faces greet us, beautiful smiles on the bus ride to a bobbing motor-driven boat, its engine throbbing noisily, where the luggage is loaded and we guzzle grapefruit punch, having shifted from cashmere to cotton shirts, from heavy boots to sandals. Peter, the captain of the boat, and the men who handle luggage are like some holy disciples of past times, ever the same, sturdily faithful in their guardianship of Paradise, their memories of our names, their sense of living always in the present. They are strong, handsome men in their fifties now, their hair graying. When we started coming here, their hair was black and they were young, as we were.

We pass pink and green and white houses and then the buoys and outer rocks and on into the deep water between the islands. Wearing sunglasses and taking deep breaths of sea air, our heavy winter coats abandoned, rumpled, cast off like airplane acquaintances on the curving deck chairs, we are home.

Our island retreat is a place of luminous light and beauty, dazzling white beaches and palms, forests and blue water, soft breezes. There are rain forests, tropical flowering plants, banana quits and mongeese, hummingbirds and turtles, sleepy cats and creatures of the mountain that rise green above the water, holding rainbows in their arms.

They are wonderful people, the islanders. Most of them own their own homes and love what they do. Acilia, who cleans the cottage where we stay, has the deep ochre-colored skin and the slow, peaceful beauty of the islands, her dark eyes quick to laughter and her work methodical and caring. Her hair is black and pulled back away from her face, her body is agile. In the morning I hear her coming, singing as she goes, with sheets and towels and often a bowl of flowers for our room, handpicked by her from some wild bush near town, wild pink bougainvillea, white star flowers, yellow honeysuckle. She admires our watercolors and when I asked her many years ago if she would care to come to New York to work for us she smiled with her eyes. Her amused silence suggested I might be a lunatic.

We arrive exhausted, as usual, and begin to unwind here in this healing place of peace. I write and read, sleep to the sound of the surf and the songs of the night birds. I do watercolors, throwing down color on paper, watching the vibrant pigments, Russian watercolors I bought somewhere on the road. I listen to the sound of the waves, rubbing on sunscreen, blinking my eyes under a wide hat, writing fragments of song lyrics that come to me in dreams, in walks on the white, ravishing beaches. I've read wonderful books here, absorbing them, pondering Thomas Merton, Katherine Anne Porter, Antonia Fraser, Iris Murdoch, Robert Massie, Umberto Eco, John Cheever, Henry James. There is time to read a novel here, to listen to the wind. I am restored, rejuvenated, my winter pale skin browned, my mind refreshed, polished, purified.

I was young that first year we came here, barely thirty-nine. I wanted to know everything. My innocence is gone and now I know too much, more than I ever needed or wanted to know. In this place where I looked at life, I look at death as well. Every prayer I ever prayed, every night I ever felt empowered, every lesson I ever studied, must help me now. All the teachers I have had—Brico, Max, my father—none had so great a lesson for me as my son. I learn it each day, every day.

Are we different? I ask my husband, knowing the answer. The waiter has just called me Mrs. Nelson. Louis laughs, knowing it is a sign of maturity that I simply smile at the waiter's words. It used to bug him when they put the room in my name or called him Mr. Collins. Our mail, addressed to Mr. and Mrs. Nelson, would make me scarlet with rage. "Don't they get it?" I would fume. I am more accepting now. So is he.

We often walk and eat alone, nodding to fellow vacationers, seeing the few friends we have come to know here occasionally. When we do, we are giddy with pleasure in their company. But on many days we don't want to break the sanctuary, absorbing the birds and the water, the light, the fish, sleeping to the sound of the ocean, waking to the light of day. There is no glitz here: others go where they can find it, but we run to our island to escape it. We are never surprised when others, people whose faces we know from the world of politics, sports, entertainment, drift off into their private worlds from lunch or dinner, disappearing as though they were only mirages. It is the kind of privacy we go to great lengths to preserve.

Watching the fish, basking in the sun, walking with Louis, I think of my old enemy. I remember meeting the black dog of depression on an island of great beauty near here, when I was younger. He made the time there a hell.

In recent years, he has been cooped up somewhere far from here, yet my fear is always that he will come back, slinking through the blue sea, shaking water off his long black fur, growling between his sharp, frightening teeth.

ഇരുഇ

Winston Churchill gave him his name, the long, lean ghostly, black dog of depression. Depression is the enemy, the monster who regularly howled at the door when I was younger. I would look for somewhere to run when I heard his paws scratching, when I heard his breath on my neck. Often there was nowhere to run, because no matter where you go, even to paradise, there you are.

My depression symptoms were always classic. I believe my son inherited them. I thought I would never look up and see the stars again. Everything went black, all sparks of joy were hidden. I plunged into a dark and hopeless place. At times like that, knowing everyone becomes depressed is no comfort.

After my son died, depression was there, my old companion, but in a different form. It was a new beast. I had, after all, every reason to be depressed, but this pain was so great that I think the black dog was afraid of it, afraid to come too near. This was something else, he must have thought, something perhaps more dangerous even, and the scent of it was too strong. Still, the black dog licked at the door after a while, scratching, breathing, sniffing.

Iris Bolton told me suicide tendencies are not inherited, but tendencies toward depression are. According to my mother, there was alcoholism in her and my father's families but no suicide. My cousin Lois, my father's brother's daughter, told me recently that there is no suicide in the Collins family that she knows of, but that there is much depression.

From childhood I struggled with the black apparition. I could feel it hover, feel its claws tighten on my throat, my heart, defying every rational thought, making a mockery of optimism, of good fortune, of anything true and valuable and real. It was as though, from time to time, the black dog had to come to be fed its share, to be petted, paid attention to, bribed to slink off or shown the back of my hand, the steel of my resolve, the smile of my angels.

Dr. Robert Marshand, a sensitive and intelligent man with a practice at Paine Whitney, prescribed Miltown for anxiety when I went to see him in my early twenties in New York. Miltown seems like such an old drug now. In the early sixties it was the new thing. I told Dr. Marshand I was afraid of being poisoned. He recommended I see a shrink, which I did. But I continued for many years to be afraid I was being poisoned. The fear would come over me like a crawling, poisoning fog.

I remember one late summer in 1967 when I had gone to sing a concert in Colorado. There was nothing particularly unusual about the trip. The weather was fine and I was alone with my guitar, as I often was in those years. I flew from La Guardia to Denver and then made the connection to

Montrose. I was already a regular world traveler, on the road for eight years. There was nothing unusual about getting on a plane and going out, like the troubadour I had become, to sing.

On this trip to Colorado, I was expecting nothing more than to do my concert, singing to the college students in Montrose, a dry, faraway city in the west. But when I got to Montrose something was wrong. The light was flat, flatter than it should have been in the late afternoon. My head seemed to be spinning. A soft haze extended over the dusty town and the young man who met me seemed to be talking in a voice stuffed with cotton. I couldn't seem to move very well. The young man took my guitar and my bag and we walked to the car, a dusty VW bus. The tall, lanky western boy in his cowboy boots and Stetson drove me to the outdoor concert arena where I did the sound check, not really knowing where I was. The whole experience was like a slow-running movie but I had no clue as to what was happening. I felt light-headed, as if I had stepped out of my own body and I couldn't get back. I was immobilized in what I began to recognize as a deep and overpowering depression that had me by the throat.

The black dog had chased me all the way to Montrose.

The young man took me to my hotel, a bland, wooden structure in the center of town. He put my bag and guitar down in the room and told me he would be back to get me in a couple of hours.

I looked around the room: plaid bedspread, pine dressing table, plaid flounce around the bed and ochre-colored towels. Maybe it was the towels that did it, their color. Or a rug that had seen much traffic and better days. Or the sink and toilet, a rusty stain in the bowl, in the small bathroom.

I sat down on the bed and put my head in my hands. The demon was on me. I went to the bathroom and put my hands and then my face in the water, trying to snap out of it. I lay down on the top of the bedspread of the hard, double bed, and realized I had to get home—now.

I had a few drinks before the young man got there, trying to get my courage back, but they failed. I had called the airport and made a reservation back to New York. I had called my therapist, saying I had to see him the next day. I called my manager, Harold Leventhal, and said I was ill. I asked him to make it right with the school.

When the young man came back to get me, to take me to the concert to sing for the two thousand young people waiting in that arena to hear me, I told him I was ill, that I had to go home.

My Montrose host, whose name I don't even know, was a perfect gentleman. He said not a word to contradict me when I told him I had to go home. He lifted my bags into his Volkswagen and held the door for me. I wasn't drunk, but I knew that if I stayed in that hotel room—or that town—for one more minute, I would die. I had to get back to civilization, to therapy, to sanity, to my home.

I never went back to Montrose, but I have been in a lot of motel rooms that looked like that one, with anonymous bedspreads and depressing walls, lonely shells far from home, smelling of cigarette smoke and fear. Some have harbored the howl of the black dog. There have been a lot of nights I thought I wouldn't make it back out of the dog's dark cave, many days when the sunlight didn't make any difference. But I have never again had to leave and come home. I learned from leaving that town that the black dog can be everywhere I am.

At the end of my drinking I was dying from my distance from God. I sought God in the bottle, where the spirit finally drowns. I sought solace, some great spirit that might heal the chaos in my life. I was on a spiritual search, driven by my physical allergy to alcohol and the terrible compulsion; it was an unenlightened search, but still a search. I went to gurus and tried to meditate, did yoga and read Krishnamurti, went to churches on Christmas and Easter. I believed in the miracle, I just wasn't sure I could hang around until It arrived.

Marianne Williamson says, "Become yourself. Seek God. No less potent steps than these will be deep enough to move you forward."

I tried to meditate as I sweated out my hangovers in the sauna at the gym and slouched through the remorse each morning. Sometimes—in lovely fleeting moments by the sea or in the mountains, listening to music or skiing or after swimming or just talking to a friend—I would drop onto the path and be at peace, feel no breath of the black dog. But those were moments few and far between. Mostly I was running from the demons.

I read *The Hero with a Thousand Faces*, listened to Gregorian chants which I had loved since my teens; I read *The Letters of James Agee to Father Flye,* whose red-brick, garden-enclosed cloister was down the street from my first apartment in Greenwich Village, and wondered in a vague way, if I were a nun, would I not drink so much? If I were sent to jail for some political action, would I get sober and find God?

I had embarrassment about admitting my spiritual search. To see auras, to wear flowers, to light incense was all right; to admit to a spiritual search might be viewed as a weakness. To go to church, fine, but to be caught praying, meditating? Very suspect.

Yet the path to meditation was always near me, like a road in the woods that parallels your wandering course, a road strewn with violets and sweet smelling buds, shimmering light and warm patches of sun; a path, beside mine, waiting, as I progressed along my own dark road.

There was God in our lives as I was growing up, though perhaps not exactly God the way the preachers preached. But we did have some deep, personal conviction that we are connected to the big thing that runs the universe, the spirit of hope that fires it, and the miracle that can happen to any one of us.

Dressed in our best clothes every Sunday, my parents took me and my brothers and sister to the white, pristine Methodist church on Montview Avenue in Denver. In Los Angeles we went to a stucco Methodist church on Wilshire Boulevard, where swallows flew in and out of the arches in the roof as the motes of dust danced in the sunlight among their wings, an image appearing holy to me. I sang in the choir and wore a purple robe and looked forward all week long to the glazed donuts they served to the singers on Sundays before the service. I would sit in my robe, staring out at my parents in the pews in front of me, my siblings lined up, faces scrubbed, eyes bright, the light pouring in from the modestly decorated stained glass windows, such a contrast to the wild, freely colorful, gleeful, gigantic stained glass in the Catholic and Episcopal churches I later came to know. I would listen to the minister in his purple robes talk about Jesus and the ethics of work and the power of prayer, and I would feel a deep relief and satisfaction in being there, in being safe, safe in the music, safe in my choir robe, safe watching my father sit quietly next to Mother.

We children were always invited to discuss the sermon over dinner, served at four o'clock on Sundays. The table was laid with the tablecloth my mother had crocheted with her long fingers in delicate white swirls, the crochet needle flying through the many hours and years it had taken her to finish it, and the silver my father had bought her when the tablecloth was done. The porcelain dishes and plates, of a red-and-blue-flowered Limoges pattern, were laden with stewed chicken and dumplings, steamed green beans, mother's vinegar-and-oil-dressed salad, bowls of celery, mashed potatoes, relishes, a second salad of aspic and Spanish pepper stuffed with green and plain black olives. The Sunday meal was a holy meal, sanctified, like the swallows.

Sometimes a relative or a friend would join us. Daddy would either praise or dispute the sermon. The conversation would fly, and God and his power or lack of it was richly discussed. I was always invited to join in, welcomed to the dispute or chorus of praise. Sundays were usually days on which Daddy was on his best behavior. An early dinner, maybe nothing at all to drink, and a quiet evening reading at home.

Heaven. I learned in those long and easy days that everything can be holy: the practice of eating a meal, the music I make, the laughter I shared with my family.

The spirits were also nearby in music. There was a dimension I reached when I sang or when I played the piano, or took a solo in the choir, a pair of angelic wings that lifted me beyond sight, beyond explanations, beyond the facts of my own life. God was in the breath, the feel, the pulse of music.

But I wanted to consecrate my life in some way, even then. In my early teens, I made a secret, secluded altar in the closet off my bedroom and prayed in some embarrassment, afraid my mother would discover me and make me dismantle my small stool, pillow and candle, which she did. Methodists have strong feelings about worshiping idols. Sometimes I think of that today as I meditate, burning candles, sitting in yoga, calling to all saints, gurus, from all religions.

Perhaps the dark place held a particular charm, a certain power over me. When I was young the habit of depression came easily: it was so vivid. Perhaps it was hormones, probably chemistry as well. In my teens my depressions ranged from mildly foggy days to the day I made an attempt on my life. The shadow would come, seemingly out of the blue, though I was perfectly healthy. I had no particular worries. I had enough to eat, plenty of clothes, friends, entertainments. We lived in a lovely home. My mother was a fine cook, my father a fine breadwinner.

I attempted confessing to a priest when I was thirteen but he refused to hear my sins. I knew Catholics had some great key we pale Methodists did not have, either the incense, or the truth spoken from lips moving behind the screen where a face is hidden, things hot and passionate and pleasant. If you could just tell someone; and then, tell them what? I hadn't sinned in the large way, not if you didn't count discovering pleasure in the darkness, not if you didn't count stealing Daddy's chocolates and Twinkies from the store on the way to my music lessons or the whispers of secrets, the ill-will I bore certain people, some of them relatives; not if you didn't count sticking out my tongue at my father, who was blind, and whom I knew couldn't see me where I paraded about in his face with my desperate anger showing on my eleven-year-old face. Of course my mother saw me, and told him. You can't win, I was sure—and maybe even you can't be forgiven? Still I hoped.

But my feeling of fault was deep. I begged in my heart to be a Catholic, or some kind of person who could be forgiven by some firm God, more successful in forgiveness.

Prayer I desired, prayer I needed. I didn't know where to look. Pope John Paul II describes prayer in the following way: "We begin with the impression that it's our initiative, but it's always God's initiative with us." In later years, the false wings of alcohol failed. The spiritual knowledge fled in the morning after, and the despair in the wearying years of trying to recapture the vision of God wore me down to the bone.

In recent years I have begun to meditate formally. The daily practice I do is a form devised by the Indian guru Yogananda, a practice called Kriya Yoga, passed on to me in her later years by my great teacher, Antonia Brico.

It seems that this practice has been hovering around me since I was ten, waiting for me to discover it. I didn't know, in all the years I studied with Brico, that she had this, at that time, peculiar habit of following a guru.

I discovered my teacher's connection to the guru and finally read *The Autobiography of a Yogi*. I connected the dots. For the first time in my life, the black dog was on the run.

There are always reasons for depression. Sometimes today a depression lives only in my dreams.

My father's drinking, I now know, was a powerful trigger for depression. People who live with alcoholics are often depressed. I lived in a certain amount of terror all the time. I didn't know how to fight the feelings, I had no tools. But I learned as soon as possible to drink. Alcohol medicated my mood swings, allowed me to be part of the solution.

Later, it seemed to me there was something romantic about depression, before it became clear it was the enemy. Depression could be a flirt, posing as intellectual curiosity, as camouflage for the reason often given for erratic behavior. Depression was a perfect excuse to get in bed with a good book and a pound of chocolates. What came first, the depression or the chocolate? Oh, for those days, without the depression, and with the chocolate!! (But for me, chocolate in large quantities is a depressant!)

I remember the romantic, confused idea I had that the dark places where sadness and negativity lived possessed charm and power, that they were moods to which we might aspire, if we were to become artists, and my friends and I wanted to be artists. Artists were dark, concerned, seriously depressed about the world and themselves. The artist was always hunted down, we thought. We were right. The artist *is* hunted down by the black dog, and many of my friends who were artists are dead, their black dog hunting them down to death.

Like most teenagers, I had moods that were sometimes difficult to distinguish from mental illness, alcoholism and even madness. The darkness is seductive. I loved to lock myself up in my room and read depressing books. I reread *Anna Karenina* a few years ago and thought, how could I have *not* been depressed as a teenager when I was reading such things? I thrust the book aside. Too depressing by far!

In subsequent years my depressions would take different forms at different times. I would wake up in the middle of the night and call my therapist and say I wanted to be put in the hospital, that I felt I was a danger to my own health. Whatever doctor I called always talked me out of my terror, making me know instinctively that part of the depression was isolation, at which I am an expert. I can isolate in the wink of an eye.

Therapists helped with my depression. The darkness must have a reason, these doctors consoled, and we worked for years to find out what it was. I didn't realize alcohol was a depressant and would contribute to the feelings of doom. I didn't know that alcoholics often want to die. The burning passion, in many addicted people, and in my own experience, is to be gone, to be dead, to be through with it.

As I struggled, I picked up tools along the way, things that helped to chase the black dog. From my midtwenties on, I knew that if I exercised, the depression would lessen, even while I was still drinking. When my heartbeat increases and I run or swim or do an aerobics class, the depression is lifted. So I fought the demon with my heartbeat, sweating it out in Mrs. Craig's exercise classes at Elizabeth Arden; lifting and bending and running in place to the Royal Canadian Air Force exercises; learning to swim and doing laps, sometimes for hours; joining health clubs before it was the fashion; running for miles; trying Pilates, Karnofsky; stretching and bending; trying desperately to lose some pounds, but mostly to shake off the black daze.

In my twenties I took pills to lose weight and, for a time, these counteracted the depression. The uppers worked for a while, pink and blue and green and yellow—purple for going to sleep—all from a happy-hour doctor who made a fortune on the longing of young women for slim figures and the lifting of the black dog with legal speed and legal sleep. In my purse during the sixties, I carried every kind of pill I could get: uppers, downers, sideways. They kept the black dog leashed, far from the house, where I could only hear his howls sometimes at night.

I abused food when I was depressed. Sex was another way to fight the demon. I was a sixties woman, freed from sexual barriers. The flower child generation discovered sex as though it were a new shore. We were like

Columbus, armed with birth control pills and new morals, finding a continent. We burned our ships and meant to stay. Sex, it was preached by the already converted, could solve everything.

But the black dog lived even on that new shore. One-night stands did not help, as I always hoped they would. Often, instead of helping a depression, they made it worse.

Drinking and the black dog lived side by side. My depression lessened the day I stopped drinking. It further decreased the day I put away the food and these terrible compulsions were removed. They were not removed by me but by God. I know negativity, fear, neglecting prayer, eating too much sugar, neglecting my own physical health can contribute to depression.

I think alcohol may have saved my sanity, for if I hadn't been able to drink in the early years, my depression would have probably destroyed me. There might have been many more suicide attempts. I settled for the long suicide of drinking, to get away from the black dog, not knowing the alcohol had the dog on a leash as long as I was drinking.

When he was fifty-five my father, the man who had taught me hope is forever, told me he had stopped hoping. He fell into a deep depression brought on by disappointment, loss, alcohol (I believe), and perhaps even diet. He told me his life was over. Perhaps my father was a manic-depressive, but no one, including the psychiatrist he saw for a few months, made that diagnosis.

What his doctor said was, "Your father will not deal with, or talk about, his drinking."

In the reading I have done, there is evidence in alcoholism and depression research that the tendencies to depression and chemical dependency can be inherited. A growing body of information about families who have this disease of alcoholism as well as the depression with suicide ideology supports the idea that these patterns often go hand in hand. I find this in my own experience, too.

Mental illness can be confusing in an active or recovering alcoholic or drug addict, because when we are using, we are acting in an insane manner much of the time. That is the nature of the disease of active alcoholism and drug addiction. Often when people detox from the alcohol, those who acted peculiar when they were drinking start acting like the rest of the planet, sometimes up, sometimes down, but not as depressed.

I know sober people who sometimes have difficulties with depression. They say that serotonin, a drug manufactured in the body naturally, is missing in the right amount in the bodies of those of us who suffer from visits by the black dog. Serotonin is also low in suicides, and in sober alcoholics. There are natural ways to increase your serotonin levels. Aerobics, meditation and physical rest increase serotonin levels. Some foods increase serotonin levels, but these, like sugar and wheat, have the after-affect of making some people more depressed. I know many people are prescribed antidepressants when they feel the breath of the black dog on their necks, the bite of his teeth. If you suffer from symptoms of depression that will not lift, most professionals suggest you get in touch with an appropriate specialist through the National Mental Health Association or your personal physician.

Medical professionals work with compassion and intelligence to help those who are prone to depression, and there are surely many times when medication for mood swings and depression is a valid course. Yet, how often after a suicide do we hear "The medication dose was not right," or "He needed more medication" or "She wasn't on the right type of medication."

A knowledge of the effects of what I eat and the role of alcohol and drugs in depression is a *must* if I want to be conscious, if I am to take my mental and physical health into my own hands. This is a relatively new concept, and most of us have depended on the medical community for so long to pull us in and out of emotional as well as physical symptoms with drugs that we feel strange being proactive in our own search for health.

For twenty-three years, I went to perfectly competent doctors who didn't know anything about alcohol and less about diet. I had to find out about exercise and mood-altering drugs and their effect on me. I am terrified of most drugs, and I am convinced there are safer ways for me to treat my depression. I don't ever want to become dependent on an outside force again, as I was so long dependent on alcohol and drugs.

While having a medical procedure I recently spoke to a doctor about his wife.

"She is suicidal," he says, "and has been for years. She is in treatment, sort of, although she doesn't want to go into the hospital. She is on some medication, but she sort of . . . threatens sometimes. Says she doesn't want to live. Her niece did it— killed herself, I mean. It was a long time ago."

I talk to him about perhaps going to some suicide survivor meetings, and then I realize there is no support group for people who suffer with the ongoing threat of suicide from a loved one. While giving me an antibiotic shot, the doctor says something that intrigues me.

"You know, this drug Prozac is very interesting. My wife suffers from major depression, where she can't move. Prozac lifts you up, gives you energy. She's tried to kill herself a couple of times on the Prozac. Do you think depression, where you can't get up, is God's way of saying, 'Don't get up right now? You might do something you won't like.'"

ॐ

With meditation and exercise and prayer I began to learn slowly how to send the black dog howling into the woods, slinking home.

Recently I have discovered Andrew Weil, the author of *Spontaneous Healing,* who talks about a particular breathing exercise to treat anxiety, saying that the deep, internal relaxation that comes from this breathing promotes emotional healing and is therefore an aid to overcoming anxiety. Singing brings that deep, internal relaxation that Dr. Weil talks about. When I have done a concert, or sometimes when I have simply been in my studio working on songs, I feel lifted out of anxiety. I also do the SRF (Yogananda) meditation form that includes deep breathing, usually twice a day. Dr. Weil also recommends taking natural remedies for anxiety—valerian root and passionflower. My homeopathic practitioner recommends a few pellets of Ignatia or Aconitum napellus for anxiety, and these have worked well for me. I like homeopathics because they are safe and nontoxic. Also, they can't interact with any other medication I might be on because the doses are miniscule, so small they can barely be detected. They are tiny but mighty. You cannot overdose on them. They only work on a symptom if they are the right remedy, and if one doesn't work, you simply go on to the next. For two centuries these tiny white pellets have been available in countries outside the United States and now can be found in most pharmacies and health stores in the United States.

Andrew Weil confirms what I have learned through trial and error about depression:

"The best single treatment (for depression) is vigorous, regular aerobic exercise, at least thirty minutes a day, five days a week." Most of the time, after I spend a half hour or more excercising, any cloud of depression lifts so completely that I feel a small miracle has been accomplished.

In the treatment of depression, Dr. Weil advises, as do other physicians, "avoidance of alcohol, sedatives, antihistamines, and other depressant drugs." After many years of not using drugs and alcohol, I can see their direct connection to the depression I experienced when I was abusing both, never happy in any emotional state, always looking for a way out. Dr. Weil also talks about dietary modification—less protein and fat, more fruits and vegetables. There are foods I know I am allergic to, that make me depressed, and I have to avoid them. Sometimes sugar, sometimes grain and wheat.

In the past years I have often used alternative medicine —acupuncture for cystitis, homeopathy and naturopathic allergy treatment for asthma. Glucosomine and chondriatic sulfate have cured my arthritis. I have a weekly massage, to keep mind and body in shape. I have my feet, hands and face done once a month. "The care of the nerve endings," Miss Rogan at Elizabeth Arden's calls these treatments. I believe they are, she says, not luxuries, but necessities. These treatments also help my depression. Lately, I see a lot more men in the salon to which I go, which wasn't true thirty years ago. Men are discovering what women have always known: that a day at a beauty salon often has more to do with peace of mind than with vanity.

Another thing Dr. Weil suggests is to "seek out others who have been healed." I have been fortunate that on the road to health I have discovered those who journeyed before me, pioneers I could trust and emulate. If someone has recovered from a symptom or a condition that I have suffered, I am eager to know how, especially if they have found a natural, noninvasive means to health.

The tools against the black dog of depression—running, swimming, meditation, writing in journals, talking, eating right, sleeping, creating—have helped me to recovery from my son's death.

Today, I don't have to stay in that terrible and dangerous place. I know I cannot afford to let a dark thought dig roots. I have tools:

I read a spiritual book.

I call a friend who has a kind word, a lift in her voice.

I think about the good things in my life.

I count my blessings, often writing them down. There is so much in my life to be grateful for.

I breathe in deeply. I look out at the sun on the river and run my hands through a plant I have nurtured.

I listen to a song I have written.

I smile with my husband, with one of my friends, with my mother, my sister.

The stars are always shining somewhere. I have only to look through the blue sky or into the black night to find them and let them shine on me. The sky will clear, my mind will clear, if I move from negative to positive. In the moment of silence between stars there is healing, there is the sound of the pulse of light, the sound of God talking to me, listening to me, healing me, bringing me strength. All I have to do is look up.

Today, I don't try to avoid thinking of the dark night my soul is traveling. I give it its due, but then I put the negative and terrible thoughts aside in order to look at the world of beauty that is around me. Like the phantom of the night, my depression cannot live today in the bright sun, exposed as it is to loving friends, healthy thoughts, healing and prayer. I run for the sunlight, I leap for safety, for friends, for exercise, for prayer, for health. Today I know where to turn for healing grace.

Finding our way through the darkness and pain of depression is the path to our brilliant days. Running with the black dog may lead us to a place of wonder and light and joy that we may not otherwise have seen.

Running with the black dog has led me to my angels.

The birds sing in clusters in the trees in the courtyard, purple finches wrapping melodies around the one-note call of the grackles, like lace around a wand, like flowers on a black pole. The days shine now, like polished stones, like jewels, like fluttering flags in a new wind. The early summer has been kind and soft, June rain washing away the soot left from the spring snows, rinsing the slush of the winter months.

There is hope in the air.

It is morning and as the sun cracks through the window, breaking like bits of glass on the tiles in the kitchen, I pour my first cup of coffee and think of my son, who loved his coffee strong and rich, as I do. In the last years of his life we would often make our coffee in these cities, he in St. Paul and I in New York, and talk on the phone while we shared the day, our plans, our fears, our jokes. He laughed as no one I knew except my brothers and sister, my mother and father, deep, full laughter, right from the toes, from the gut, from the heart. My brother Denver laughed like that the other day, at a joke I told him. It made my heart sing to hear him laugh as none of us has laughed for a long time. The coffee is still strong and good, the laughter is still deep, deeper for the tears, more treasured for the sorrow that has come into our lives.

I pray to be healed by laughter, and by memories.

11

Daybreak: The Wedding

In 1993, a year after my son's death, Louis had to have an emergency appendix operation. The surgery turned out to be very serious. For a week, my life partner hovered between life and death.

We had been living together in everything but matrimonial bliss for sixteen years. I spent each day praying for Louis's recovery, reading to him, hovering over his hospital bed, talking to doctors, signing papers, trying to be as cheerful as possible.

At the beginning of the second week I was visited with an irresistible urge.

"I think we should get married," I said, rubbing his feet. Louis didn't respond at first.

Then the handsome, bearded Norwegian managed a smile from the Demerol fog in which he had been dozing. "Getting married won't keep me from dying," he said, and laughed, and grimaced. It hurt too much. "But yes, of course, if that's what you want." He adjusted his hospital robe. "That's what I want, too." A smile again. "This isn't the way I wanted this to sound," he said and closed his eyes. I imagined he passed out from shock, but I think it was the Demerol.

Later, when he worried about his obtuse reaction to my proposal, I told him it had been perfect. Being Norwegian, he probably didn't realize it was also very funny.

His toes were bare, and his ankles and calves, where abundant hair curled, were also bare. The hem of his hospital gown had shimmied up above his knees. Above the gown I could see a lingering smile on his lips. Every orifice of his scantily clad body sprouted clear tubes that found their way to the tall stand—a sort of medical hat rack with beepers, blinking lights and bags of clear fluid. A nine-inch incision on his abdomen, open to the air, was healing from the inside out. It looked like a cut through a mountainside, complete with archeologically vivid details of past millennia showing through the pink, raw flesh of the surgical incision.

Three days before, Louis's surgeon, Leon Pacter, had taken out Louis's appendix, at which time he discovered that the appendix had ruptured at least a year before. Louis's body had thrown up an abscess, holding back and containing the infection after the first rupture occurred. Dr. Pactor said the condition was quite rare and it was miraculous that Louis had survived the infection.

I clearly remembered the night of the earlier incident, when my stubborn life partner had been running a high fever, suffering much pain, but refused to go to the hospital. It was the same night of the Anita Hill–Clarence Thomas hearings.

This time, I had rushed with him to the hospital where the doctors delayed operating for twenty-four hours. "Why?" I asked, hounding the surgeon for facts and getting at first a blank stare until he understood that I wasn't going away, until he became aware that I thought he was a genius to have saved Louis's life. When they saw the shape Louis was in, the medical team told us it would be at least a week before they knew whether Louis was going to make it. He wasn't yet out of the woods. All I wanted was for the doctors to say everything would be all right. They told me they couldn't say that, because if it wasn't true, they might be in jeopardy of a malpractice suit.

Louis had never in his life been in a hospital if you don't count birth. He is a workaholic, an industrial planner and artist and designer by profession. His work is beautiful, his grace in design, from the brightly colored skis he had designed for Head skis in the sixties—purple, yellow, violet and pink polyester—to his latest work, which, even as he lay in the hospital, was continuing: the design for the new Korean War Veteran's Memorial Wall to be erected on the Mall in Washington.

For all the years we had been together, we had avoided the discussion of marriage. Both of us had been married before, and neither of us felt the need for the institutionalization of our relationship. I am devoted to Louis and I assumed, as a feminist, a humanist, a liberal, a free woman and my own person, that I didn't need to marry him to prove it.

But now that I had almost lost him, and since Clark's death, I had felt some inner shift, some deep change in my opinions about all kinds of things. I knew what I thought before, and now, I know next to nothing.

The buds were beginning to come out in Central Park. As I drove back and forth to New York University hospital every day for those two weeks, Louis hovered on the verge of what we didn't talk about. Spring blossoms clustered on the limbs of the cherry and apple and plum trees, tulips in white and pink and orange and yellow and fuchsia spilled out over the green median strip in Park Avenue and out of the building-front gardens on Fifth Avenue, like tubes of watercolor pouring out of breast pockets on tidy businessmen's suits; the big magnolia trees burst with pink and white buds, and the sparrows sang furiously in the trees. I prayed furiously, constantly, counting the days, watching for signs of Louis's return to health. If he got well, we would get married. All the flowers celebrated with me. He would get well, they said.

I couldn't bear the thought of losing him. In the years before, there had been a tumultuous, sexy, brilliant, shining list of men, but no one is Louis, none of the others are in the least like him.

Joni Mitchell once said to me, "Judy, I don't believe you're still such a romantic!" She is right. In a way, the most romantic part of my life started after the sixties and seventies, after the flowers and the promises, after the heady days of peace signs and free love. It began after the crowds had gone off to do other things—find out about stock options and put away tie-dyes and hang up peace signs for teenage children to frown at and ask questions about.

In the years we had been together, Louis and I, for ourselves as well as for many of the friends who know us, were living proof that you don't have to be married in order to be committed. I quite liked that idea, of being the ones who didn't have to do "it." When one or the other of us would muse about whether we might get married, it was usually alighting from a taxicab in the middle of winter, hurrying through the cold, or going out the door to a party. Clearly, neither of us really wished to discuss marriage seriously, yet we wanted to signal that if the other were in some need of that "security blanket," as I was wont to call it, the other was certainly willing.

I called Louis my life partner for most of our time together, and by the time five, then ten, and then sixteen years had gone by we assumed that we had better *not* get married—simply because it might ruin the truly wonderful relationship we had. We had been tested in the fire.

There had been the first few fights, emotionally heated, but then they died down and we rarely fight anymore. We were happy, happier than I remember ever having been with anyone before Louis.

When Clark died I was told that many couples' relationships, married or otherwise, do not survive the death of a child. The average is not good. Louis went to great lengths with me, going to therapy sessions, committed to our relationship and determined, as I was, to find a way to stay together and to grow together; he was able to grieve with me, and more important, he allowed me to grieve the loss of my son in my own way. He was there for me in a way that was both tender and understanding. Louis had kept me going and supported me and mourned with me and prayed and wept with me. We had lived through a tragedy and had survived. If we could get through something so difficult, we could, I hoped, get through anything.

At the hospital for the next two weeks, while Louis hovered among tubes and prayers and I hovered over the papers I had to sign, telling official people what to do with his body parts if he should die, I was experiencing feelings, I have to admit, that were very "married." Louis had been there for me from the first. He was the best. It even looked as though he might finally quit smoking, with the help of a Demerol drip.

I was not about to let him get away.

◌◍

And so, on a day in February 1996, I stand in front of the mirrors of the second-floor showrooms at Vera Wang on Madison Avenue, looking at wedding veils, emerging from my cocoon, trying the light, trying my wings, not at all sure of their strength.

Vera Wang is a place I had never in a million years imagined finding myself. Famous for its dresses, veils, bridesmaid's outfits and chic costumes for the bride and her wedding party, the salon is a haven of brides-to-be. Here I am, at almost fifty-seven, a bride-to-be.

Around me, yards of white lace and silk dresses flow out of dozens of dress racks, their skirts like the sails of galleons ready for long voyages; glittering headbands of diamonds and pearls double themselves endlessly in the mirrors along the walls. Darker shades of satin, plums and violets, long dresses for maids of honor and bridesmaids, flower girls and matrons, hang in adjacent rooms, so as not to break the flood of white that flutters and pouts and crushes together in every inch of hanging space.

Murmuring conversation can be heard from the adjoining salon, where I can see the reflection of an eighteen-year-old with a twenty-inch waist posing in front of a woman my age dressed in a Chanel suit. An uncomfortable-looking older man, obviously the father of the bride, nods mutely in the corner, glancing over at his white-clad daughter nostalgically. She is cocooned within yards of satin, her shoulders bare, her eyes glowing, dreaming of wedding cake and church bells.

I feel a pang. I will never see my son standing shyly in the corner of a smart salon watching as his daughter and her mother pick out a wedding dress. It is four years and a month now that Clark is gone. These thoughts go through my heart like a dagger, when others speak of their grown sons, or when I see young men and their families on the street, looking happy.

Like all those other moments, this one passes, more easily than similar moments six months or a year before. I am getting better. I will never be over it, but I am living my life.

Now, the rebel, the flower child, accustomed in previous years to bell-bottoms, Mexican wedding dresses and buckskin, is looking at herself in a white suit with a sweetheart neckline, and gazing down at her white satin shoes.

They already hurt my feet.

The saleswoman brings out a long, light-studded veil—and what a veil it is! From the hairline around my face the lace flows down my head and shoulders, down to my ankles, then out on the floor for another seven feet.

Every inch of it sparkles. On top of the veil is a garland of pearls and rhinestones, a tiara that shines and dances as I turn in the mirror to get a better look at myself. My friend Ellie, who has come with me to Vera Wang to give me moral support, looks admiringly at the results. There are dozens of veils, but this one speaks to me, calling. The tiara, the white duchess satin coat over my long-sleeved, full-length concert dress, are my "something old, something new." Even in my wildest dreams I had never conceived of myself as a bride again. I will have to find something borrowed, and something blue.

I remember my first marriage on a warm afternoon in the offices of the justice of the peace in Ft. Collins, Colorado, having just had a haircut and a fight with my husband-to-be. Very different, this wedding.

My friends are giddy, my family making plans for hotels, airline tickets. Louis and I are in a frenzy of activity, strange after all these leisurely years together, hurrying as though I were pregnant (and I am, sorrowfully, decidedly not pregnant!), choosing the right caterer, the right location, the right limos, the right hotel, the restaurant for the rehearsal dinner, as though afraid of being late to our own wedding. All our friends and family will be coming. Our granddaughter, Hollis, she will be our ring bearer.

Little Hollis is eight, blond and beautiful, with a charm and loveliness that remind me so much of Clark that when I am with her, for the first day or so, I find it hard to bear, so sweet yet painful. She moves her head in the same way he did. She says things that are intelligent and tender, as he did. She gets it—life, the wonder, the recovery, the mystery. She *is* mystery and joy personified. More and more quickly I see her as her own complete and unique person, so much like my son but so much more like herself. I have a deep bond with her that is growing as she grows.

When we go skiing in Colorado with my family, she whirls down the mountain in the sunlight, a flash of goggles and bright pink parka. At Christmas in the mountains, seeing that everyone is exchanging gifts, she creates personal presents for all the family, sharing in the way that Clark could share, in the way her mother Alyson has taught her to share. Alyson spends time with her daughter, reading, doing projects, at all times interested, with an intense patience I find breathtaking, and impressive. Hollis comes to New York to stay with us in the new room I have made for her, filled with her toys and art and animals, and there are play dates and theater and eating together, pizza and movies, seeing friends, and healing laughter. Talking, talking, talking. I sing to her at night, lullabies we make up. I love just sitting and watching her play.

Hollis knows how to be still, and she knows how to laugh. She has an incredible sense of humor. Her mother does, and Clark did, so she comes by it honestly. She and Louis have the same birthday and now they share a party every year, some of her friends, some of his friends. Hollis has a tender heart and a fine mind and a sweet spirit like her father. I call her one Sunday and she tells me a family friend who knew her father is coming to see her. They have a daughter a bit younger than she is. I ask her to give them my regards, I haven't seem them for a long time. "I have two presents for them, one will be from you," she says.

She is beginning to be able to carry the tune on her own when we sing rounds together. Sometimes she will look at a picture of her father and say, "I remember Daddy singing to me, I remember him laughing." She told me she believes in the Buddhist philosophy, that her father has reincarnated. My granddaughter is comforted that her father is in heaven, and also that he is in the world with her, loving her, guiding her. She is wise. She sees no contradiction.

While the organ plays in the great church outside of which, one February day so long ago, her father surrendered and put the possibility of her beauty into our lives, Hollis will be with us.

Louis and I will be married at the Cathedral of St. John the Divine, where the Dean, Jim Morton, will do the ceremony. Dorothy Papadakos, the fine organist at the cathedral, will play Mozart and Beethoven and Collins. We will have a trumpet. (We *have* to have a trumpet, Louis said.) We will invite all our friends, and family. We will be married on a Tuesday, at high noon, exactly eighteen years since the day we met.

Last night I dreamed of veils—veils of tears, veils of mourning, wedding veils.

It had all happened so fast, yet I was moving in a dream, a slow-motion version of a whirling dervish, I thought, turning in front of the mirror, admiring the gown, the veil, and my nerve. I had, after all, been the one to propose.

≫≪

The wedding is getting closer by the minute. Louis and I went shopping for our rings, looking at Buccellati (wildly overpriced), where I was embarrassed that my nails look, as Lenny Bruce once said to his father at Mr. Kelly's in Chicago, as though my gardener did them. We looked at Cartier (only twice the reasonable price) and Tiffany (exactly the right price!). We ordered the engraving—"Judy and Louis, April 16, 1978"—the day we met, and somehow knew we were in it for the long haul.

In the words of married friends, whose words I previously derided as sentimental, there is really a different feeling now that we have made the "commitment." It is a strange and wonderful time.

My two best friends from high school, Marcia Pinto and Carol (Cas) Shank, gave me my first wedding shower in 1958. Now, my friends Muriel Lloyd and Eugenia Zukerman are hosting showers, and I feel the abundance of my women friends, supporting me, loving me, holding me up. At my first shower there are many New York friends as well as Marcia, my old friend from Denver. Marcia lives in Tacoma now and is married to a Lutheran minister named Dick Moe. I know that under the veneer of a seemingly restrained woman is a girl I went to school with, a girl with a funny, quirky mind, a girl who says things occasionally that shock me, leaping like fish out of water, a story that only she would think funny, a comment that I wouldn't make but she makes for me. That is what friends are sometimes for, I think, to say and do the things we long to and can't.

I tell Marcia and the other women about being shocked that I had to find my divorce decree to get married and how scared I was I wouldn't be able to locate it. Marcia tells one of those incongruous stories about herself. She and Dick had lived together for about five years when they decided to get married, and it was then that she had to tell Dick, to his great consternation since he was minister in a somewhat proper Lutheran community, that she had never bothered to get divorced from her first husband. It was such a Marcia thing to do, a wonderful thing to do.

Among these women I feel safe; we giggle and talk and share as well as cry, as I open gifts—lingerie! At my most flower-child stage, bedecked in tie-dye (always velvet!), I never wore lingerie. I could never have imagined that now I would have these lacy, lovely things that smell pretty and make my skin feel like silk. Who would have guessed?

Announcing the wedding allows our friends to celebrate the "us" in who we are. The wedding is for our friends, in a way, even more than for us. These wedding gifts are "ours," not mine. This partnership is "ours," not of my making only. Joining our lives together is a sort of defiance of cynicism. To live together for eighteen years and THEN get married—rather than never, rather than separating—I like that. It defies the cynical nature of our times, and I am, if anything, bound to do things differently if I can find a way.

I am writing songs again and have started a wedding song.

ॐ

My dressmaker, Leon Schneiderman, is from Kiev, Russia. Bent and overworked and about seventy, he is an artist, a genius with the scissors and thread. He talks about the "look" of clothes; everything must have a "look." He cuts fabric with no pattern, moving the scissors like a paintbrush. He is making little Holly's dress of lilac silk charmeuse and more lilac silk shawls for the girls in case it is cold in the church.

Everyone is coming, including mother's sister Jeanette, and her nieces Pam and Betty. Betty is the one who gave me our great-great-great-grandmother's quilt, connecting me again to my female, artistic ancestors.

Coincidentally, as though the Goddess really does have a sense of humor, I *could* get pregnant. Possibly. Estrogen replacement therapy *can* do that, make the body willing, if not able. Not very likely, but what the hell, there's the chance!

We've come to the country for a few days over Easter weekend. The crocuses are blooming, the birds are singing, the willows are already yellow, their branches fuller each day, the swans gliding elegantly on the lake. The snow yesterday was falling on buds and robins, on the lake and the mallards, on the pines and squirrels. A foot of snow fell around the calm stone Buddha who sits in our garden, a gift from my brother Denver and his family.

Louis and I read the scriptures, Mathew, Mark, Luke and John, aloud. I could use the Resurrection story every day.

It rains on Easter and I have a profound depression brought on by the sudden realization, once more, of Clark's absence.

He *is* here with us, Louis reminds me, but I want him *here*, sharing in the celebrations of each and every day. I miss my boy and find, upon waking, that my cheeks are damp with tears.

I had my second shower at Eugenia's a week and a half ago. What amazing women I know! Talented, soulful, productive! Many of them came to this shower—Letty Pogrebin, who introduced me to the Clintons; Gloria Steinem, Barbara Quinn, Harriett Vicente and Esther Kartiganer, Maureen McGovern, Ilana Rubenfeld, Joyce Ashley, Susan Cheever, Muriel Lloyd, Lucy Simon—therapists, musicians, writers, producers, agents, healers. And gifts came from those who didn't come—one from the First Lady.

In the pretty packages, rapturous underwear and a silk robe; Hillary sent her gift with a three-page, handwritten letter, telling me that she and Chelsea had put on incognito clothes and gone down one night recently to look at Louis' Korean War Veteran's Memorial and how moved she was, once more, by seeing it. Regretfully, she and the president would not be coming to the wedding because they are going to be in Japan. Otherwise, she says, they would be here. Their loss!

I have realized more and more that our friends are all very excited about our wedding. They put on the weddings of their children, or their friends' children, going to events where they don't know many people. This wedding, for all of those we love, is a place where they will know friends and be with people they have been with for years. Everyone feels as if the wedding is something that is happening for, and partly because of, them. They are right.

All during that week, and the following, there are plans, food and clothes, and talk about the prenuptial agreement, which I see is the only protection women have against becoming, as a result of the act of marriage, chattels of the state. Without the prenuptial, anything the state has to say about your separation rights goes—regardless of personal beliefs, systems of sharing or separate financial status.

A week of wedding pampering: facial, massage, pedicure, hair coloring. All of the nerve endings.

Imagine: parties, and plans, and more dresses and fabric and now, I try to decide whether my gift to Louis—a kimono of black silk—should be lined with fuchsia rather than gray.

April 13, en route, New York to Orlando
Four days to go!

We are almost ready, gifts for the family bought—silver bookmarks engraved for the men and the moms, pretty porcelain boxes for Holly and my nieces Corrina and Natily. My white wedding coat is finished; tiara, veil, flowers, food, order of the ceremony—most important, my wedding song for Louis—are ready. I will sing it a cappella.

Hopefully, without my glasses.

April 14, en route Orlando to Boston
I fly home from my concert in Boston with Chuck Berry. The rehersal dinner is tomorrow and I dream of wedding cake and rock and roll.

The entire family, by this time, has been in New York for a few days, going to museums and theater, shopping. It is my brother Mike's wife Kathy's first time in the city so Mike shows her the town.

The van and limo pick everyone up and bring them to the church and there we are, the whole family, walking through the ceremony with Jim Morton leading us. It's cold in the church, but not as bad as I thought it would be. The flowers are on the iron sconces, the white orchid sprays among the ferns, and the stained-glass windows glimmer on all sides.

That night I sleep like a bride and when I wake it is pouring, a rain that is said to bring great good luck. The morning splendid—I have my bagel and honey, relishing the moments before the house is awake. Then, I wake Hollis. Louis and I, in the old tradition, are kept apart, not seeing each other before the wedding—he showers and vanishes into the kitchen, he and Hollis giggling, she hiding me while he goes in to get dressed. Louis, who usually makes me prompt, goes ahead to meet his gentlemen in waiting. The girls come at nine-thirty to dress. What a thrill to have them all here! By eleven-thirty Holly Ann, my bridesmaid, Louis's sister Dorothy, Corrina and Natily, my nieces, and Hollis all look like lilac blossoms in their violet silk dresses, their hair shining with white silk flowers, long white opera gloves above the elbows of the older girls, and we go down to the limo and to the church, barely on time.

The flowers in the garden around the big statue of the god of the sun are blooming, as is the pink cherry tree in front of the synod where we will have our reception at the church, we sweep up into the robing rooms, and there is my husband-to-be, looking stunning, splendid in his morning coat and pink tie that vibrate with the lilac from the girls' dresses.

"Don't look at me!" I say, all the while staring at my husband. How handsome he is, standing next to my handsome brothers, everyone smiling.

Dean Jim Morton welcomes us. He and the other priests put on their multicolored, vibrant vestments amid the two dozen roses from Leonard Cohen and the note that says, "It's about time, with much love, Leonard." Leonard, now a monk of the Buddhist faith, who wrote so many songs that lifted me through the early years. Stained glass, candlelight, white roses and white orchids pour out of every nook, every crevice and tall vase, every corner and surface of the church.

We start up the aisle with the organ and trumpet playing Mozart, the procession in front of us. Hollis is dressed in her long lilac silk dress and Lucy's velvet purse around her neck, bearing the cargo of our Tiffany rings.

"To qualify for communion, you must be breathing," the program said, and nearly everyone did and was. Louis stood to read his poem:

We climb to the roof to see the new comet —
In mountains, she river-walks in glacier streams
With poles in her hands and Hollis in her steps.
On an Idaho highway, we sing rounds of "white coral bells."
Home. Listen. The sound in the trees.
Bird calls and peepers.
Wind chimes in the woods.
Shhhhhh! Listen.
Together, walking where bombs fell,
She brings laughter to crying children —
Joy to crowds of teenagers.
They sing for her amid the scars of war.
In a far place that I remember with pain, we visit with families.
Boys in the hill country giggle as I place blossoms in their hair —
Pose silly with smiles in their eyes for my camera.
A girl gives me flowers she picked from the field.
A bird called. I pick up the phone.
Four years ago Clark left us.
He let go of her. Of them.
Of me.
Some of you were with us.
Three years ago
When tubes came from my body,
She held onto me.
She brought me crystals, and a cross, and smiles and you.

I hold the tears back, gritting my teeth. I must sing my song without weeping. I take my place before the gathered friends and family to sing my wedding song.

The night before our wedding I dreamed of falling stars
And all the souls that I have loved
came bending to my window

A galaxy of wishes as far as I could see
I thanked the Gods and Goddesses for bringing you to me
And it's time to celebrate our wedding
After all these many years
To celebrate our lives together
I'll marry you for love
I'll marry you for laughter
I'll marry you ever after
Once more the comet flies
   after eighteen thousand springtimes
Over our ancient vows
Like a shining pearl
Sorrow may come again
But the joy will keep returning
Love can do anything
Love can change the world.

White and lilac silk, my mother in peach with a peach hat, smiling. Faces of the family I love, of friends I love. The light from the stained-glass windows pouring on us as we say "I do." The recessional, preceded with a trumpet blast from great organ pipes, one of which bears Clark's name, in his memory, a gift from Louis after Clark's death—a commemoration. The renaissance musicians, leading us out of the church, everybody dancing. We circle around to rejoin the family for photographs, skipping, giggling. Louis's father sitting in a wheelchair, looking lost in happiness; Ingrid, Louis' mother, looking found.

At the party after the wedding Max, my teacher, bent and smiling, growing old, said to my brother Denver, "I was looking for an older man." Then he said, "When we met, you were small, and now look, I am small!" Max, smiling, light dancing in his glasses. The long receiving line lasted all afternoon. Back at the house, rooms full of family. I remembered that morning, eighteen years ago, the night after I met Louis, sick from drinking—I came out into the dining room and there was my nephew Kalen, nine months old, sitting in his high chair, and I thought, there is nothing in life that is worth anything except this beautiful child, my sister's child. Kalen's was the only light shining then. Now, Kalen is twenty and the light shines from every crevice, every cranny.

It was magical, and I am married.

We took our honeymoon in Montauk, at Gurney's Inn, where we knew we could just jump in the car, roll out there, get into comfortable clothes, run on the beach, have massages, eat fish and dream, and write in our books and make love and talk and exercise and do our meditations and walk—and think. About everything. About nothing.

We stayed in Bridge Cottage, one of four cottages looking out onto the beach. Bridge is like an eagle's eye into the weather, waves falling like lace ribbons up and down the long, sandy beach—waves breaking into pearls of white thrown into the sky, falling back where sand and sea meet, the sky emerald, violet, deep cerulean blues, the water green, then pale, then deep and dark, ruffling into bigger white foamed waves out at sea, waves that catch at the edges of the sky, pulling them down to the water. Storm coming, stirring the waters, stirring my memories.

I used to watch those ribbons of white, that dance of sky and sea when I lived out here in the summer of 1972. At the other side of the rolling dunes that run from Montauk southwest to Amagansett along the Atlantic, on this same glorious beach, I rented the sea house just behind the sand dunes, its broad porch the full length of the house and its floor-to-ceiling windows facing the beach. A thousand years away, light-years ago. The fishermen of Long Island were sometimes my only companions, plying their nets and their trucks out on the long beach that rolled at my front door.

They don't fish like that anymore, with the big nets. Not this season, anyway. But that summer they would toss a five-pound fish into my arms thirty feet from my front door and I would bake the bluefish and serve it to friends who dropped by for dinner. I played the piano that I had brought out from New York. I would get up every day and practice. I wrote a few songs. One night I slept with a famous poet and perhaps we had sex, but more likely we didn't, or couldn't. It was often thus. In the morning he brought me a new potato from the fields of Long Island and I cooked it for lunch and it was the most wonderful thing I ever remember eating. One morning in a hangover I dropped the Venetian blinds on my toe. Sitting here having my feet done at the spa at Gurney's twenty-four years later, sitting next to the man I married on Tuesday at high noon, in our wedding, I can still see that wound.

The ocean rolls and sparkles right outside our window. Last night as we went in to dinner I told the maître d' at the restaurant that our names were Collins and Taylor; I have never before done that. From deep in my lost memories, the name of my ex-husband, Peter Taylor, popped out of my mouth, unbidden. I felt foolish. A few weeks later we went to dinner one night with Helen Frankenthaler and her husband, Steve De Brul. Helen used to be married to Robert Motherwell. That night, as the four of us left the restaurant, Helen turned her head and said, "Bob, darling, wait up." Realizing what she had done, she clapped her hand over her mouth and looked to see if Steve had heard, then looked at Louis sheepishly like a schoolgirl.

Walking with the wind on my face, I look out at the waves and think of how fortunate I am, what a life of blessings God has given to me. My beloved family is healthy, my siblings are thriving.

I see my family often, plan family reunions, spend weekends with them when I am on the road, have them here to the city. I feel my family is like a mosaic that is always in motion, that is, I am always trying to be with them. When I am with my family, I am more myself than I am at any other time.

And so, on this wide, white beach, the water at my feet, the sun above me, I feel overwhelming, total gratitude: for the path I have come, for the beauty of those who share my life with me. I don't come to my second honeymoon without memories. That is the interesting thing about time, how it stands still now while my hair changes to silver (which Agnes my hairstylist colors with brown and blond streaks), and I have to wear more and more powerful glasses to read, to look at television, to sew, to watch the world. My vision may be blurred, but my memory is keen.

I dream of Clark behind the glass at what appears to be a Buddhist retreat, his face clear-eyed and at peace, looking out at me.

I am married, but not settled—more stirred up, I think. Still rebellious, still searching for inner peace. I see how death has troubled my relationship with Louis, has increased the joy and gratitude, and how life has molded our partnership; how living with and loving this man has surprised me, has turned out to be something I never expected. There seems to be more intensity and clarity in our lives today.

I am surprised to be alive, now that nothing really matters. Yet everything is more essential and matters terribly, painfully, achingly—more, even, than it mattered before. There is a fire in my heart and brain that burns and burns, transcending, singing, sailing, vibrating with energy.

ᔆᦓᧉ᧊

Louis and I are a thousand times blessed. In the sun and in the darkness as well, we can be happy together.

There were storms I could never have guessed, never have dreamed. I sail in their wake as though I am on some pirate ship on a vast sea, like a mariner, sunset before me, sunrise before me, the water clear or cloudy, the day bright or dark.

Married, I am happy.

Married, I am free.

𝔅𝔒𝔠𝔈 Dear Clark,

I went to the sea to heal and to find some peace. I swam, counting the hours and minutes you had been lost to me, feeling your presence in the sea.

At night, when I remembered the sea and the way that it healed me, I remembered you at the sea as a child, running in the waves, laughing in the water. Now you are in the sea, in the water, in the rainbow, in the dance of the music of the spheres, comforting, smiling, radiating.

Perhaps you were closer to me there than anywhere, looking at me in the light of the sky, shining in the rainbow that reached from one side of the sea to the other, talking to me in the sound of the birds' songs at night, and in the sound of the rain when it fell.

At night, looking at the stars above, a million stars in your sky, you were as rich and bright as the star-filled sky. The wind was wind in your hair, the water felt like silk on your skin. I was enveloped in your memory; no, not in your memory, in your presence.

You are the rainbow, the stars, the earth, the sea. You are the music of the spheres now, in your death, even more vibrant now than ever.

I am enfolded with your spirit, with your beauty. The sea bathed me in your music.

12

Harmless with Nightingales: Bosnia and Vietnam

At the end of Paulo Coelho's book *The Alchemist,* there is a scene in which the young hero, having searched long for his treasure, is finally digging in the desert to find it. Exhausted, weeping in frustration and sorrow, he listens to his heart, and it tells him to dig where his tears fall and he will discover what he has been seeking.

In November 1994, I made my first trip as a UNICEF International Ambassador for the Arts. I traveled, with Louis, to Bosnia-Herzegovina and Croatia. The journey, coming two years after Clark's death, was at an early stage of my own healing. I was still terribly vulnerable and often shaky, struggling to accept what had happened to me, and struggling to find the joy in my life.

In the former Yugoslavia, as in Vietnam, to which I traveled the following year, everyone is trying so hard just to live, just to breathe, just to eat, just to exist. There are hard realities and each day is a challenge. For me, traveling in these countries, the lessons were many. I knew that I had been given this gift of visiting countries for UNICEF so that I could see something I needed to see, people poignant and courageous, full of determination to live their lives no matter what. The journey allowed me to see how my story was, in many ways, just another story of loss and survival. In their losses, the people I visited were filled with joy in the moment of living, which is what I was learning, one day at a time, to do.

Louis traveled with me for UNICEF, even joining the Vietnam trip as a special representative. Before our first trip to the former Yugoslavia, we read as much as we could, including *Black Lamb and Grey Falcon*, Rebecca West's remarkable book about the region, in which she dedicates her pages to "all my friends in Yugoslavia who are, or will be, dead or enslaved." Even from her vantage point of 1937, before the creation of Yugoslavia, West was not optimistic about the future.

By then most of us had seen the newsreels of the death marches and mass murders, the snipers on the hills of Sarajevo, bombs smashing the beautiful old city of culture and art nearly into the ground; streets filled with murder and desolated children, a community isolated, cut off from the rest of the world, the only access to safety a nearly mile-long tunnel in which one had to crawl on hands and knees. I read of refugees pouring from town to town, with no water, no food; of children with wide eyes, starving.

The world had watched, seemingly helpless, as bombs smashed the elegant twelfth-century bridge in Mostar, a centuries-old city in Bosnia. The bridge of lacy stone turned to flying particles of death before our eyes, glued to television sets around the world.

Now, we were there to witness in person the destruction as well as healing in the midst of war. When we arrived, bombs were falling, snipers were firing on Sarajevo and security was tight. The war was in its third year. We headed through the countryside, north to Mostar, not far from artillery action, in the white UNPROFOR minibuses. My eyes roamed the fields and lovely hills that rolled on either side as we traveled over pitted roads, past bombed-out houses our guides referred to as "ghost houses," once country homes, now with barely a wall left standing. All along the mountains and among grape arbors and fields of untended crops, dry and brittle under the November sky, skeletons of houses stood, silent witness to the refugees who have fled along these same roads we are traveling, carrying whatever they could, on their backs. The newsreels do not do justice to the devastation of houses with their walls, roofs and inhabitants bombed away. I kept my eyes glued to the facts, trying not to weep, but the tears kept falling.

Our entrance into Mostar was a shock, and a line from Lawrence Durrell's poem, written in Sarajevo in 1956, came to mind:

Promise us a peace . . .
harmless with nightingales.

Lining every street there were shells of buildings once tall and fine when Mostar was a stop on the tourist routes: buildings that once housed tourist bureaus and chic dress shops, vegetable markets and high-rise offices, lining European-style streets behind rows of tall poplar trees bending in the summer winds. The winking, blind eyes of these empty buildings were everywhere held open by fragments of walls, with nothing left of the interiors. Street after street was bombed, shattered, as though we moved down a nightmare from both world wars. The insides of the buildings were dumped in piles of rubbish; in vacant lots debris was heaped like monuments to despair.

From time to time a child, scantily dressed, with wide, knowing eyes, peeked from behind a building at our passing faces. The silence inside the car as we drove was profound. I couldn't speak, and had no questions, the devastation around us answering every one. It was worse, they later told us, than it had been a week before.

Suddenly the van came to a stop at a corner and Louis leapt out to take a photograph of a stop sign with the figures of children crossing the street, the sign itself riddled with bullet holes. Tom McDermott, the regional head of UNICEF in Zagreb, jumped out of the car after him, shouting for him not to walk off the road for fear of mines. This was my first exposure to land mines. Tom told us that every industrialized country in the world makes land mines.

"You can buy an antipersonnel mine for three dollars," he said, "a used one for one dollar. It takes a thousand dollars to remove a land mine. The estimate to clean up antipersonnel mines worldwide is thirty-three billion dollars.

"There are estimated to be more than seven million mines in the former Yugoslavia," Tom went on. "Antipersonnel weapons around the world kill and maim twenty-five thousand people each year, ten thousand of them children. There is one mine for every twelve children in the world. The number of mines in the world is growing every day."

ЗꙨꙨ

The city of Mostar is a jewel in the crown of Bosnia-Herzegovina, a city divided by a shining blue-green river that runs under an ancient, arching bridge of red and pink stone. Before the war, the bridge was anchored to delicate, peak-roofed stone buildings with tiny windows in their uppermost floors, windows that winked like eyes out over the mountains of violet and lavender. Today in the center of Mostar a fragile replacement bridge of rope and wire swings high above the river, threatening to disintegrate at any second.

In a young people's center later that day we heard a young man named Peter sing a song, strumming his guitar, called the "Bridge of Broken Hearts." Teenage girls danced on their long gangly legs, smiling from ear to ear. A rock band played for us, the children raised their voices on the choruses of rock songs. It is the same insistent and lively beat as rock music in the U.S.A., with the same purpose: forgetfulness, joy of the present moment, movement and laughter and singing to take away the sting of living.

Later that day we made a visit to a UNICEF program in the local high school where children bearing flowers and singing songs greeted us. I sang for the children, "White Coral Bells," "I Dream of Peace," and "Amazing Grace." We visited children in schools, orphanages and classrooms. In a bombed-out basement room in a school in Mostar, surrounded by rubble, we met children of twelve and thirteen having their lessons as we heard the explosions of tank and gunfire in the mountains close by. Their voices sang, while their blue, black and brown eyes shone. The children ignored the sounds, making drawings, guided by the gentle, recorded voice of Rune Stuveland, a Norwegian teacher who developed a method of dealing with war trauma in which terror becomes art for a moment. The children's drawings and paintings were eloquent, their loveliness like a healing grace. In their midst, singing in the storm, drawing in the shadow, smiling as the bombs fell, I felt the power and courage of these children, survivors of war.

In Bosnia I learned, again and again, the lesson of creativity: the painting I make today, the drawing I do today, the poem I do today, is meant to save my life today.

ဿာလ

Before going to Bosnia, I had written a song based on the book of drawings and children's words called *I Dream of Peace*.

> Blood in all the streets, running like a flood
> There's nowhere to hide, no where that I can go
> I reach out my hand, touching death itself,
> Just a holy day in Sarajevo
> I can feel my heart, pounding like a clock
> Hiding from the planes and from the bombing
> Fire in the sky burning down my life
> There is no more love and no more longing
>
> *But when I close my eyes, I dream of peace*
> *I dream of flowers on the hill*
> *I dream I see my mother smiling*
> *When I close my eyes, I dream of peace*

In Dubrovnik I met one of the children whose picture had been included in the book *I Dream Of Peace*. Mario was thirteen at the time he made his drawing in a refugee camp outside Dubrovnik. Now he is sixteen, a strapping, handsome young man with a haunted look in his brown eyes. He and I sat on a terrace overlooking the sea outside the old wall of Dubrovnik. Together we looked at his drawing in the book, an elegant and terrible one of soldiers and guns, bullets flying and planes dropping bombs, of fire pouring out of buildings, of refugees filing out of a city they had abandoned. He wept at the sight of his drawing. He told me most of his friends were dead or orphaned or exiled. Mario's life was shattered, his plans postponed. He told me he only wanted to be a teenager, to have back the life that had disappeared for him. He would become a sailor, he said, and go out on the sea, and not return to his beautiful Dubrovnik, for there was nothing there for him now.

♥♥♥

There are other images from Bosnia: lunch with the Serb, Croat and Muslim mayors of the divided city of Mostar, along with Hans Koenig, the mediator from the European community. I had just come from the drawing class and showed pictures the children had drawn, spreading them out on the table on which no welcoming cups of tea or coffee had been placed. We were, after all, visitors from the outside, hostile world. Hans Koenig was charming, and, of course, neutral in these strained circumstances in a city in which he had come close to death the previous week, when the Serb mayor had tried to have him assassinated. I watched the look on the mayors' faces as they looked at the children's drawings of fires, guns, refugees and bullets. The men seemed totally surprised, as though it had never occurred to them that their children might be affected by the war around them.

In Dubrovnik, we watched seven-year-olds being taught about anti-personnel mines in a classroom in front of a table covered with fifty different types of mines including those made to look like candy wrappers and coke bottles, intended to blow the hands and feet off unsuspecting children.

After lunch with the mayor of Dubrovnik, a generous meal that consisted of sparkling water, white fish, delicate pasta and fine white cake, the handsome, war-weary man gave us a foot-tour of the ancient city behind the pink walls, pointing out shrapnel holes in the old stone, the bombed-out insides of elegant buildings, while he talked of bringing tourism back to the Dalmatian coast, his dark eyes troubled.

At night in the square of Dubrovnik hundreds of children and adults serenaded and danced for us on the last night of our visit. In their traditional costumes, they raised their voices in music that made its way through the night sky over Dubrovnik, over the black sea on which the boats once brought the bombs. We needed to sing, we needed to dance, they said to me, and I sang with them and our voices filled the square and filled the night air with music.

After the songs and shared meals, laughter, and tears with children and adults of great bravery, there a was feeling of hope. But I understood the war no better. I had met Serbs, Muslims and Croats. They were each beautiful in their way. I went to the seaside town of Dubrovnik and sang in the square with a thousand children. I watched children draw pictures, turning their pain into art. We all need healing.

We all need a place harmless with nightingales.

𝒷❧𝒸

In 1995 I made my second trip for UNICEF, this one to Vietnam. I was excited about going to Vietnam. It seemed to me that during all those years of fighting against the war I had been very close to these people even though they had been considered our enemy.

I found I was still in a rage over Vietnam. Why did they not speak out? Johnson, McNamara? Johnson, who we now know was tortured by his conviction that we were doomed in Southeast Asia, just as all of us out on the streets outside the White House and on the great Mall before the Washington Monument knew, with our shouting, singing, crying. McNamara, whose hesitation doomed so many. While we were hurling insults at the gates of the White House, being tear-gassed and murdered at Kent State, it turns out that many inside the White House thought just as we did.

Landing in Hanoi, we flew in over blue water, meeting a seahorse-shaped land of breathtaking greens. Our wheels touched down and slowed along the haze of water and trees and yellowed, rotting airplane hangers. The sun blazed outside the barracks in which the North Vietnamese planes had sat between bombing runs in the war between our countries, Jacob and the Angel. It is as hot as predicted, a hundred and twenty-five degrees in the sun. Humid, a place for orchids and water buffalo.

I sweated through my jacket and perspiration formed on my face. The formalities began—smiling, bowing, meeting everyone. Our spindle-thin hosts, utterly beautiful, were dressed in white silk shirts and long black pants, fuchsia on the women, their eyes dancing. In the reception area in the airline terminal in Hanoi a little girl in a red dress and bright red lipstick named Gwin gave me a huge bouquet of red and yellow flowers. She danced and bent, laughing easily and stretching, like a ballet dancer. Her mother hovered, smiling.

We drove to the hotel, past tall, thin houses, like narrow, multilayered cakes, different flavors on every level, delicate balconies at the top. How do they stand so narrow and tall? Tea plants folded over the soft hills, dark rich green alongside the paler greens of rice in the lower paddies, a rich fabric of deep color. Cone-shaped hats bent and nodded between the rows. The exhilaration of being there cut through the exhaustion of the trip from London, over Europe, India, Bancock and China, into the dawn, but that night I slept like a baby.

In the hotel, my brother Denver, Louis, and I had three rooms together, where we could talk easily, move about, have our quiet mornings. Denver (who had come to film the trip) and Louis and I rose at six A.M. the following morning. My brother and I love our coffee, and the French influence has assured that the Vietnamese make sensational coffee—strong, even better than Starbucks, even better than my own coffee. Over coffee and shortbread, which I had brought with me in case I reacted badly to the foreign foods, we watched the morning images outside the windows: beautiful men and women doing tai chi, running around the lake outside our hotel, bicycling. Everyone was moving, the streets were dense with thin, brown forms, faces full of light and energy, all doing a death-defying dance against the odds that plague the country, as though the movement and the energy could conquer the enemies of children and adults alike: polluted water, parasites, malaria, encephalitis and land mines.

Despite the conditions, Vietnam is the only country in the world that has a government agency that is solely devoted to children. The children are all, even when maimed, even when sick, beautiful. I suppose all children, to some extent, have this blessing of beauty. Many are tiny, dwarfed by malnutrition. Most families live on $240 a year. There is disease and a lack of clean water. UNICEF's big job in Vietnam is what they call "Wat-San," water and sanitation. The opening of a new well and a party and parade for the opening of a new latrine in a northern province are the things that are most joyously celebrated. One hundred percent of all children in rural areas have parasites and most everyone suffers from malaria although, thanks in great part to UNICEF, polio has been almost totally eradicated around the world.

ॐ

Outside the post office near one of the ever-present statues of Uncle Ho, which is what the children call Ho Chi Minh, we bought copies of Graham Greene's masterpiece *The Quiet American*. Writing in the fifties, Greene captured it all: the temperament, the sweetness of the Vietnamese, the horror, the violence, the transcendent character of these warrior people who have survived every one from Genghis Khan to General Westmoreland.

Warren Christopher had been in Hanoi three weeks before for the opening of diplomatic recognition between our two countries for the first time since the war ended. George Bush was coming the following week for Citibank.

ॐ

One afternoon I went to the Swedish Hospital to sing for a little group of children suffering from Down's syndrome—aged from three to nine. Their eyes lit up when I began to sing, and a little nine-year-old stopped eating her rice and green beans. Her serious dark eyes looked at me and then she smiled and we all began to sing and, when we finished singing, clapped like mad for each other.

There were a number of Canadian veterans, working with the children. They told me about the problems of encephalitis, carried by mosquitoes. The Japanese have the vaccine, but it is too expensive to bring in the quantities in which it is required.

At a press conference the next morning, the first question was asked me by a young, determined-looking woman with a glint in her eye. "Ms. Collins, what do you think of the arresting of the monks by the government?" The monks who had been taking part in a rally about agricultural problems and famine in a province in the South, had been put in prison. I said I thought the government's actions were a disgrace. The comment made the headlines and upset people in Geneva at UNICEF's headquarters. UNICEF exists at the invitation of the local government and is apolitical, expressing no opinion on matters of government. I had to do some explaining, but what the hell, I am the original rebel folk singer, what did they expect me to say?

❧

There are still twenty-five million craters from bombs the Americans dropped on Vietnam. Though they are all covered with the green, green growth, the land on which they lie cannot be farmed.

There are land mines everywhere. More casualties among American soldiers occurred from American-manufactured antipersonnel mines than from any other cause. In sixty-eight countries around the world, nearly one third of the planet, there are an estimated 110 million antipersonnel land mines. In Cambodia, crops are left to rot because no one can get to the fields and forests due to the proliferation of antipersonnel mines.

❧

The Vietnamese appeared tall because they are thin and have an elegant way of carrying themselves. The men wore white bright shirts—plain, shining, gleaming white over slim trousers. The backs of men and women alike were straight as they rode in twos and threes and singly on bicycles at a pace that was beautiful—quick but not too quick for the cars and taxis that honked and honked. The women wore cone-shaped hats or plaits in their soft dark hair. The wind billowed their clothes and the tails of their tunics flew as they pedaled their bikes, turning their heads in unison, trios and couples, like fish or birds, all at once. Here there were three slender fine-boned faces, the white, blue, pink, red, green silk of the clothes below them flowing, gently flying, behind. The street was a mass of pedaling legs; across the road, there were elephants in the park, draped in mirrored, brightly woven blankets. There was music, there were voices singing, faces intent, horns honking, rain on the lake, bass jumping.

We walked the wide, French-designed streets, with Gna, a lovely, gentle Vietnamese woman in her early twenties who had been on the UNICEF staff for three years. Gna bargained for my purchases, a few lovely stones fired at high temperatures to make them shiny and colorful; some boxes inlaid with mother of pearl for my mother and sister. Jade is expensive, but I bought Denver a white ivory Buddha, for far too much money, according to Gna.

I asked Gna what her name meant. "Ivory," she told me. A Vietnamese beauty with long dark hair and delicacy of face and figure, Gna asked me who Denver is. I told her and she looked at him, flirting, her eyes coy. My brother was dressed in khaki shorts and a dark silk shirt, leather thongs on his feet. He was photographing everything, absorbing everything with that keen, intelligent energy of his. Gna smiled, looking at him from under her long black eyelashes. She asked me then who Louis was, and I told her. She glanced over at my life partner, knowing the boundaries, then her eyes cut to me. I slipped into the car and sat in back with Louis so Denver could sit next to Gna on the way to the hotel. Their heads bobbed together and I could hear their voices. Their two heads moved closer and I heard my brother's lilting laughter. Yes, he is something special, my brother.

A haze covered everything as we drove through the twilight of Hanoi, through the nearly tropical heat, and even the evening light simmered in damp, floating like a mirage over the pagoda in the middle of the "Lake of the Reemerging Sword." The bicyclists pedaled and their garments, the *áo dais,* floated through the light behind them and the horns honked and the dazzle of brown handsome faces moved in a constant rhythm.

In Hanoi that night there was a ceremonial dinner at the People's Republic house, and entertainment. The ethnic minority musicians, dressed in vibrant green and red silk costumes, playing unusual-looking instruments. I asked them to join in on "Both Sides Now." It was psychedelic, almost, and total musical chaos. I sang in Western harmony while they followed in twelve-tone antiphony, a meeting of East and West.

As we drove through the countryside each day, visiting UNICEF programs, wells and clinics and schools and medical facilities, the heat was horrendous and we dripped as we listened to the children sing and I dripped as I sang. It was a bit like giving concerts in a sauna. Wherever we traveled, the horns honked, the ducks wandered alongside the roads, and cone-shaped hats bobbed among the green rice. Among the shimmering green fields, the smoke lifted from burning chaff and the rice moved in waves in the wind. Our driver had to blast the horn every few seconds, dodging bicycles. We passed open-air markets, baskets of fish and fruit, water buffalo wandering at their slow pace by the road, with children, armed with a book and a long stick, often tending their progress. In a rice field near Saigon where we stopped to see the installation of a fresh-water well, a very old woman told me I was beautiful, held my hand, looked into my eyes, wanted an autographed picture.

On our third day in Hanoi, we headed north, traveling toward the province of Yen Bai, driving on the narrow, rutted roads. All along the sides of the road the fields of rice were delicately, almost luminescently green, floating in the wet, never-entirely-sunny sky. The greens were magical—the deep forest green of the tea plants and, pouring forth from the sea of rice, the soft pale greens and blue-greens shimmering in the damp light, aquamarines that lifted from the land, layered in shades of color toward the gently vibrating horizon. It was a sea of beauty. The fields were planted in intentional, careful rows and separated, one field from the other, each distinguished by immaculate borders. Each person, head topped by a pointed bamboo hat, seemed as autonomous as his or her rice field among the green flood of light and color from the rice and from the vegetables planted anywhere there is room. I was very moved by this relationship of the Vietnamese to the land and the rice fields on which they live, eat, breathe, and die. It is primordial, succinct, perfect. In many fields, there was a small stone monument, a burial site, where the previous tenant rested after his long, hard life of grueling work in the fields.

While the soft rain fell, we stopped at a small café in a tiny town near Yen Bai where the sanitary facilities consisted of two footrests alongside a hole in the floor behind a curtained cubbyhole.

In the restaurant, I drank sweet dark coffee while Maurice Apted, our traveling companion and the head of UNICEF in Hanoi, smiled over his glass, stirred with his spoon, and then held the spoon up in the air, saying, "Guess what this used to be? A B-52!" I looked around the room at the glasses of strong coffee, all with metal spoons in them. The Vietnamese have the most extensive method of salvaging and recycling metal in the world.

ಲೌ

In Yen Bai we visited a community where Mrs. Sao, a woman who looked seventy but probably was closer to forty, smiled a brilliant smile, dressed in her long purple and black tunic. Her teeth were black from betel nuts, like Bloody Mary in the musical *South Pacific.* The dark stains upon her teeth are considered a mark of great beauty. Mrs. Sao told us of the four generations who lived with her in her small, bamboo-thatched stilt home; pouring tea into tiny cups upon the bamboo mat where we sat cross-legged, she explained how she and the fifteen other women in the program sponsored by UNICEF were spending the thirty dollars a year they were given in microeconomic loans from UNICEF.

"We buy pigs and chickens," Mr. Ting, our driver, translated, "and ducks." Mrs. Sao nodded toward the livestock running under the trees, around the house, ducks and chickens nesting in baskets atop ceramic pots three or four feet high; "I give my children pork and chicken and shrimp to go with the rice."

Mrs. Sao was tiny and so were her children, so that we could not tell how old they were. Malnutrition was evident, for Mrs. Sao's ten-year-old looked five, from so many years of no pigs, chickens, shrimp, or ducks.

I sang "Bread and Roses" for the gathering of Mrs. Sao's friends, and they laughed and clapped and sang me a song as well. We were not sure of the translation, but I thought it meant, from the smiles on the women's faces, "We are happy to see you and we love you." "We love you" was in their eyes.

Outside, Louis made friends with some children of indeterminate ages who kept giggling and bringing him flowers. Louis was flying helicopters in

Germany in 1961, two hours short of the time needed to fly Huey helicopters. Hueys and their pilots were being sent to Vietnam by then. Their life expectancy in the air was thirty minutes.

Louis finished his tour of duty for Jack Kennedy as a captain in the Army and came home to go back to graduate school at Pratt. Now, standing in the rain under a bamboo stilt house two hours north of Hanoi, Louis put his hand out to a gaggle of brown-faced, smiling children and they put their hand on his, then he on theirs, until they built the international, nonlinguistic game that every child around the world seems to know: "hand on hand on hand." He put a flower into one girl's hair, and the girl giggled and brought more flowers.

He took pictures of the children and they smiled happily at the handsome man with the gray beard and dancing blue eyes.

My brother Denver stood by the stilt house, looking up at me as I sat in the window of the bamboo balcony. It could have been any time, any place on the earth where time was standing still. These people have nothing, and yet they have everything. Their beauty and generosity of spirit was evident—you felt it although you didn't intend to, there where the rain dropped on the bamboo roof and the birds sang melodically from their nests around the bamboo housetops.

Later, I told Gloria Steinem about this feeling in Yen Bai. She had just come back from a trip to the edge of the desert in Africa, to a far-flung tribe of beautiful and distant people. "It is as though, while we were working out the outer space, they were always working on the inner space," she said.

We saw women and children, but few men. Those we saw were hovering in the background, as though ashamed to appear. Or they were hanging about one or two of the shops out on the narrow highway, drinking tea. Most of the men, Mrs. Sao told us, were in China, sent north to be in the work crews. They sent money home, or maybe they didn't.

A memory that stamps Yen Bai forever: over the tops of the rice fields and mountains, in the rooms of the primitive bamboo thatched-roof houses, figures glittering on the screen of television sets, Judy Woodruff speaking from so far beyond this world, in black and white on CNN.

Saigon is such a different city from Hanoi! More pollution, millions of motorbikes, more noise, more signs: Coca-Cola, Kodak, Citibank. We thought back on Hanoi almost with nostalgia, for the beauty and simplicity of the people, their elegance, their uniformity.

The waiter who brought my coffee in the hotel restaurant in Saigon had beautiful brown hands, slender fingers, a quick, ready smile, a gentle voice. He floated into the room, understanding exactly what I said, replying in perfect English. I spoke Vietnamese, hello, good-bye, cheers, thank you. He had already forgiven everything.

In the afternoon we traveled to an outlying province near Saigon where we wanted to see a Buddhist shrine. On the way we saw the Cao Dai temple—the Cao Dais worship Christ, Buddha, and Victor Hugo!

The Buddhist temple was, amazingly enough, never bombed during the war. The monks gave us tea and took us through the maze of candlelight and shining Buddha figures. I lighted candles and said prayers for my son and remembered the story of the wise man who told the king he wished him these things: that he should die before his son and that his son should die before his grandson. The natural order.

By the time we arrived in Saigon I had been eating mostly rice and shortbread, afraid of the water, afraid of getting sick. I felt comfortable about this, smiling a great deal when our hosts passed other delicious-looking dishes. It was all right that they thought I was weird. I felt fine, the rice everywhere was very good, but my small supply of Walker's Shortbread, brought with me as an insurance policy against not being able to find anything that I could eat for breakfast, was running out.

After our visit to the temple, at the ceremony in the beautiful French quarters of the local communist government, lunch was served. There was a crispy, round fish like the fish I had in Israel at Ein Gev, on the Lake of Galilee, a fish they call St. Peter's fish. Here, the white fish was prepared with almonds stuck into its sides like medieval points of armor and then flash-fried in oil so that a flaky brown crust coated its outsides; there was a thick soup from which divine vapors rose; a dish of mixed, tossed mushrooms, and other vegetables that steamed from their bowls. I dug in, greedy and eager, and stuffed myself with fish and almonds, soup and vegetables. My rice fast over, I sipped tea with a satisfied look on my face. I let go, I was really there at last.

In Saigon we stayed at a floating hotel on the river. There were Pepsi-Cola signs along its banks, rushing traffic, the noise of horns and a million or so motorbikes. It was the festival of the century, the celebration of the fiftieth anniversary of the independence of Vietnam. Their constitution was taken in part directly from our own—life, liberty, the pursuit of happiness. Ho Chi Minh had come to the United States to seek an audience with Truman in the early fifties. His request for an interview was denied.

❧

The head of the U.S. Committee for UNICEF, Dr. Gwen Baker, was with Louis and that night, as we made our way from the restaurant back to the hotel the streets were jammed to the sidewalks for the anniversary with people on motorbikes and bicycles, sometimes five, even six to a bike, an entire family, tiny babies clinging to the shoulder of a mother, or father. A tiny boy with bare feet—perhaps five years old, but it was hard to tell—attached himself to Louis like a shadow, moving alongside him without touching him, just floating as we walked. Practically invisible, he put his little bare brown hand, open and flat, against the side of Louis's trousers. Like a pilot fish he kept up with our slow progress for a couple of blocks. The child was not begging, he did not seem to want anything. Perhaps he just wanted to be near the tall Western man, making his way from the densely crowded, hot, humid, mosquito-infested streets of Saigon into the cool, cleaner air of the Majestic Hotel? Perhaps he had been told by his mother to find an American and stay near him or jump into his pocket. Perhaps he just was going our way and wanted shelter from the crowd, a sturdy leg, a man eight times his size, to accompany him across a street filled with motorbike traffic. I will never know, but eventually the child peeled off, flowing in the direction of the traffic, moving across the mobbed road in front of the Continental Hotel, lost in the legs, arms, wheels, *áo dais,* honking horns.

It was a strange image, that small boy at Louis's side. Louis looked like so many of the big, graying men who have come to Vietnam to make peace with their memories. We saw them from time to time, walking among the thin brown people, so distinct, working in hospitals, working in clinics. They have come back to do what they can. They can sleep at night now, even here in the sweltering heat, these former American servicemen, since they have come back to put their nightmares to rest.

The richness that I have in my life is made up of a double journey, the one into the past and the one into the future; the destination of those two streams is always the present.

Each time I write a song or a poem or a piece of prose, each time I sing a concert and remember the good things, the touchstones, the moments; each time I make a painting, putting the color on the paper and watching the magical, one-and-only fusion of color, I am living in the present, a river fed by the tributaries of the past, moving into my future.

The things I know about today, my grief and my joy, my heartache and my ecstasy, are in those streams; I see them in the past and they flow into the future. My frailties are there, my disappointments, my guilts and griefs, and the thing I am beginning to see is that they, along with my strengths, are my own. I own my failures, they are pebbles in the bottom of the stream on a day of clear straight-through sunlight, when the whole stream is revealed, with its rapids and its ripples and its living, moving flow. They flood the present. My son's death, and his life, are in the stream of the past and the future, and in the beauty of the present.

I pray for the streams of my life to carry me always into the present, into its reality. There is no other reality, and now that my streams run clear I can see straight to the bottom, through the sun-lighted water, into now, into the present, that flows forever.

13

Politics and Presidents

Yesterday, Louis and I took a boat ride with Lucy Portlock, the marine biologist at our island retreat. We motored to Sandy Spit (My Island, I have dubbed it), a tiny dot of sand and palm trees in the Caribbean, and, at Jost Van Dyke, swam with a school of fifty or so eight-foot-long tarpin, their mild, sweetly shining gray eyes following us in the water.

President Clinton, Hillary and Chelsea have also been snorkeling here this week. Lucy was their guide, too. Everyone knew the Clintons were on the island, and the resort was atwitter with rumors of the presidential couple's plans and their private trip with Lucy.

Louis and I are fortunate to have been to the White House a number of times. I have always felt comfortable with the president and first lady and am fond of them both. So it was a bit as though some friends had dropped down to our hideaway. Over lunch at Turtle Bay, we gossiped about the presidential visit with Michael J. Fox, whose snorkeling date with his family and Lucy was preempted by Bill and Hillary. Michael was totally forgiving. It isn't every day you can give up your snorkeling instructor for the president.

Lucy regaled us with the details: The president arrived with Hillary and Chelsea in a big boat to board Lucy's tiny craft. A dozen Secret Service men began throwing towels, drinks, food, snorkel gear and supplies at Lucy. She found places for the towels and the people and then the head of the Secret Service handed her a particularly compact, very heavy bag.

"Set that somewhere safe from the water," he said. Lucy looked surreptitiously at the black box, knowing as she stowed it under the wheel that here was the "button" we all know about, never more than a few feet from the hand of the president. Then, she thought, "My God, I could start World War III from here! Or stop it!"

There were the dozen Secret Service men with the president, as well as Chelsea and the first lady, in a tiny boat meant for six, tops. Lucy says the president looked terribly hassled, tired and almost gray. He put on his life preserver and Chelsea showed him how to inflate it, blowing in the air tube.

"Are you required to wear that?" Lucy asked the president, pointing to the puffed-up pink article of water wear that now extended almost to the president's elbows.

The president looked over at the senior Secret Service man, who shook his head in the negative.

"Then take it off," said our bold friend the biologist, who was about to dive down, as she does every year with Louis and me, bringing up sea cucumbers for our inspection, pointing out octopuses and barracuda. "You look uncomfortable."

After an hour or so of riding the soft surf and looking at the brilliant fish, she said, the president, his wife and daughter with the black box close by, actually seemed to relax a bit.

I think of Bill Clinton flashing through the shafts of sunlight as I do, under my mask and bright pink fins, my arms stretching out to embrace the water, the deep, caverned rocks, the waves above me flooding over and over again, murmuring, "There is no death here. There is only life. Only life after death."

꿈꿈

When I first met William Jefferson Clinton, in 1991, he wasn't yet the president of the United States. I had been doing my usual summer tour, and in September I was booked for a concert at one of my favorite concert halls, located in the Chautauqua center in upstate New York. Chautauqua is an old Bible-study community near Lake Erie. The center, with its quaint, gingerbread houses and old trees and gardens, had been a gathering place for spiritual retreats earlier in the century. William Jennings Bryan spoke there, and John McCormack sang, in the open, wooden auditorium whose acoustics always ring well with my voice. I looked forward to the concert. My schedule was tight and I only had time to fly in, jog around the beautiful grounds in the afternoon, have dinner at the theater, sing, sleep, and catch the plane the next day for my next stop. The weather was rainy, but that was fine, because the open-air auditorium at Chautauqua has a roof. The rain might fall outside, but inside, within the finely crafted walls that ring with the echoes of those glorious voices, I could sing all night.

My friend Letty Cottin Pogrebin had been leaving messages on my machine in New York telling me that she was coming to Chautauqua to attend a conference on women's and children's issues. Letty, a well-known writer, would be there with her husband Burt, a New York lawyer. Letty and Burt would be bringing a few friends backstage, a couple by the name of Clinton. He was, she said, the governor of Arkansas, and his wife, Hillary, was a "good egg" and a real advocate for children. Letty had known her for years through her work with the Children's Defense Fund. Letty and Burt and the Clintons had become closer at the Renaissance Weekend that summer, and Letty's messages said she looked forward to bringing them backstage to meet me after the concert.

The weekend turned out to be extremely rainy and the travel long and arduous, through many airports. We got into Chautauqua late in the day, in time only for dinner and the show, not for the jog. Nevertheless, it was, for all the rushing and the lateness in travel, a good concert for me. I always hear the sounds of history at the Chautauqua auditorium, voices of intelligence and wonder, poets and thinkers, and the karmic company makes me happy as I sing. The rain let up that evening and the bugs were somewhere else. All in all, the evening was a pleasure.

After the concert I slipped out of my long beaded jacket and silk dress, wiped off my pale lipstick and took out the combs from my hair, pinning it up on top of my head. I was about to sponge off my makeup and head for the car and the hotel room when Letty and Burt arrived, flushed and excited and still bubbling from the concert, their friends in tow.

I was introduced to a tall, good-looking man with a lot of great hair and a wonderful smile and a look of sheer rapture on his face. I was only aware peripherally of Letty trying to tell me something. This, she was saying, was the future president of the United States.

Not at all sure I had understood her properly, I shook the hand of the attractive blond woman with him, whom Letty whispered confidently would be the future first lady.

"You're better than ever," Clinton said enthusiastically, pumping my hand before I could quite put this all together. It was still months before he would announce his candidacy for president, and his face, though handsome, was not as familiar as it soon would be. I was tired after a long day of traveling, and though I sensed Letty and Burt and the Clintons would have liked to go out, for drinks, or coffee, or just to chat, I was just not up to it and said so. Politely but firmly, I took my leave of the president-to-be and his wife. I thanked him for his kind compliment, packed up my bags, and headed off for the hotel, bidding the future president and his wife farewell, delighted to have had such an enthusiastic audience and such a good time singing.

In May of the following year I met Clinton again. The New Hampshire primaries were over and the debates in progress. I was in Santa Monica, staying at the Miramar Hotel near my sister, Holly. Sometimes we would bring her middle child, Aidan, who was then one and a half, to the pool to cool off, and we would order wonderful lunches and let my beloved nephew trash the room and rummage in the minibar and push my wheeled luggage carrier around the room. We spent one terrifying ten minutes there after Aidan ran for the elevator and managed to get in and push the button. The door closed before Holly got to the elevator. Her heart in her mouth, she took the next elevator down and found Aidan standing sheepishly by the door on the main floor, perfectly safe. She brought him upstairs. Too relieved to punish him, she watched as he punished himself by tucking his little blond curly-haired head down and walked around for an hour or so, his face tucked between his shoulders like Pooh Bear after an embarrassing situation. It was so sweet, his embarrassment so evident, his face as beet red and as foolish as he had probably ever been in his short life.

That day I checked into my favorite room, admiring the big old fig tree by the entryway and thinking as I always did about how familiar Santa Monica feels, with childhood memories brought up by the damp sea air from the ocean. All of a sudden I heard Bill Clinton's name—he was also a guest in the hotel. I sent a note to his room saying I was there and would love to see him.

By then my fog had lifted. I was slowly coming out of the depression that followed Clark's suicide, little by little relearning how to live and how to use things like memory. I thought of Letty's words each time I glimpsed the governor's handsome face on every television show in the country. He was on the campaign trail by then, and the camera crews and news media were eating him up.

In a few minutes the bellman came back with a request that we join the governor in his suite. That day my nine-year-old niece Corrina, brother Denver's daughter, was with us. Holly and I went up, the blue-eyed, bright Corrina with us, Aidan in his stroller. We all spent an unforgettable half hour or so with this electric, energetic, forceful and bright man.

Bill Clinton's open, accessible personality makes you feel like family, like he's your best neighbor, your closest friend. He told me which of my songs he loved the best and which of the records, which was flattering. He spoke of things close to our hearts, comfortingly of the loss of my son, about which he seemed to have known. It was still only a few months since Clark's death. I experienced first hand the amazing gift of Bill Clinton's ability to remember and comment upon intimate, personal details in the lives of those he has met in the past, the words always appropriate, the sentiment always on target. The longtime habit of his five-by-eight note cards with names and facts and bits of personal information, started when he was in college working political campaigns, was working in his life in a natural, automatic way. It's more than just good politics, I believe, something you can't fake. You either have that touch of class and humanity or you don't, and Clinton has. It is charming and unusual.

He offered us a diet Coke, laughing easily at our nervous humor, dressed casually in a polo shirt with some animal crest on it and soft, light trousers. He introduced all his bodyguards and personal associates, who hovered about, but not too close. Then the governor and Holly, Corrina and I just talked. We sat on the couch and Clinton alternately paced in front of us like a big, wild cat and sat with his legs thrown over the arm of a chair, on cozy terms, as though we made it a habit to drop by for diet Cokes and conversation every afternoon at the Miramar with the president-to-be.

When we made our way down the elevator to my floor we were walking on a cloud. "He's amazing," my sister said and then added, "He's also the sexiest man I have ever met in my life."

"He's going to be president," I said with assurance. Nothing would have convinced me otherwise.

In May 1992, a few months after our meeting at the Miramar, my brother Michael called me. Our conversations are often taken up with the most recent of our reading journeys, but today the conversation was not about books.

"Do you know what you're going to wear?" he asked, opening the conversation.

"What do you mean?" I responded, totally in the dark.

"Clinton says that if he is elected, he will have a big parade, and he will have you sing." Mike laughed. He had read this in *Rolling Stone*. "I'm going to come to Washington, too, if you sing." I read the *Rolling Stone* interview, thrilled that a man who had a good chance to be president knew all my songs and would invite me to sing at his inauguration. It was, as my zany friends would say, "cool"! In the *Time* interview that followed the *Rolling Stone* piece a few weeks later, Clinton said he and Hillary had named their daughter Chelsea after my recording of Joni Mitchell's "Chelsea Morning." When asked what album he would save if his house were burning, the president-to-be named not only my 1973 collection, *Colors of the Day*, but all the songs on it. I was impressed.

This was a man who had stood on picket lines, as I had. He was roughly of my generation. He had refused to fight in the war that had shaped my conscience and the consciences of my peers. He liked people, he was easy to talk to and he was incredibly smart. He was, if not my friend, a man I had spent some time talking to and getting to know. It was remarkable to me that someone as smart as he was had survived the rigors of politics and was willing to take on the big race. I would support him. I would work for him. I knew he would win.

I had been involved in many political campaigns in my life. In the seventies I had worked on the campaign for McGovern, I had sung at the Women for McGovern rally at Madison Square Garden with Jane Fonda and Shirley MacLaine. I had worked for Mondale and Ferraro in 1984. I had voted for Jimmy Carter, and prayed against hope for Dukakis. So during the 1992 election I happily worked on the effort to get out the women's vote for Clinton. In Washington Square Park, the scene of so many protests during my early years in New York, women met in a candlelight march to tell their stories. It was a scene reminiscent of the long-lost but never-to-be forgotten sixties, that time when we all had hope that each rally, each election, would solve it all. In those early years, most of the rallies I went to were events in which we begged Congress to bring our troops back from Vietnam. Bill Clinton and I had stood on the same side of those fights. And when Clinton won the election in November 1992, I felt as many did a kind of exuberance that seemed to have been waiting thirty years to arrive.

During the four days of the inaugural festivities in Washington, I felt a comfortable familiarity everywhere I went, a sense of balance after two decades of standing on the outside of the White House and the Capitol, protesting, marching, singing. I now walked freely through the halls of Congress, where I was once arrested during a Redress of Congress action against the war in 1972 for which I spent a night in the Washington city jail with some well-known fellow protesters: Yale president Kingman Brewster, poets Kenneth Koch and Cynthia Macdonald, producer Joe Papp, playwright Tennessee Williams, author Francine du Plessix Gray. Radical and chic, as certain cynical writers would later call it, along with Leonard Bernstein's fund-raiser for the Black Panthers. It was simply that well-known people, too, were fed up with the war.

Louis and I attended every inaugural party and event we could squeeze in, hurrying from place to place. My brother Mike, true to his word, came with his wife Kathy to the inaguration, and we were glad to be together at the auspicious event.

Mike is a speech pathologist who has a large and successful practice in Wisconsin, in which he often works with stroke patients and Vietnam veterans with head wounds that affected their speech. He is enormously well respected in his field and writes, publishes, and often travels to speak at conventions on aphasia, which is his specialty. He also reads voraciously, as most of us Collins kids do. I was thrilled that my oldest brother and I were at this great event together, and thought often of our father during the festivities.

I sang "Amazing Grace" at the Presidential Gala the night before the inauguration, with the Philander Smith College Choir from Arkansas, a hundred incredibly beautiful young people singing behind me, after which the entire audience joined us, including the new president of the United States, William Jefferson Clinton.

From where I stood on the stage, I could look directly into the eyes of the president. I had already sung for him at a fund-raiser for the Democratic Leadership Council the previous December, so I knew how much the man loves music and how enthusiastically he responded. Clinton listens with his whole body, his whole being. A good saxophone player, all those all hours of practicing and a natural gift gave him the ability to appreciate the music of others. That night I looked right into his eyes, singing with a deep sense of joy and celebration. Clinton was a friend, not just a friend to me, but to the nation. For once, we were going to be represented by a man who would do the things we had all dreamed of and prayed for, who was also a musician! What luck!.

We all felt so exuberant, so full of hope on that night. There was a sense of destiny in the country. The president was going to take on difficult issues, make a difference, balance the budget, pay the United Nations bill, get education moving for children and help them become literate. He was going to continue to work on health care, liquor and cigarette lobbies, handguns, gay rights, support for AIDS research, international trade and a ban on land mines. We were going to fly.

Many times, over the next four years, we did fly.

The night of the gala, all of this was in front of us. The huge, drafty backstage at the arena was filled with stars. Annie Leibovitz, the great photographer, took portraits of each of us for a big spread in *Vanity Fair*. It was an astonishing collection of musicians: some of whom I knew: Michael Jackson was gracious and lovely. Barbara Hendricks and I spoke nervously to one other: "Just another concert?" I asked. "I don't think so!" she said. We laughed together, sharing the anxious moment, and I told her she looked too beautiful to be nervous. Warren Beatty, the man Annette Bening finally tamed, and Richard Dreyfus, a good, caring soul whom I am particularly fond of, were there. Barbra Streisand came to the backstage area wearing a coat over her face so that the press (and we?) couldn't see her without makeup. Fleetwood Mac was there in a refreshed nineties ensemble that sounded terrific and so was Dan Fogelberg, who had once recorded my song "Since You Asked."

The next day we made our way to the grounds of the Capitol for the inauguration itself. It seemed that everyone I knew was in Washington for the big event: friends from New York, fellow performers, congressmen and -women—even Bella in her hat!—all in high spirits. Graham Nash and I went through the security check outside the Capitol. He took my elbow, speaking in a soothing voice. "This must be very strange for you," he said, "the tragedy of your son's death coming so close to this triumph for the country and for you personally." I nodded, tucking my chin deeper into my heavy black cashmere coat to keep out the cold air that followed us. Graham always was a sensitive man and on that day he was more than right. It was very strange, the combination of fates, but I knew that someone, something other than me, was in charge. There was celebration too in my life, the irony of it all.

Maya Angelou's poem and Marilyn Horne's voice set the stage for the moment when the president took the oath of office. I had never experienced personally the extraordinary sight of the old regime passing peacefully into history as the new comes into power: President Bush, leaving in his helicopter, having turned over the keys to the White House and the kingdom. And what a new kingdom! Our new president dancing through the night at every ball, playing the sax at the Arkansas ball, dancing with the First Lady in her amethyst, jeweled dress.

On the wall of my office are letters from Clinton when he was still governor of Arkansas, thanking me for participating in the Women Light the Way campaign and the fund-raiser for the Democratic Leadership Council. There are letters after he became president, thanking me for participating in the inaugural, both the gala and the ball.

We began a correspondence of notes, sometimes even phone calls. One night, when Louis and I were at the lake, the phone rang and the voice on the line said the president of the United States was calling. "*Who* is calling?" I said. "The president," she said. I nearly fainted.

I had written the president a note telling him his first one hundred days were going well. He was calling to thank me. We chatted for a while. I remember it was raining, and Louis smiled at me as he lit the fire in our fireplace. Then I called my mother.

Oh how we wanted him to be perfect! I had liked most things Clinton did, with the exception of his backing down on the gay rights issue in the military in those first few weeks. I found that disappointing even though editorials and friends said he had been trapped into making an untimely and, I felt, unfortunate decision. It was the beginning of realizing the man was human, not perfect.

A few weeks later I was back in the Capitol to sing at an event for the women in Congress, many of whom were my friends, heroines and mentors. I worked on Patricia Schroeder's first campaign for Congress in 1971 in Denver and did fund-raising for a number of other women candidates, including Diane Feinstein, Barbara Boxer and Patty Murray. These are some of the women who shake up the men in the government. There are so few, and they make such an enormous difference.

It was another of those sunny, shining afternoons in Washington and I got settled in my suite and ordered tea. I watched the people wandering down the street in front of the White House and running, walking and sitting on the benches in Jefferson Park, the verdant tree-filled park of gardens and curving paths. I was about to take a nap so that I would be fresh to perform when Betty Currie, secretary to the president, conveyed an invitation from the president. Unfortunately he would be unable to hear me sing, but after my performance, would I and my husband like to come to the White House for dinner? I explained Louis was in New York, and Betty suggested I come anyway. The president would wait dinner till I arrived. Would I like, also, to stay the night in the Lincoln Bedroom? Amazing!

I put down the telephone and gasped. I called Louis.

He said he was sorry he couldn't be with me. We weren't married. Would that be a problem?

The concert went well and when it was finished I was driven by a chauffeured limousine to the White House with my suitcases and the coffeemaker I always travel with. I was greeted at the visitor's door to the White House by the housekeeping staff and Chelsea's nanny, Helen Dickey, and the woman who took Bill Clinton to his first Judy Collins concert, Malinda Bates. Clinton had asked them to greet me. He was in meetings, and the First Lady, I was told, was still in Little Rock. Her father had taken a turn for the worse and she would not be coming back to Washington that night. I was disappointed because I was eager to spend social time with the First Lady as well as the president.

The White House is dazzling, filled with beauty. In the entrance to the private quarters there is a magnificent mural on which soldiers from the Revolution stand at the ready, uniforms sparkling, horses prancing, troops lining the hills. Each room is furnished with paintings, antiques, glass, and marble. Statues greet you at every turn. Each corner is a delight to the eye, an education, resonating with the stories of the people who have come through this house with their different tastes, the gifts bestowed on them by other nations and grateful citizens of the United States. Hillary had begun to show American sculpture in the garden near the visitor's entrance and each piece was a tribute to American artistry. In the main entrance are works by Remington, paintings by the Hudson River Valley painters, others by Mary Cassatt. In the powder room downstairs, portraits of Eleanor Roosevelt, Rosalyn Carter, Barbara Bush and all the presidents' wives are gloriously rendered in oil. Paneling and poetry, bronze and pots of fresh flowers, everywhere is history, everywhere beauty.

I was taken to the private quarters of the first family and shown to the Lincoln Bedroom.

In actuality, Lincoln did not sleep in the Lincoln Bedroom. But he signed the Emancipation Proclamation in this historic room. Helen and Malinda explained where everything was and how I could order coffee or anything I might need. They told me the president had ordered dinner for the two of us and that he would join me in the family dining room.

I said I had to call my mother and Louis.

Next to the antique bed on a small table were White House stationery, a pen, a silver tray for cards, and a telephone. When I got Mom on the phone, I told her I had finally made it to the White House. She told me she was proud of me, and that my father would have been proud, too.

And then I looked around: Lincoln's desk sits near a window overlooking the Washington Monument, as do all the rooms on that side of the White House. I looked out at the long park that cradles the White House, magnificent, filled with old, gnarled trees and lawns somehow still green in the March cold. It was dark by now, but looking out the window I could see the perpetual light that burns at the memorial. I could envision, to the right and down the Mall, the steps leading up to the seated bronze figure of the man who had signed the document above the desk at which I was standing. I could also imagine, to the right and left of the Lincoln Memorial, the Vietnam Wall, and opposite that, the site where the new Korean War Veteran's Monument, being designed by my husband, would stand in a few years' time. The Lincoln Bedroom, situated at the end of the family quarters and used to accommodate guests of two centuries of presidents, overlooks remembered history, past and present. On that Mall I had marched against our dark war, the war no one had wanted to commemorate or remember. In the dark I imagined I could see the ghosts of the dead from that terrible war, so many who had not come home.

I unpacked my bags and set up my coffee machine in the bathroom. Later that night, preparing my morning coffee, hurrying to get to sleep, grinding beans and drawing water from the tap, I tipped the whole machine over and had to clean coffee off the pristine white tiles. I did a good job, thinking to myself this is how the shanty Irish come to Washington, on their knees. At least I was inside!

A black-suited gentleman valet came to take me to dinner with the president—my second dinner with a president, counting my dinner concert for President Kennedy. I was older now, and maybe wiser.

The chief of state greeted me warmly in the living room, giving me a hug and asking how my concert had gone and apologizing for not having been able to come. He was dressed comfortably in a suit and looked tired as we walked into the dining room together. He apologized again for Hillary's absence and told me her father was, at this point, probably not going to make it. We sat down at two settings and I looked around the blue walls of the dining room at the circular painting, a beautifully rendered landscape. I saw little of anything. The president's energy was returning at the prospect of food and we chatted over salad. He asked me what I thought about Mario Cuomo and would he be a good choice for the Supreme Court and would he accept the nomination?

Yes, I said, Cuomo would be great, and I hoped he would accept, but I doubted if he would, having heard many rumors to that effect.

We talked about the gala, Clinton said he had loved my singing, and I told him again how grateful I had been to be a part of what I considered an historic moment. When we had met in Santa Monica, Clinton had extended his condolences to me about Clark, and now we talked again about my loss. He asked how I was doing, and how Louis was doing. I was again made aware of Clinton's sensitivity about people, who they are, who they love, and how they feel. We talked about suicide and alcoholism. He said he knew something about that, since his father had been an alcoholic and his brother as well.

I was impressed with a sense of being with a real human being. There is something dazzling about a man who is brilliant and also accessible, human and vulnerable. This quality is part of Clinton's great charm. I have met many men who are only brilliant or only vulnerable. My husband is both these things, which is why I married him. But it is rare. And Clinton is funny, with a good sense of humor.

Once Louis and I went to a reception at the Waldorf Astoria for the United Nations, after Louis had undergone his appendix surgery. When we reached the line to shake the president's hand, he looked right into Louis's blue eyes (what a sight, four beautiful blue eyes!) and said, "How are you feeling? I know you just had a serious operation." Clinton knows how to be with you where you live. He can do this in an instant, with a single glance. He looks you straight in the eye and you feel appreciated when you are with him precisely because he is interested in what you are saying. Many men who think they have power speak above, around, through and beyond us mortals. Clinton is real and smart and funny and likable. In a man of such power, that is an amazing trait. He is too impressive to need to impress you.

I didn't much like dinner, which was beef, I think, with some kind of heavy French sauce. I thought to myself—but of course didn't say—that they would soon switch to a menu with less butter and lighter sauces. As though reading my mind, the president told me he and Chelsea and Hillary often would come in to cook their own meals, simple things like omelets and salads, sending everyone away, so that they could be by themselves. He also said they were feeling overwhelmed by the constant pressure and company of the office. We had decaf and I refused dessert. He didn't, though, and we continued to talk as he lived up to his reputation of loving sweets and carbohydrates. I watched with envy!

Then, the president of the United States took me on a tour, showing me the huge oak desk in the room above the Oval Office with the balcony overlooking the Washington Memorial: the president's personal war room, in which Roosevelt's cabinet met to vote on going to war with Japan and Germany, the Cabinet members tucking their notes into the little drawers around the edge of the table; the table on which were written many of the letters in the great exchange of correspondence between Churchill and Roosevelt, Churchill begging Roosevelt for tanks and guns.

When the president told me he had never had so much closet room, I remembered that the Clintons had never owned a home of their own. He showed me the pair of blue suede shoes that the traditional maker of presidential shoes had crafted for him. He was as tickled with those shoes as a twelve-year-old! I was struck with how much like all of our homes this was, with pictures of friends, the three Clintons together on a beach somewhere with wind- and sunburned faces. Pictures with his mother, Virginia, with Hillary's parents; photographs of Chelsea, pictures of Socks. The guy was a regular person!

The president said that the Arkansas crowd would be arriving soon and that we would have more coffee and drinks with them.

Diane Blair, the historian, and Kaki Hockersmith, the interior designer helping Hillary redecorate the White House, were the first to arrive. While the president was off to more meetings (although it was now about ten-thirty, I believe), we talked and talked, of the work to be done, of the excitement in Washington and the country about the new administration, and of the future.

The living room of the family quarters soon began to fill up with men—Vince Foster was hard to miss, tall and good-looking, with his reassuring manner. The president grabbed my hand and brought me over to Foster, introducing him to me as his oldest and best friend. Bernie Nussbaum, whom I had met briefly before, nursed a drink, smiling, and Webster Hubbell, as well as a number of others, wandered comfortably, talking among themselves, collaring the president and speaking confidentially. George Stephanopoulos arrived and was introduced to me again. These were obviously people who both knew and liked each other and felt at ease.

At some point the president, shyly, looking around at the gathered crowd, suggested that I might, if they asked nicely, sing a song. They all said, "Oh please, would you?" and of course, I did, sitting down nervously at the piano. I sang "My Father," and I remembered the words, thank God, and my fingers didn't slip off the keys, and I got through the song. I found myself very teary, thinking of my father, and of being here, and of how much he had done to make this moment in my life possible, possibly inevitable. There was much clapping, from the president and everyone, and I felt very appreciated.

Sometime later that night Kaki and the president and I went downstairs to the Oval Office to look at the new rug. Being in the White House in the middle of the night with the president, down on my knees looking at the brilliantly colored circular rug with the bright eagle that had just been put down that night, was something out of a fairy tale. I was awed by the room—

and started to find myself there. As we rode the elevator back upstairs, Kaki and the president and I remembered that the president runs every day of his life when he can.

"I'd love to join you for your run in the morning," I said.

"Sure," he replied, peeling off for the far end of the family quarters and bed. "About six-thirty. I'll pick you up."

I gulped. It was late. Six-thirty would arrive all too soon. I waved good night and embraced Kaki and Diane, who were both overnight guests as well. I shut the door to my bedroom, where I prowled about, looking at each piece of furniture and examining the fading writing on the Emancipation Proclamation very closely and looking out the window at the light shining in the Washington Monument, standing sentry out there in the dark. Alone, in the historic room, I felt privileged and just a little giddy, like a schoolgirl.

But I slept well, never once hearing the ghost of Lincoln walking, as some who sleep in Lincoln's room say they do. I awoke at six and hurried to get ready, throwing on the jogging outfit I usually run in, a pair of white pants and a white jacket over a black leotard. I rang for coffee, having abandoned my coffee-making attempts—the bathroom was now pristine and I wanted to leave it that way! I drank the rich brew quickly—who knew the White House could make such good coffee—and the president knocked on my door. I was a bit shocked to see the chief executive in his running shorts and jacket. I asked if he had heard how Hillary's father was feeling and he said there was not good news and that he would probably leave for Little Rock sometime that afternoon.

Then we were off, down the elevator from the family's quarters. I heard the security guard say into his intercom, as we stepped into the elevator, "The Eagle is moving." Honest to God.

A security guard handed the president a thermos of coffee and we stepped into the limo that was to drive us to the top of the running course set out for the president. We each sipped coffee from cups bearing the presidential seal and continued to talk comfortably—about what, I have no idea. I was still dazed by the whole idea of being there. We got out of the car and started to jog.

I had seen the president jog all during his campaign and so had the rest of the world. He had been photographed on the morning news running with people all over the country. He had run in Central Park in New York, exciting the imagination of all of us who run for fun and for competition. I knew he liked company on his runs, and would often see a half dozen Secret Service men with him on the morning news, as well as friends who might or might not have high profiles.

But I was expecting an anonymous and silent jog. Instead, we chatted all through it, which was not on my breathing plan. There we were, it was very early in the morning, barely a soul out and about in the parks and streets of Washington. It was hard talking while running, but I run nearly every day and have worked out many times a week for years, so I was able to keep up as we ran past the reflecting pools and I talked about Louis's wall. More and more, though, he talked! And I, by now, tried to keep up.

We talked about the struggle to end the war in Vietnam and our marches against that war. He seemed to have Lincoln on his mind that morning and spoke about the second inaugural address of Lincoln, which he said was his favorite. A few veterans in khaki and a couple of wide-eyed tourists parted to let us by, smiling at the sight of their new president. One hollered, "Good morning, Bill!" We ran directly to the Lincoln Monument and up the stairs. By now I was ready to collapse, panting. He was fine. He runs about a seven minute mile. I don't. At the top of the long flight of steps we stood together in front of the massive sculpture of Lincoln, seated, looking out across the city, across the years, witness to our changed world. We paused, silent, in front of the great man's statue. My breath slowed down and my heart stopped beating so hard and I said a silent prayer to the running Gods. We turned right and stopped in front of the panels of Lincoln's second inaugural address. Standing next to the president of the United States, Secret Service men to our right and left, I read the text on the wall, as do so many visitors to the monument.

> With malice toward none; with charity for all; with firmness in the right, as God gives us to see the right, let us strive on to finish the work we are in; to bind up the nation's wounds; to

care for him who shall have borne the battle, and for his widow, and his orphan—to do all which may achieve and cherish a just, and a lasting peace, among ourselves, and with all nations.

The Secret Service, a small group of men dressed in running clothes with wires in their ears, clustered about the president. I had caught my breath when we started back down the stairs of the Lincoln Monument, and the Mall in front of us seemed to have suddenly filled with people. As we headed down the other side of the Mall, coming out from the stand of trees at the end of the pool, there were a half dozen photographers. They snapped, and the picture of me running with the president made the papers. At least I was still on my feet!

I stopped then, feeling my lungs were really giving out. The air, no matter the crisp morning, was full of city diesel fuel, and I was having trouble. The president could have gone ten more miles easily. He was barely panting and was sporting about it, saying I had done a good run. He said he would catch up with me back at the White House, that the limousine would take me. He ran on for a few more miles and I settled into the limo, thanking God for small miracles.

Back at the White House, I showered and got dressed, and then had breakfast, a bran muffin delivered to my room. I went downstairs to thank the president. He had spoken to Hillary to tell her that I had sung the night before. I promised to come back to sing especially for the first lady.

The family quarters were quiet when I went back to pack my bags, except for the sound of a vacuum in a nearby room. I sat down at the piano in the living room and began practicing, a few scales and an exercise and then "The Blizzard." It always used to be my dream to give all my friends pianos, so that when I visit them I could play them a song. A housekeeper, dressed in a soft gray skirt and white blouse, her hair pinned up on her head, began vacuuming the lush gray-blue rug in the room next to the one in which I was playing. When she became aware of the music, she turned off the switch and came into the living room and stood listening. Some of the other people who work in the family quarters paused, came nearer, and listened. A man cleaning the brass around the fireplaces, a guard who was standing near the elevator, a woman who was watering the plants, stopped what they were doing and listened.

I played on. There seemed to be a special grace about that moment, with the noise of the vacuum cleaner stilled and the audience of six or seven men and women who have worked in the service of this president and other presidents listening quietly. Outside these walls, all around us, Washington teemed, I was sure, that morning as every morning, with opposing opinions, controversies, each side coming up to the podium with a passionate viewpoint. Soon the tour groups would be starting through the White House rooms downstairs, being told the stories of the paintings, the tapestries, the sculptures, the presidential seal. In the gardens new flowers were being planted. In front of the Capitol a group of protesters, their banners high, had once called for a nuclear freeze. I trusted there would be other groups outside, with new banners and new chants, a huge group petitioning Clinton to sign a worldwide ban on antipersonnel land mines, people of all colors marching for the dreams of a better world.

Inside the quiet living room I continued to play the fine Steinway that Truman had probably played, a piano that had probably accompanied President Clinton as he played the saxophone to relax.

When I finished singing "The Blizzard," I stood up and the spell was broken. I had had an experience I would never forget.

The housekeeper, a bright smile on her face, gently put her hand on my arm.

"We needed your music this morning, Miss," she said. "It gives us a lift."

Another Thanksgiving without Clark. I awake with his presence in my consciousness. All night I have been dreaming of him. The tears come frequently through the day. It is ten months since my boy's death, and his face looks at me from the hallway, from my dressing table, from the glass tables in the entryway. He is eight; he is twenty; he is thirty, married; he is thirty-three. Forever.

Thanksgiving, and I am devastated, and at the same time grateful. How can these two emotions be in the same heart? Saint Augustine says miracles are not contrary to nature but only contrary to what we know about nature. It is a miracle that I am breathing, walking. I make the traditional meal, a twenty-pound turkey, thinking of Pilgrims, of new shores, of this new shore of grief and my travail here.

Across the continent, the phone calls fly, brother to brother, mother to daughter, sister to sister, granddaughter to grandmother, father, cousin, uncle, son. Clark's absence echoes like a vast and windy plain, a terrible hole that vibrates with pain. We talk of his beauty, and ask again and again, Why? There is no answer. We share a festive meal and I search for comfort.

I pray for the courage to meet this landscape of pain like a courageous pilgrim. I pray for miracles. I pray for peace. I pray for release.

14

Singing Lessons

Clark was thirty-three when he died, the magic age, the age of mystery. Of all the lessons I have learned in my life, some of them bitterly hard, my son's death was the hardest.

When Clark was five and I was twenty-five, I met Max Margulis and started my singing lessons. It was a time of hope and bright visions, when I was sure that nothing stood in our way: that the weather of the soul would always be bright.

In 1964 I moved from Greenwich Village to a new apartment on the Upper West Side, so that I would have more room for Clark and me. For months I had been asking people about singing teachers in New York. Although I had been singing since I was a child, in operas and choirs, choruses and solo performances, I had never seriously studied singing. I was losing my voice often when I sang, not knowing how to pace myself through the growing number of concerts and recordings I was doing.

As I asked around for teachers, many people suggested Max Margulis: Harry Belafonte's accompanist Ray Boguslav; Mordie and Irma Bauman, who ran the Indian Hill music camp in Lenox, Massachusetts. These people, who knew good music and all the teachers at Julliard, Mannes College of Music, NYU and other institutions in the city, told me that Max was the one with whom I should study. They emphasized his knowledge of the voice, and said he knew more about singing than all the others put together, and that he would not take away from what I had, but only add to it. I was convinced and wrote Max's number down a number of times, but had never called him.

A few days after moving into my new apartment, I called Max, introduced myself and asked if I could come to see him. He said yes and I asked for his address.

In a coincidence even the most cynical might suspect of having been preordained, it turned out that the man who would be my singing teacher for the next thirty-two years lived next door to my new apartment.

I walked out my new front door, turned right, walked about eight steps, and there Max stood in the doorway, his angular face tilted, his bright eyes looking at me through his glasses, inquisitive as a bird.

"Yes?" he greeted me as he invited me in. I repeated that he had been recommended to me as the finest teacher of voice in New York. His eyebrows rose, his eyes twinkled.

He led me to the piano and asked me to sing a few notes. As I sang, he hesitated, as if he had been caught by something he heard but was not convinced of what he thought. Then this gentle man with small hands and thick glasses said he wasn't sure he wanted to take on any students right then. I think I begged him, actually. I know I would have gotten down on my knees if that was what it would have taken. I was desperate. I was about to go on tour and wouldn't have my first lesson until I returned. But I knew I had to get into his doorway, into his apartment next to mine, into his life. Finally, he agreed to take me on.

When Max found me I was ready to be molded. My voice was deep and natural but breaking and cracking, unable to find its way out of the rough material of the lower register through to higher, clearer realms on its own. In thirty-two years, Max carved, in lesson after lesson, for hour after hour, for week after week, with repetition and care, consistency and wisdom, an instrument that will move easily through three octaves, has a shimmer in its overtones, and usually does what I want it to when I want it to. My voice has kept its resilience, as Max promised it would do. Max always said you don't need to be psychoanalyzed, that if you work with the voice, you can change and form your whole being to the best that you are. Although I continued to see therapists as well, my lessons with Max probably saved me a lot more than money. In the end, they probably saved my life.

Max knew the human voice, the phrasing of the English language, intimately. My studies with Max arched through the years, with times of intensity and times of absence, but always in my mind was the technique Max taught, of clarity, simplicity, directness of phrasing, the long, unbroken line of the voice, an almost unreachable ideal at first, and the thing toward which he struggled, and in the end toward which we both struggled.

There is something of Pygmalion and Galatea in the journey of a teacher and a student. As we traveled together over many miles and many years, Max was determined to remake a part of me, and I was always resisting, relenting, opening up, and shutting down. An intimacy of this kind, like a love affair, cannot be a steady going up or going forward. There are lapses, pauses, just as there in are in music itself. Mozart said that rests can be the most important part of a piece of music. Max used to compare the process to reaching a certain plateau, staying there for a while for comfort, even holding on rather than letting go, then shifting to climb to a new plateau, sometimes reluctantly moving to another level.

❧❧

Max was born in Milwaukee on September 1, 1907. His father was a singer with the Chicago Opera. The family moved to New York when Max was five. He studied the violin and loved literature and writing. He graduated from De Witt Clinton High School in midtown, which is now John Jay College of Criminal Justice, a white and rose-colored building that has been newly restored. Today, its Art Deco architecture, with its curlicues and rose angels and faces of distinguished men in stone, softens the dirty, noisy sounds of traffic on Tenth Avenue across from the elegant new entrance to Roosevelt Hospital, where I would last see my beloved teacher.

After De Witt Clinton, Max went to City College, and then continued studying the violin and played, taking many trips to Germany in the twenties on which he played in the ship orchestra. He used to tell me stories about the musicians on these trips, the card playing and the joking. During these years he also went to work for Bell labs, where they were doing research projects on the voice. Max was often given paintings and sculptures by his friends Arshile Gorky, Willem de Kooning and Joseph Solman. Max met de Kooning in Chelsea soon after the artist had arrived as a stowaway. Max owned an overcoat and de Kooning didn't, so the two men shared the garment, one going out in the overcoat while the other stayed indoors, thus making it through the cold months. De Kooning used to call Max his brother. After his marriage, Max consulted with de Kooning before selling the portrait called *Max*, painted by de Kooning. With the profits from the sale, Max bought a Gagliano violin. He was never forced to teach everyone who came along and chose his students carefully.

Helen, Max's beautiful and young-looking wife, is like a thin, lovely waterbird. He met Helen, who was from Texas, on one of her New York visits and married her. When I first met Helen, she wore her long black hair plaited, in a bun on top of her head. She played the cello and the piano beautifully, sometimes accompanying me when I sang a song. She tended and cooked for Max, caring for this diminutive genius.

Max wrote for many publications, including the *New Masses* and the *Massachusetts Review*.

In 1939, the year I was born, Max, along with Alfred Lion and Emanuel Eisenberg, started Blue Note Records, a company which recorded, in its beginnings, "Basic Negro New Orleans Music." Max worked with Blue Note for eight years, often writing record notes for the albums, in part because his partner, Alfred Lion, spoke no English. When the company began to move away from the original idea of the blues, Max resigned his interest and his partnership and left the company.

Max's name has been subsequently irradicated from Blue Note's history, for unknown reasons. Max always refused to defend his history with Blue Note, feeling that time would be his testimony. A very detailed history of the company, compiled by Michael Cuscuna and Michel Ruppli, in 1988, called *The Blue Note Label: A Discography*, does not mention Max's name as a founder. Max's apartment was filled with photographs of black jazz musicians at sessions, including one wonderful photo of Max with Pete Johnson, after his cutting of "Kansas City Farewell"; in the photo are also

Abe Bolar, on bass; Alfred Lion, his partner at Blue Note; and Ulysses Livingston, on guitar.

Helen was always shocked at the way in which Max was treated by his old partners. She started sleuthing and discovered the original documents from the founding of the company in the New York Office of Records:

Bus Cert. 3918
1939
Certificate of
Max Margulis
Alfred Lion
Emanuel Eisenberg
Conducting Business Under the Name of
  Blue Note Records
  235 7th Avenue
Filed by Davidson & Mann
  122 East 42nd Street
Fee paid, $110.
3/25/39
Filed Mar 25th, '39
New York County Clerk's Office

Having lived with the story of Blue Note for all these years, and having mentioned Max's name to many people who would know about Blue Note, including Bruce Lundvall (who now runs Blue Note for Columbia Records), only to be told they never heard of him, I'd like to set the record right: Max was one of the trio who started Blue Note. I can only now surmise it was either jealousy or spite that stole Max's involvement with Blue Note away from him. Max never received his due. Now, at least, he will be honored as the founder of one of the truly great and important record labels in the history of recordings.

I sent the information with Max's history to Blue Note Records and received a letter in return from Bruce Lundvall agreeing only that Max was a silent partner in Blue Note Records. Helen said that this was absurd, since Max was *actively* involved for at least eight years: writing liner notes, attending recording sessions, and helping to choose the music and musicians that became the foundation for the renowned label.

May I suggest in the name of truth and history that Dan Morgenstern—jazz historian at Rutgers—Michael Cuscuna, and Michel Ruppli update their discography of Blue Note Records in order to honor Max's memory and contribution to the label's history. One hopes that, knowing the facts, all who are concerned about Blue Note Records will recognize Max and reinstate him in their history, retrieving him from his mysteriously imposed oblivion.

∾꧁꧂∽

Max taught voice to many great performers. He taught Laurence Olivier how to sing for *The Entertainer.* He taught Sigourney Weaver, who used to say people would laugh when she mentioned she studied singing with Judy Collins's teacher. She may not be a great singer, but she speaks like an angel even in the *Alien* movies. I introduced Stacy Keach and Harris Yulin to Max, and Susan Crile and her brother, George, a producer and writer. Max also taught Louis, my life partner, spending hours with him reading James Joyce and T. S. Eliot. Today my husband is a fine public speaker, engaging, with a lilting voice that has plenty of range and flexibility. After his long studies with Max, I never miss a word of what Louis says, and Louis has a lot to say! He says Max had an ulterior motive in teaching him. He wanted someone close to me to know what it was that I was learning, so that Louis, when Max was no longer around, could point out whether my singing was crystal clear or muddy. Louis has learned the lesson well.

Even at the beginning of our lessons, Max said he wanted to see me every day. I was filled with mistrust. In order to get where Max wanted me to, I would have to trust completey. After two years I knew that there would be no finding anyone else who could do what he was doing. I listened to early Pavarotti records, where his silk voice cuts through the air like a magic flute, with brilliance that took my breath away. Always strive for the top, they say.

Max had many old LPs in his vast collection. There was Adelina Patti, who died in 1919. In 1904 she recorded one of the first records ever made; Gigli, the great Italian singer; and Jenny Lind, who Max said had a quality something like mine, were singers to whom we listened.

Max taught Italian classical singers, none of whose names I recognized, but who were very famous on the European concert circuit. They would arrive from Rome and stay for two weeks at a time to study with him every day. He would throw them up to me, trying to get me to study more faithfully. We listened to singers together, relishing their triumphs, worrying about their problems. Once we studied Pavarotti's jaw and listened to the end of his notes, noticing a troubling tremor and wobble. We were concerned, and so was Pavarotti apparently. Soon after this he spent a number of months away from the opera and concert circuits, studying intensely with his own teacher in Italy. When he returned, the voice, once again, was healthy and steady. Max and I were relieved.

Max and I saw each other at least a few times a month. Sometimes we didn't sing at all, but just talked, about food, about clothes, about books. He told me how he, Gorky, and de Kooning received installments of *Remembrance of Things Past* as it was being published in France in the twenties, and read them in the original French, aloud, to one another. Max told me he had pointed out to de Kooning the artist's difficulties with drawing, which resulted in many wonderful drawings, sketches, oil paintings, and portraits of Max in which his old friend attempted to prove him wrong. Helen told me that once, in 1983 at the Whitney Museum, gazing at the portrait called *Max* that he had sold many years before to buy his violin, Max muttered, "The hands still aren't right." De Kooning's wife, Elaine, also did a beautiful portrait of Max in the eighties when Helen and Max visited the couple. The years were slipping by, and the two men had shared the memories of their glorious youth together, in New York, in the ferment and yeast of a new time of art and politics. "My brother," de Kooning said when Max entered his door again.

Max also taught me more about literature, an education begun with my father and the fine teachers I had in high school in Denver. Max introduced me to *Les Liaisons Dangereuses* in the late sixties, long before the play or the movie. He suggested I read *Fantomas,* an intriguing French novel about a mysterious, ghostly and magical character at the time of the French Revolution. He shared with me the story of Yvette Guilbert, the French chanteuse whose long, black-glove-clad arms and leonine body were the model for posters by Toulouse-Lautrec at the turn of the century in Paris. Guilbert was a very successful singer of popular songs who turned her back on her popular successes to become a scholar, studying French folk songs and writing novels and memoirs. Max gave me a copy of her memoir in French. We talked of writers while we listened to music and read poetry—John McCormack, T. S. Eliot, Shaw's *Man and Superman.* The voices of Dame Judith Anderson, Laurence Olivier, Dylan Thomas and Enrico Caruso floated into the room and out the window, winter and summer. Max said that all of this was pertinent to good singing. Good singing, good art, and good writing are intertwined, he said. To sing well meant to speak well, and vice versa.

Max was endearing, but he could also be infuriating. I spent much of our time together thrashing under his perfectionist drive to go over every line in every song I was planning to sing, but the outcome was always to make the singing better. Once I took him to California to be with me while I was making *Who Knows Where the Time Goes.* We spent intense time on the songs, the phrasings, the smoothness of the lines. Other times in my studies with him I would go off and do something on my own for a few weeks. When I returned he would usually pout and we would have what amounted to a fight. He would accuse me, once again, of unfaithfulness, as though we were lovers. My faithfulness was always in question over the years, yet, in truth, I was faithful. I always knew he was right.

My lessons with Max were sometimes like moving through thick water, and getting to his apartment might seem a lifetime journey in an afternoon. Occasionally, especially after I moved uptown, I would be late for a lesson, I who am usually on time for everything. In the blue-rugged apartment with walls covered with Gorky and De Kooning, I would look beyond the reflective light of Max's glasses as he sat at the piano, through the light that filtered through his pink, thin ears, out across the roofs of the buildings to the

playground on the block in the next street. There were often children playing and their laughter would drift up on spring days through the open windows.

In 1970, Helen got a parakeet whom she named Papageno after the
character in *The Magic Flute*. Papageno would sing and chatter and talk when
I sang, and we would laugh when Papageno would suddenly burst out with
"To be or not to be," and "Cute thing" and fly onto the water faucet when
Helen filled the kettle for my tea. She would pour my tea, put it out on a tray
with a little chunk of sweet ginger or a menthol drop and some bread or fruit,
offering me lunch, which I usually refused. I would sip tea as Max and I
talked and gossiped and went through lyrics and as he would tell me, always,
that I should have started earlier on that song or that lyric or that concert or
that record. Max, if all were known, really wanted you to have started studying before you were born, and gone on ahead before meeting him! It was a
charming and maddening trait.

I would stand in the harp of the piano, Max would be seated at the
piano, his face tipped my way, his chin turned a bit. He would look intently
at me through the sparkle of his glasses.

"Ah," he would sing, his voice starting low and rising to a high pitch,
then descending, stretching the vowel, in one long sweep up and down the
scale.

"Ah," I would repeat, clearing the hurdle of three octaves safely on one
long, extended vowel. This was not a scale, as others might teach—do, re, me,
fa, and so on, although there were times when we did scales as well. This was
Max's own brand of learning what he called clarity. After studying with him
for many years, I thought I should know how to clear this hurdle.

"No", he would say. "There is fuzz in the voice. The vowel is not clear.
The bell quality is missing. Think only of the vowel."

"Ah," I would sing again, bringing the bell quality finer, rising to the
pitch and down again, meeting the challenge. This time I would hear the difference. The note would be clean as a bird sound, and would, if necessary,
travel all the way to the other side of the block and back.

"It's not volume, you can't shout to be heard at the back of the hall, at the end of the street. It's clarity, clarity, and the pitch rising that brings the sound to the level you would like it. Shouting only makes you hoarse."

I would leave a lesson with a clear, bell sound throughout the three octaves of my voice.

I would think of the old singers, think of my father when he warmed up at home, with no microphone; I would think of singers clear as lovely bells, singing in beautiful halls, each phrase like crystal, hanging in the darkened audience, piercing the heart. Max sometimes spoke critically of contemporary singers, both opera and popular singers.

"They have fallen into poor habits because they listen to each other, and learn each other's bad habits." He would shake his head and sip his tea. "The voices wobble, the vowels all sound the same. "Oh tho so o tho lo," when it should be "Oh the song of the lark," each vowel clear, and singing the phrase, always singing the phrase. "In the early days it was easy to sing more beautifully," he said, "because everyone around you was crystal clear, they had to be heard in those vast and fine halls. If they had shouted, they would have lost their voices— and their audiences." He would shake his head. "Nowadays, nobody cares."

Max's face would go sad, the lines around the mouth matching the lines around his eyes, only upside down. Most of the contemporary singers, Max said, could not sing at all, with all their marketing, all their fame. Pavarotti, yes. Carreras, yes. Caballé—"Now *there* is a singer!" Pop singers drew mostly frowns. But Max praised singers with clarity and simplicity in their phrasing, singers like Johnny Cash, Julie Andrews, Frank Sinatra and Jacques Brel.

"You see," he would say, naming a favorite, "you understand the lyrics, you know the phrases, so you hear the words. The beauty of the voice comes out when you can hear the words, the phrases!" Few passed muster. I prayed to convince him I had learned, and studied to be understood.

We read aloud quite often. Max would pull out a volume of *A Portrait of the Artist as a Young Man,* and I would read a passage aloud to him.

"Oh the wild rose blossoms on the little green place."

"That was very nice, very good," he would nod in approval at my lilting phrase. "Now, sing it, make a melody. The melody should convey the lovely phrase you just sang." I would sing, "Oh the wild rose blossoms," and sometimes I would get through the entire phrase, and we would go on, reading the great Joyce. Max would chuckle.

"Joyce was quite a singer, you know, quite a singer!" he once told me. He described a singing contest in Dublin in which Joyce competed against John McCormack.

"Joyce wore thick glasses—like bottle tops, they were," he said, "and the first part of the contest in Dublin was singing something he knew by heart, and Joyce won that part hands down!" Max clapped his hands in delight, and looked at me as though he could see Dublin and the lovely hall where the singing contest took place.

"And the second part of the contest was sight-singing." Here, Max looked at me as though I might explain the insanity of having a contest that included sight-reading. I myself had always been a terrible sight-reader in music, so I felt I knew what he meant.

"But Joyce refused, said it was not possible to give a truly artistic reading of a song if you had to read it, that it must be sung from memory!" Max nodded enthusiastically as though this put the finishing touch on any attempt to sing from music. I always assumed Joyce's refusal was based on the fact that he wore heavy glasses and couldn't read the music very well. But maybe not.

When I first started going to Max I was hoarse, with a low and rumbling sound in my voice, and a painful break between the lower and upper register. I stumbled over a B going to a C above middle C as though I had run into a large piece of furniture. The hole was so big I practically fell into it. I despaired of ever being smooth as silk, nearly wept over the pain of it.

Max smiled. He was sure of me, even though I wasn't.

"You take the clarity from the very top and you move it down to the lower reaches of your voice." From top to bottom, without a break. I would sing the line, on *oh,* on *ah,* on *oo,* on *e.* Crack and fall, run into the wall, but at last I began, as he had promised, to get from one end of the phrase to the other, and to sing a line that was smooth as silk, no break in the register from lower to middle, from middle to top. We worked on the songs, going over and over the phrases.

"Isn't it rich?" I would sing, from "Send in the Clowns."

"Isn't it *rich?*" he would repeat, clearer than I. And so on, each line of each song. We studied the lyrics, underlining the way the phrase could go.

"You must sing to the end of the phrase," he would say. "Don't stop in the middle as if you had run out of interest. 'Send in the clowns,' right to the end of the word *clowns.* Don't say 'Isn't it,' and stop there! Or 'Send in the,' and drop the phrase. Sing it right through to the end, let the note ring, let the word finish. 'Send in the *clowns!*'" It was grueling, but it worked. I began to be able to sing to the end of the phrase.

If you ever listen closely to birds singing you'll know what Max meant about singing to the end of the phrase. In the space between the end of the note and the beginning of the repeat, you can almost count the pulses in the air, as the bird prepares to sing again. That's what Max meant.

I also think Max, though he would have refuted the accusation, was teaching something spiritual. We are here, living. We just climb on board. When we are dead we stop singing, but the pulse of the note, the spirit, goes on, and when we are ready, we just climb on board again. We are just singing, and we will sing again.

Max would have liked that thought, and I doubt I ever said anything like that to him, though I often thought it. Max was not a believer in God or Karma. His funeral was held in the acoustically perfect wooden auditorium at the New York Society for Ethical Culture. Helen had a difficult time deciding if I should sing "Amazing Grace," succumbing only when it occurred to her that it was not merely a religious song, but also an appropriately timeless one.

"You're singing now," he would say. "Just open your mouth and join in the sound, with no bumps and no racket in the throat and the mouth, just smoothly get on board." He would laugh when I got it right, as though he had told a very funny joke. "You are singing right now. Most people don't do that."

Once he said to me, "If I am speaking in another room, far away from you, you will understand what I am saying if the phrasing is clear." We tested it out and he was right. If the voice in the other room was whispering or mumbling or the vowels were covered or the music of the phrase was not there, I would not understand. If the phrase was lyric and smooth and the vowels clear, the walls were no impediment.

"And," he would say triumphantly, "if you understand what is being said, in speaking or in singing, you are speaking and singing correctly!" None of this placing the voice in the toes or in the head or in the kitchen for Max. It was clarity, pure and simple, clarity and phrasing.

"Trust the lyrics, put your time into the lyrics, that they should be understood. Don't fuss about the melody, once you know it. If you plan to sing the 'Star Spangled Banner,' you are not going to accidentally suddenly burst into 'Yankee Doodle Dandy' by mistake!"

We would both laugh so often, and Helen would smile in the kitchen, puttering over our cups of tea, and Papageno the parakeet would whistle contentedly.

On a rainy day in December in New York in 1996 I was riding home in a cab through Central Park when the light, suddenly brilliant, cut through the afternoon mist of thunderous clouds and rain. I had been Christmas shopping at Tiffany's, feeling particularly sad and discontented. There was, of course, the reason there always is: that Clark is no longer here to share the weather of the soul. But then I remembered that Max, too, was dying.

I had managed to put completely out of my mind for a few hours my visit with Max in Roosevelt Hospital that morning. He lay with his eyes closed, a small, shriveled person, a shadow of himself, breathing with the help of oxygen, his inhalations barely moving his shoulders, his eighty-nine-year-old frame clad in a hospital robe, his bones protruding from the thin material. Morphine dripped into his arm every four hours. He was in no pain and out of this world, following whatever gay and bright dreams were flitting through his ever-inventive, creative, brilliant mind.

That morning when Helen called to tell me how he was doing, she fell apart on the phone. She said, her voice shaking with sobs, that he would probably not live another day, and that I had better get there if I wanted to say good-bye. "I cannot imagine that this is happening," she said. "We have no children, and of course we were all to each other, and it is so short a time since he was my young lover."

I called to tell my brother Denver John, who, along with all of our family, was like family with Max, knowing over the years this amazing, gentle, smiling, thorny, bright, blazingly intelligent man. My brother remembered things I didn't or had forgotten. He was deeply saddened to hear of Max's leaving, sad for himself, sad for me, for Louis, and for Helen. When I told him of the morphine drip, he said, "God, I hope he isn't having the monkey thing!"

"Monkey?" I ask.

"Remember when they gave him morphine for that terrible sciatica he had? He hallucinated monkeys crawling all over his Steinway."

Arriving at Max's hospital room I leaned over my teacher's pillow and put my lips on his frail head. I told him that I was grateful that he had taken me for his student, grateful we had these years together. I thought, Max cannot be dying, this must be some other old and deflated man. I thanked God for the tapes I have of our lessons, fragile, crumbling, from the seventies mostly. Having them means I will still be able to hear his voice, talking to me about art, talking to me about phrasing, that favorite, that perfect, that impenetrable thing he knew and loved and made me love.

The man in the bed next to Max had a huge purple Barney balloon his grandchildren had brought. I brought Max a teddy bear with a heart balloon attached to a bottle of red and white candies which I hoped Helen would like. The balloon said "I love you."

Max, I was sure, was remembering playing the violin, remembering that I was a difficult student, remembering, I prayed, that I was his favorite, or at least his favorite after Harris Yulin.

We would all miss him, but none of us as much as Helen. She was young and lovely when he brought her from Texas to New York. "Just imagine," she said, "I have been so lucky! I could have married some Texas hick! Instead I married this brilliant, knowledgeable and creative man and he brought me here to the greatest city in the world." Tears in her eyes, she hugged me, and we parted. I left the hospital room humming the "Star Spangled Banner." What a man, what a gift. I doubted I would see him again.

I said to myself, Max is still singing, he is still speaking. He was so important to my life, to my son's life. He appreciated Clark's intelligence, his keen mind, his eagerness to learn and to do everything. Even his voice, which Max said was a very fine, natural voice. I can hear both their voices, they are together somewhere. Singing.

Just listen.

꧁꧂ Dear Clark,

The weather is freezing and there are ice patterns on all the pine trees and a frost of feathers in the air that bites my nose as I breathe in, and puff out steam as I breathe out. I breathe carefully, aware of the distinction between life and death, between what is and what has been and is not, between breathing and not breathing. You loved the snow, and I see you shoveling, breathing your vaporized breath out into the air on a cold night. I see visions of you bringing in a pine tree for the holidays in New York, of you as a child in the snow in Connecticut, your bunny suit buttoned to your chin and your eyes shining, you in your heavy winter coat in Minnesota, shoveling the walk of your house, hauling in the pine tree from the crystal, falling flakes. It snowed the day of your funeral, and I cannot stand to see the snow this year. How dare the seasons continue to come, each in its proper sequence, when your dying was out of order and contrary to nature?

Nature brings me signs, and the snow does fall, covering the bumps, the angles, the dirty ground. It shines white, white, and the vision of salvation comes to me even in the bitter taste of snow crystals on my tongue. Your life, your vigor, your energy, are gone.

Let me pray for the solace of nature and watch for messages in the wind, in the river, in the trees. Your spirit hovers everywhere in this winter night, calling to me like a wild bird.

It is almost six years now since Clark's death. I feel an abundance and a beauty in my heart, a solace from some inner, deep place that has only come recently. There has been, as teachers and mystics promised, a rebirth, a transcendence in the aftermath of my son's death. In order to live, I have had to move from the dark place of self-doubt and fear into the gift of survival—light, joy and freedom.

As my life has moved through these deep waters I have kept up the song. Perhaps the rocks in the river are what makes the river sing.

This morning the sun dances on the river, sparkling on the water as it moves north along the Hudson. I look at Clark's photographs, pictures from the past, from the future, from the present: Clark on our friend Terry Williams' boat, the Mississippi River, sun on his face, a smile wide and brilliant, the big Twin Cities Bridge behind him; Clark at his wedding, polished-looking in a new haircut, grinning from ear to ear, his tux shining, his eyes shining; Clark at six or seven, his hand holding his cheek, his eyes looking up at me.

I still think sometimes, perhaps there has been some mistake.

But the mornings are better now.

The alarm rings at seven-thirty and I open my eyes to the new day, rising from the depth of my feather bed. I get up quickly, breathing in deeply, shaking the wisps of dreams from my head. At the edge of my bed, I look into the face of the standing Buddha who guards me, one hand lifted with the fingers bent in a sign of peace, the other hand stretched out, open palmed, toward the future. There are other Buddhas, one from Vietnam, of red and gold; one from Thailand, a small, golden Buddha; and an inlaid cross, a statue of St. Francis, angels on the walls, porcelain, papier-mâché, needlepoint—all of them protecting me as I go to armor, suit up, show up for the battle. The struggle to keep from slipping back each day must be fought. I cannot let the darkness win. I must flood my life with light.

Last night I threw the I Ching. The coins gave me the reading: "Be not sad. Be like the sun at midday." Life in these past few years has become rich even through the pain. I feel a new dimension of change. I have learned many lessons from the loss, the grief, the mysterious gift of my son's death, a gift that makes me want life even more; for myself, for him, as though it were in my power to live my own life and also to somehow live the rest of his, that part of his that was unlived.

In this journey I have learned more deeply the lesson that even the darkest day has its bittersweet song. Even the darkest day has its sunlight.

I have learned there is a bond, like a heartbeat, between loss and victory, between singing and weeping, between losing and healing.

I have learned that the lesson of love is the most important lesson of all.

I have learned that there is a gift of victory in defeat.

And I have learned the truth in Camus's conclusion: "In the midst of winter, I discovered that in me there was an invincible summer."

꩜ *Yesterday I went to the river where, so many seasons ago, we scattered your ashes. The Mississippi ran in the bright sunlight, April swallows swooped over the place where we let you go free, into the river. The sun was bright, the river smiling, and Terry and Chris and I got our feet wet in the river scattering red and yellow rose petals on the water, where they drifted out into the middle of the river, like flower boats headed for New Orleans, headed for the Gulf of Mexico. We walked between two big cottonwood trees near Hidden Falls where I will put a bench and a plaque bearing your name:*

Beloved Son
Clark Collins Taylor
Jan 1959–Jan 1992
"Deeply Mourned—Free at Last"
Rejoice

It will be a place we can go and sit by the river, your daughter and your friends and your family, watching the swallows fly, the sunlight dance, in the years as they come and go, remembering you in all your beauty.

My beloved son, I feel your spirit in my heart, where you will live forever.

Acknowledgments

$\mathcal{I}$ want to extend special thanks to the following people: my editor at Pocket Books—Mitchell Ivers, Susan Cheever, Loretta Barrett, Lynn Nesbit, my sister Holly Collins, Katherine DePaul, my entire family, and especially to my husband Louis Nelson. All were enormously helpful in giving me advice and courage to finish the book.

As I was finishing this book, my nephew Luke Taylor died from an overdose. Clark and Luke were extremely close: cousins, friends, angels together, forever.

Guthrie, Woody, 129, 138
Guys and Dolls, 48

H

Hair, 154
Hall, Robert (Judy's stepfather), 15
Hamer, Fanny Lou, 130
Hamilton, Susan, 111
Hammond, John, 106
Handicap, of Judy's father, 25–31
Hazelden Renewal Center, 12, 81,
    195–96
Healing, xv, 21, 103, 243, 245
    process of, 124, 140, 201, 221
Hellerman, Freddy, 106–07
"Hey, Nelly, Nelly," 127
Holden. *See* Bowler, Holden (Judy's
    godfather)
Holt, Will, 120
Holzman, Jac, 106, 110, 118–19,
    124, 126, 145–46
Homeopathic remedies for anxiety,
    241–42
Hope, Bob, 64
"How Are Things in Glocca
    Mora?", 35

I

I Dream of Peace, 273
Ian, Janis, 125, 147
Idaho, University of, 30–31
"I'll Be Home for Christmas," 36
"I'll Be Seeing You," 171

In My Life, 144–45
"In the Hills of Shiloh," 128
"It's a Long Way to Tipperary," 137

J

Jac. *See* Holzman, Jac
Jackson, Mississippi, 129–30
Jacksonville, Illinois, 87
Jazz, 64, 72, 143
Johnson, President Lyndon, 275
Joplin, Janis, death of, 152
Judith, 171, 175
Judith, in Bible, 23, 27
Judy Collins #3, 127
*Judy Collins Christmas at the
    Biltmore*, 206
The Judy Collins Concert, 138

K

Kartiganer, Esther, 258
"Kathleen" ("I'll take you home
    again"), 26
"Kathleen Mavourneen," 23, 35
Keach, Kalen (Judy's nephew), 18,
    178, 262–63
Keach, Stacy, 52, 164–68, 170
Keats, John, xiii
Kennedy, President John F.
    assassination of, 128–29
    meeting, 119–20
Kennedy, Robert, assassination of,
    151, 154
"The Kerry Dancer," 71